I GOT A MONSTER

I GOT A
MONSTER

- - - - - - - - - - - - - - - -

THE RISE AND FALL OF
AMERICA'S MOST
CORRUPT POLICE SQUAD

BAYNARD WOODS and
BRANDON SODERBERG

ST. MARTIN'S PRESS
New York

First published in the United States by St. Martin's Press, an imprint of St. Martin's
Publishing Group

I GOT A MONSTER. Copyright © 2020 by Baynard Woods and Brandon Soderberg.
All rights reserved. Printed in the United States of America. For information, address
St. Martin's Publishing Group, 120 Broadway, New York, NY 10271.

www.stmartins.com

Library of Congress Cataloging-in-Publication Data

Names: Woods, Baynard, author. | Soderberg, Brandon, author.
Title: I got a monster : the rise and fall of America's most corrupt police squad /
    Baynard Woods and Brandon Soderberg.
Description: First edition. | New York : St. Martin's Press, 2020. |
Identifiers: LCCN 2020002705 | ISBN 9781250221803 (hardcover) |
    ISBN 9781250221810 (ebook)
Subjects: LCSH: Baltimore (Md.). Police Department. Gun Trace Task Force—
    Corrupt practices. | Police corruption—Maryland—Baltimore.
Classification: LCC HV7936.C85 W66 2020 | DDC 364.1/323—dc23
LC record available at https://lccn.loc.gov/2020002705

Our books may be purchased in bulk for promotional, educational, or business use. Please
contact your local bookseller or the Macmillan Corporate and Premium Sales Department at
1-800-221-7945, extension 5442, or by email at MacmillanSpecialMarkets@macmillan.com.

First Edition: 2020

10 9 8 7 6 5 4 3 2 1

*This book is dedicated to all the defense attorneys
fighting for the Fourth Amendment.*

AUTHORS' NOTE

The account of the Gun Trace Task Force (GTTF) in this book is derived from wiretaps, body camera and surveillance footage, jail calls, and other recordings; transcripts, audio, and video from numerous trials on both the state and the federal level; hundreds of interviews; and thousands of pages of documents. When dialogue comes from audio recordings and video recordings, it is verbatim. Other dialogue between characters is reconstructed from the participants' memories. There are also conflicting versions of some events. For a full discussion of the materials informing each section, see the endnotes.

CAST OF CHARACTERS

GTTF

WAYNE JENKINS: police sergeant, criminal mastermind; pleaded guilty

MOMODU GONDO: police detective, drug dealer; pleaded guilty

JEMELL RAYAM: police detective, burglar; pleaded guilty

DANIEL HERSL: police detective, bruiser; found guilty

MARCUS TAYLOR: police detective, star runner; found guilty

MAURICE WARD: police detective, paranoid; pleaded guilty

EVODIO HENDRIX: police detective, thief, hard-pressed father of five; pleaded guilty

THOMAS ALLERS: police sergeant who oversaw GTTF before Jenkins; pleaded guilty

JOHN CLEWELL: police detective; not indicted

GTTF Collaborators

DONALD STEPP: drug dealer, Jenkins's friend; pleaded guilty

KYLE WELLS: drug dealer, Gondo's friend; found guilty

ANTONIO SHROPSHIRE: drug dealer; found guilty

ERIC SNELL: drug dealer, Rayam's friend, Philadelphia cop, former BPD; pleaded guilty

Victims

JAMAL AND JOVONNE WALKER: arrested by Jenkins and Gladstone, 2010; case dismissed

UMAR BURLEY: chased and arrested by Jenkins, 2010; case dismissed

WALTER PRICE: arrested by Jenkins, 2014; case dismissed

OREESE STEVENSON: arrested by Jenkins, Hendrix, Taylor, and Ward, March 2016; case dismissed

DAVON ROBINSON: arrested by Allers, Gondo, Hersl, and Rayam, April 2016

RONALD HAMILTON: Detained by Jenkins's GTTF, July 2016; never charged

APRIL SIMS AND DAMON HARDRICK: arrested by Jenkins's GTTF, July 2016; case dismissed

ALBERT BROWN: arrested by Jenkins's GTTF, August 2016; case dismissed

DENNIS ARMSTRONG: arrested by Jenkins's GTTF, August 2016; case dismissed

ANDRE CROWDER: arrested by Jenkins's GTTF, September 2016; case dismissed

GREGORY HARDING: arrested by Jenkins's GTTF, October 2016; case dismissed

Lawyers

IVAN BATES: defense attorney representing the Walkers, Stevenson, Hardrick, Brown, Crowder, and Harding

DEBORAH LEVI: head of the Office of the Public Defender's Special Litigation Section, which went through all GTTF cases

NATALIE FINEGAR: former deputy public defender, defense attorney

ANNA MANTEGNA: former assistant state's attorney accused of being GTTF leak

LEO WISE: assistant U.S. attorney, prosecuted GTTF

DEREK HINES: assistant U.S. attorney, prosecuted GTTF

Other Law Enforcement

KEITH GLADSTONE: BPD sergeant and Jenkins's; pleaded guilty

KEVIN DAVIS: BPD commissioner, July 2015–January 2018

DARRYL DE SOUSA: BPD commissioner, January 2018–May 2018; pleaded guilty

DEAN PALMERE: BPD deputy commissioner who oversaw BPD plainclothes units

ERIKA JENSEN: FBI Special Agent; investigated GTTF

I GOT A MONSTER

PROLOGUE

BALTIMORE ALMOST HAD a revolution.

On an April morning in 2015, Baltimore Police officers tackled a young black man named Freddie Gray and pulled him screaming into a van where his spine was broken and his throat was crushed. His death kicked off weeks of protest and one day of rioting that ended with cop cars and pharmacies in flames, an illegal curfew, and National Guard troops and police occupying the streets. To many people in the embattled, deeply segregated, postindustrial city, this uprising had been a long time coming.

When the city's top prosecutor, Marilyn Mosby, brought criminal charges against the six officers involved in Gray's death, the nation briefly saw Baltimore as a beacon of hope for police reform. After that, though, the story goes, cops got scared, slowed down, "took a knee," and stopped making arrests. Some cops said they were afraid they might be charged with a crime if anything went wrong, and others didn't want to be the "next viral video."

Soon, the city's murder rate rose to crisis levels, and the police commissioner was replaced by Kevin Davis, a savvy cop from the county who needed both to stop the bloodshed and to address the concerns of furious citizens traumatized by decades of illegal policing.

Davis's response to 2015's near revolution was a cop counter-insurgency in the form of re-emboldened plainclothes police squads, known as *knockers* or *jump-out boys,* who prowled the city looking for trouble.

Plainclothes were directed by a newly created War Room, where BPD commanders, elite operations units, and federal task forces shared information enabling them to target the people they thought were most likely to pull a trigger, even if they could not prove that those people had actually committed a crime.

The war in Baltimore had been going on for generations. The War Room made it official. And because it was a war, where all is fair and stakes are high, police command and politicians looked the other way as long as plainclothes units racked up arrests and brought in the statistics that assured the public that, however bad things looked, the "good guys" were winning.

On the streets, these counterinsurgency techniques did little to stop the violence, and, by targeting violence-intervention groups and disrupting the underground economy of the streets, they often engendered it. Afraid of criminals and cops alike, more and more Baltimoreans armed themselves for protection.

In this environment, one plainclothes squad thrived: the Gun Trace Task Force (GTTF).

Sergeant Wayne Jenkins ran the GTTF like a war machine. He did not take a knee. He took territory, guns, and drugs, and police brass loved him for it. He was the kind of guy they'd all grown up watching in war movies and cop shows—a hard-charging hero who was willing to break some rules and cause some chaos to bring in the bad guys. For years, high-ranking allies covered for Jenkins, helping him escape scrutiny coming from what they considered minor infractions.

Jenkins had been using his squad as a front for a vast criminal enterprise. It had been a nearly flawless scheme, going back nearly a decade. Robbing drug dealers was lucrative and safe. They weren't going to call the cops—and if they did, no one would listen.

Defense attorneys were among the only people who had been

listening to the complaints about these officers and fighting to expose the corruption. They weren't likely to tell a judge, "Hey, my client actually had a lot more cocaine than the officer claimed," but they pointed out illegal stops, illegal searches, illegal detentions, and illegal tracking of citizens.

Every defense attorney in town has the cop they think is just a little worse than the rest of them. For Ivan Bates, that cop was Wayne Jenkins. In 2010, Bates thought he figured out Jenkins's MO—stopping someone in a car and making up a reason to get in their house and robbing them—and since then, he had been in what he called "a battle" with the cop who some called "the prince of the city."

A year after the death of Freddie Gray, when Jenkins rolled up Oreese Stevenson, a drug war veteran, who Bates came to represent, their familiar battle would be waged in new territory, for higher stakes than either imagined.

BOOK
ONE

- - - - - - - - - - - - -

**"THERE AIN'T NO LEGITIMATE
BUSINESS ANYWHERE."**

ONE

SERGEANT WAYNE JENKINS was going the wrong way. He steered a silver Malibu full of plainclothes cops against traffic on a residential street, rolling past brick row houses with white trim and pitched roofs resting atop dappled hills spotted with resurgent spring grass. He was looking for a monster.

Jenkins, the only white man in the car, was the driver, and he was the boss, the officer in charge of this brutal, four-man squad. Detective Marcus Taylor, the runner, sat in the front seat beside Jenkins, ready to jump out and give chase. In the back seat, Maurice Ward, the unit's steady hand, and Evodio Hendrix, the squad member most often burdened with completing the paperwork that would legitimate the baroque kind of bust about to play out on Jonquil Avenue, a one-way street in Northwest Baltimore.

These men in tactical vests, cargo pants, and running shoes, part of the Baltimore Police Department's Special Enforcement Section (SES), knew as much as anyone about the city's underground economy of guns and drugs and the desperation that drove people to them.

"Sarge," as they called Jenkins when they weren't just calling him *Wayne,* was always further indoctrinating them into his philosophy of hot-rod policing, wrinkling his forehead with two big creases folded horizontally above a nose slightly too narrow for his wide, doughy face as he squinted and gesticulated, giving orders,

never just saying but emphasizing—yelling, whispering, condemning, cajoling.

The words of Wayne Jenkins were actions.

Over his thirteen years on the force, he had studied the habits and customs of the drug trade and developed an arcane set of
rules about how the game is played. Acura TLs, Honda Accords,
and Honda Odysseys were "dope boy" cars, he explained, and
stopping them often paid off. Driving the wrong way on one-
ways added the element of surprise. Pulling up fast on a corner
and popping open the passenger door and chasing whoever ran
did too. He called it a "door pop." It was a numbers game. The
more people they stopped, the more likely they were to get drugs
or a gun.

These rules were all variations on a principle Jenkins had
learned well: Don't let probable cause get in the way of a good
arrest.

Another rule: Stop and search anyone over eighteen years old with
a backpack.

So when Demetrius Brown, a thirty-six-year-old black man,
jogged out of one of the row houses with a camo backpack and
got into a minivan idling against the curb, Jenkins hit the gas. His
prowling, weaponized midsize sedan rigged with a siren and flashing lights sprang forward and then stopped short, inches from the
van's front tire, at an angle, just close enough that there was no
way the van could pull out.

Oreese Stevenson, the van's driver, saw SES detectives fanning
out of the car, heavy black vests flashing POLICE in white letters,
a burly, bulldog-like white guy and a thin black guy with a flat-
top coming up on each side of the van, and right behind them, two
more. One superfast, nervous and wormy, and the other bearded,
older looking.

They did not draw the weapons hanging from their waists.
They didn't need to.

"How much money you have in the box between your feet?" Jenkins barked in his Baltimore white-boy accent—part Philly whine and part Southern drawl with smashed, elongated vowels tempered by the black slang he'd picked up on the streets.

"What money?" Brown asked, moving the backpack that held a Quaker Oats box packed with $20,000 out of view with his feet.

Stevenson, a thirty-six-year-old black man with the bulk of an over-the-hill linebacker—or an ex-con—said little, stoic in a minivan on a suburban street at 3:30 in the afternoon on a cloudy spring day, March 22, 2016.

"You don't have a warrant," Brown said, tightening his ankles around the backpack on the floor of the van. "You can't search me."

There was no legal reason for this stop, but the two black men were not shocked to see the cops come jamming up the wrong way and block them in. The city was at war, had been ever since they could remember. People said police had been lying low since Freddie Gray. You couldn't tell it from these guys.

Hendrix said something about how Stevenson's windshield was tinted—that always looked good on paper, even if the tints weren't dark enough to violate the law.

Ward slid the van's door open and saw another backpack, zipped shut in the middle seat. He unzipped it, found a half kilo of coke, and said something to his squad about the Steelers, the hated Pittsburgh rival of Baltimore's beloved football team, the Ravens.

Steelers was code SES used to announce drugs or guns.

"Don't move. Put your hands up," Jenkins said.

They pulled Stevenson and Brown from the car. Taylor handcuffed them. Jenkins patted them down, took their keys and their cell phones—Stevenson had more than one phone on him—and read them their Miranda rights.

"At any time being questioned by myself or another officer, you have the right to answer questions or refuse to answer questions," Jenkins said.

He usually rushed through the words, impatient and nearly poking the culprit in the chest with his restless, stubby fingers, annoyed to have to go over all of this again by rote.

Taylor filmed the ritual with his cell phone. Smart cops created and controlled video. Always be aware of how you tell the story, on paper and later in court, and always make sure you're the one with the footage, and don't fuck up and forget about a security camera up on a pole or let bystanders take their own video that might contradict you.

A woman came out of the house they'd seen Brown exit. She had her phone out. Taylor saw it too and rushed right past her and into the house. She turned to follow Taylor, and Jenkins snatched her phone so she couldn't record or call for help. Inside the house, Jenkins started asking her questions. She was the mother of Brown's children. Taylor went upstairs and looked around for drugs, for cash, for guns.

Nothing. They walked back outside.

Jenkins had to work fast. A serious gambler, he often got lucky, but he wasn't lucky enough to pull up on a cocaine deal in a residential neighborhood by accident. This was more than investigative intuition. Jenkins had studied up on Stevenson, researched his history and the federal drug case that had snagged him a decade earlier. He had shown Ward the news stories about Stevenson and all his high-powered, politically plugged-in associates who had been charged. Now many of them were back at it, and he was watching them.

"This is a big one," Jenkins told Hendrix.

He followed a procedure: Tell Stevenson he could go free if he'd flip and give them another name—his plug or a rival dealer. Jenkins would work his way up the ladder that way. All that stop-snitching talk was bullshit that applied only to testifying. On the street, most people were more than ready to talk if it meant that they could walk and nothing ever went on paper, especially younger guys who would give up their own mama if it helped them out.

Jenkins put Stevenson back in the van, in the middle seat where the coke had been, and got in beside him.

REARED UNDER THE equally strict regimes of Stop Fuckin' Snitching and Zero Tolerance, Stevenson and Jenkins had more in common as enemies than they had with anyone out there in the straight world.

In the early 2000s, after getting out of prison for manslaughter, Stevenson was running a dope shop for a crew that the feds dubbed the Rice Organization in the Park Heights neighborhood in Northwest Baltimore. Howard and Raeshio Rice and their crew funneled $27 million in heroin into the city. Stevenson helped, and when they got snagged in a federal investigation, he got caught on the wiretap, which was enough for RICO Act conspiracy charges.

Stevenson pleaded out to a state charge to avoid federal time on the RICO claim, but he stood tall and didn't rat on nobody. He was home in 2011 and got a truck-driving job, lost it, and eventually ended up here, sitting handcuffed in a van, about to be questioned by a wily jump-out boy with big dreams.

When the Rice Organization case began in 2003, Jenkins was just a skinny, shy-eyed rookie on the force. While Stevenson was away, Jenkins transformed himself into a supercop, a star of statistical policing, scooping up guns, making arrests, getting numbers. He broke the rules sometimes and wrecked a lot of cars along the way, but that was the culture.

In 2009, Jenkins made an arrest that led to the headline BALTI-MORE POLICE MAKE LARGEST-EVER DRUG SEIZURE. He and his partner turned in forty-one kilos of coke and $11,000. Jenkins said the dealer didn't want the detectives to disturb his mom, so he led them straight to the massive bricks of blow stacked in the unlocked bed of his truck. It was that easy. No one questioned the story.

Top brass loved all that coke laid out for news cameras, and Jenkins got a Bronze Star for the bust.

Other cops marveled at his prowess and joked that Jenkins could nab the lowliest street dealer with a single gel cap of heroin one day and have the kingpin supplying the raw the next day.

Now these two old soldiers, each more than a decade deep into the endless drug war, sat in a minivan together on a leafy street, Stevenson saying nothing at all, and Jenkins running through his tricks.

He would try to level with a target first, talk real low about "keeping it a hundred" with him, floating freedom in front of him in the form of a question: "If you could put your own crew together and rob the biggest drug dealer you know, who would that drug dealer be?"

It wasn't exactly snitching if you were answering a hypothetical question about a robbery.

He told Stevenson that he was a federal agent, one of his most common lies. The coke deal had come across a wiretap, he claimed. They knew who Stevenson was working with and who he was talking to, and now they had his phones, and since Stevenson wasn't the target and they were after someone bigger, he should give up his connect.

Jenkins asked Stevenson where he lived. He gave them the address on his driver's license, on Presstman Street in West Baltimore. They knew that wasn't true. They said they had been watching his house. He lived on Heathfield Road in East Baltimore.

"Where do you live, sir?" Jenkins asked again.

"4100 Heathfield, sir," Stevenson said, giving Jenkins the wrong street number.

Both men were strangely formal like that, calling each other *sir*. It was an act that had to play out even when everyone was lying to each other.

Jenkins mentioned Stevenson's actual address on Heathfield, where he lived with his wife, Keona Holloway, and their kids. He told Stevenson that they had a team there right now, executing a search warrant. They had taken his keys and would use them to prove he lived there. They might end up arresting his wife. Stevenson didn't give anybody up, but, Jenkins said, he copped to his stash—coke, cash, and guns. That was enough.

The interrogation ended.

Jenkins hopped out of the van, excited, his thick frame electrified. He called a wagon to come and take Stevenson and Brown to Central Booking.

They had two addresses for Stevenson, Jenkins announced to the squad. It made sense to check the Presstman Street place first. It was a plausible dope pad. Jenkins said he would call a sergeant from the Northeast District and tell him to go sit on the other house, the one on Heathfield Road, and make sure none of Stevenson's boys got anything out of there before SES arrived.

Jenkins didn't call the sergeant. He called Donny Stepp, a bail bondsman, cocaine dealer, and longtime Jenkins family friend.

"I need you to come to this address as quick as you can," Jenkins told Stepp, giving him the Heathfield address. "I got a monster."

STEPP, CUE-BALL BALD, with a giant gold cross hanging from a thick chain around his neck, knew what Jenkins meant by a *monster*—it was one of Jenkins's favorite words, an honorific applied to dealers really worth robbing.

They'd had this kind of arrangement for years. Jenkins would tip Stepp off to a stash or deliver stolen drugs to him, and they would split the profits. They would sometimes watch a guy for months. Stepp bought all sorts of specialized equipment through Double D Bail Bonds, his bail bonds company.

Stevenson had not been one of their shared targets, so Stepp wasn't sure what Jenkins knew, but, generally, he wouldn't leave the house unless it was a big job. Some $20,000 pissant robbery didn't do it for Stepp, but if Jenkins had a monster, he was in.

Jenkins gassed Stepp up some more over the phone, told him Stevenson was a "drug lord."

"There's a quarter million dollars on top of a safe in the bag, there's $500,000 inside the safe, and there's ten kilos in a closet six feet from it," Jenkins said. "I got the whole squad here so they don't know."

Jenkins assured Stepp that no one was at the house and directed him to pull his truck up in the alley and break and enter through the back door and clean the place out.

"You can throw the safe on a dolly, throw it in the back of the truck, and drive out," Jenkins said.

According to GPS, it was a twenty-minute drive from Middle River in the county where Stepp lived.

Stepp sped off, headed into the city, thinking of a score that would bring him, if he did his math right, about $1.75 million. He'd never made that much from a single heist before, but he believed it was possible. Calls like this were why Stepp always answered the phone when Jenkins called.

Jenkins and his crew cut southeast toward Stevenson's house on Presstman. He would try to hold his squad there and buy Stepp time to get to the other house first.

. . .

STEPP PULLED UP to Stevenson's house and saw a young man—a kid, really—running out the back with a bag.

They made eye contact.

Someone was already in the house, cleaning it out.

He called Jenkins and told him about the kid. Jenkins told him to make sure he was looking at the right house. Go back out front and look at the address and count how many houses it is from the corner and then count again in the alley. Just get inside.

Jenkins could only stall his crew at Stevenson's other home for so long. The rickety two-floor row house on the West side was pretty much empty except for boxes and boxes of adult diapers inside. The house was about to be turned into an assisted living facility. Jenkins couldn't keep them there much longer, so Stepp had to hurry.

Stepp hung up. As a bail bondsman, risk assessment was his job, and this wasn't worth the risk. But the stash of a supposed "drug lord" still tempted Stepp so he decided to stick around. He parked half a block away and watched Stevenson's house through binoculars.

A few minutes later, Jenkins, Hendrix, Taylor, and Ward arrived. Jenkins wanted to get into the house for an exploratory, pre-warrant excursion he called "a sneak and peek." The trick was to do it without leaving a trace. Witnesses, cameras, or alarms could show he'd entered without a warrant. So when he saw a neighbor looking out the window of the house next door, Jenkins created a complicated ruse that would allay the suspicions of any nosy neighbors.

Jenkins told the squad he would go knock on the neighbor's door and start talking to her and then Taylor would yell about a suspect running from the back of Stevenson's house. Jenkins would dash off to act like he was helping Taylor give chase. Then

Jenkins could come back to the neighbor and ask about the phantom perp out back.

It was a riff on a technique called "chasing ghosts"—making up a foot chase to justify a stop or a search.

"Out back!" Taylor yelled, right on cue, as Jenkins talked to the neighbor. He darted off.

Then Jenkins returned to the neighbor's door with Taylor, breathing heavy as if they'd been chasing a fleeing burglar.

The neighbor, a retired teacher, cracked open the door cautiously. Taylor took out his phone and began recording the charade.

Jenkins asked her if she had seen anybody running.

"I didn't see anybody," she said. "I only saw you guys walking up my walkway."

"Okay," Jenkins said, interrupting.

"Which is why I came down," she said, her left hand on the handle of the screen door, keeping it shut.

"Didn't you see us take off running?" Jenkins asked.

"I did," she said.

Jenkins kept talking, transforming a fake foot chase into a real one, nudging her to confirm on camera that they had run off after someone, peppering his leading questions with "ma'am."

"Did they have any young kids? Because this boy was about sixteen, seventeen, with a book bag," Jenkins said.

"Oh, no," she said. "They have two little ones."

Jenkins leaned his weight on the row home's formstone façade and said it all one more time to her, for the camera.

"He was on the back porch, and he had the screen door open when we passed there," Jenkins said.

He casually grabbed the side of her storm door and edged it open. She snatched it back and gently shut it.

"My detective said, 'Out back, out back.' That's why we ran," Jenkins said. "Obviously I was having a conversation with you and left you, but I just wanted you to know that's why. I wasn't trying to be ignorant and just leave you, but my detective had somebody running."

Then Taylor started talking.

"That's why we ask," Taylor said at the foot of the steps, still recording. "Because he, the individual, when we was trying to talk to him, he was like, 'Uh-oh.'"

Taylor's voice faded into a mumble.

"Ma'am, thank you so much for your time," Jenkins said.

"Thank you very much," Taylor said.

Stepp watched through binoculars as SES walked over to Stevenson's house. He took a picture as Jenkins opened the front door—he was often taking photos and videos of Jenkins, for "insurance," he said.

Jenkins walked inside Stevenson's home, a nice place with hardwood floors, leather sofas, and African art on the walls. He hurried down the carpeted stairs into the half-finished basement and into a sort of semifinished rec room, with an overstuffed white leather reclining couch and a flat-screen TV. The other side of the basement was unfinished, cold concrete floors and walls, a washer and dryer. Near the steps, there was a cooler full of kilos and cash—two black Glocks in there too.

Jenkins dug down into the cooler and proudly pulled out a kilo of cocaine, wrapped and packaged as the squad came down the stairs.

"When was the last time y'all seen one of these?" he said.

He kept searching.

In a small closet under the stairs, Jenkins found a safe, haphazardly hidden under a mountain of shoeboxes. He told his guys he was going to run out to the car to get a ram and a pry bar so they could open the safe up. He walked up the stairs and outside, with two kilos stuffed down into his police vest.

"He come out the door looking like Santa Claus," Stepp said. "He was protruding from the vest, so I knew—I was thinking it was the ten kilos that he was talking about and the quarter million dollars that was on top of the safe."

Jenkins stashed the kilos in the trunk of his Malibu. Then he called Stepp and asked where he was.

"Look up the street," Stepp said.

Jenkins told Stepp to drive to a cross street nearby.

As Stepp eased his truck up the street, Jenkins came flying up behind him. They both pulled over. Jenkins opened the passenger door and threw two kilos into the truck.

"Where's the other eight?" Stepp said.

Jenkins told Stepp that Taylor had seen the eight kilos, so he had to bring it to evidence control.

Then he told Stepp he was about to go on vacation.

"Can you get me $5,000 within this week?" he said.

"Yes," Stepp said. "I ain't got a problem."

Jenkins told Stepp to drive the speed limit and, if he got pulled over, call so Jenkins could come and fix it. Though he was nearly fifty and bald with almost invisible eyebrows, Stepp still looked like a kid, especially around his mouth when he got excited, and as he drove away, he was as giddy about the score as a child on Christmas, even if he was a little disappointed in the end that the fat man hadn't brought as much as he'd promised.

On the slow drive home, Stepp got to thinking. If there was a quarter million on top of the safe, he had not gotten a cut. He was the one risking his life here. Either Jenkins double-crossed him or Stevenson's people had already taken everything. Or both. Stepp was accustomed to Jenkins's exaggerations and deceits. It amazed Stepp how many schemes Jenkins could hold in his mind at one time. He could never be straight with anyone. And that was dangerous.

"He knew someone was in the house," Stepp recalled. "Had I kicked that door, I probably would've been killed."

Still, Stepp wasn't going to complain too much when he was driving away with two kilos of coke. A kilo went for $30,000 wholesale, and Jenkins would give it to him for $15,000. Since he sold grams for $100–$125, he could net nearly $200,000 off today's quick trip into Baltimore.

WITH STEPP GONE, it was time for Jenkins to get a search warrant for the house they had already entered and looted. Jenkins took Hendrix and Taylor with him to get the warrant and made Ward wait there alone to watch Stevenson's house.

Ward was stranded there without a vehicle. All he had was his service weapon. If Stevenson was really as big-time as Jenkins said, any crew he sent to raid the place and take the safe would be much better armed than Ward, and he would be dead. Depending on how much money was in the safe in the basement, that was a very real possibility.

There were three entrances to Stevenson's house, and no way he could watch all of them. This was sneak-and-peek purgatory. Ward sat down. He got up. He checked the front door with its cut-glass window in a flower shape shifting the light. He checked the back door. The door in the basement. That one was the worst. Anyone could park in the alley and roll through.

Back in 2015, when Jenkins had asked him to come over to SES, Ward happily accepted. It was an honor when Jenkins wanted to work with you. The position promised an 8:00 A.M.–4:00 P.M. schedule, no nights or weekends, plenty of overtime, and ample opportunities to steal. Ward had stolen plenty—he and Taylor had lifted a little cash together before they'd worked with Jenkins, and he had taken money with Momodu Gondo, who was now a detective in the Gun Trace Task Force. When cops stole money together, it brought about a new level of trust. When he was in patrol, Ward had believed such trust was the only way to make it into a plainclothes squad.

When Ward joined Jenkins's unit, he became fast friends with Hendrix, who also skimmed a little money here and there. Hendrix was a workingman with a family. He had five kids to support, and his wife was a full-time student, so he'd fill in the gaps, buy little things here and there, with the proceeds filched from a dope boy's pocket.

That was where Ward was when he'd joined Jenkins' new SES unit—a serious cop who took care of his family and was not above making a few extra bucks. He quickly realized Jenkins played for much higher stakes than that. Almost immediately after Ward joined, Jenkins pulled over a car with two trash bags of cash in it. It had seemed like a random stop at first, but then Jenkins told Ward he'd already tracked the car back to its owner's house in the county. At first, he talked about going into the house and finding an excuse for a warrant and then calling in the county cops. Then he changed his tack.

"You guys willing to go kick in the dude's door and take the money?" Ward recalled Jenkins saying.

Ward, Hendrix, and Taylor all hesitated. No one knew what to say. Jenkins let it drop, but not long after that, they rolled up on a weed deal at Belvedere Towers, an apartment complex stuck between the tony neighborhoods of Roland Park and Mount Washington, where Jenkins, Taylor, and Ward took $15,000 and about thirty pounds of pot from two men. Jenkins told the dealers he was a federal agent following up on a wiretap, and he was confiscating the drugs but would not make an arrest. When they left, Jenkins started weaving in and out of traffic, taking Ward and Taylor out to a park, where they left their police vests and their phones and radios in the car and got out and walked into the woods and split the money, like in a movie.

Ward asked Jenkins what he was going to do with the weed in the trunk of his car, and Jenkins said he was going to take it home and burn it. Then he changed the subject and demanded that they all go out and party.

Jenkins liked to celebrate success, whether it was a bust or a robbery. Another of the weird rules one learned quickly working with Jenkins was drinking a Twisted Tea, the alcoholic iced tea, together at the end of the night. He called it "teatime," and he expected everyone to join in.

After stealing the weed and the cash from Belvedere Towers, Jenkins insisted that they stop by a strip joint in the county.

Ward sat at the club sipping a drink while Jenkins threw money around, got a lap dance from a dancer, and then took her out to the car, where, it seemed to Ward like his new boss straight up robbed a stripper.

That night, Ward never retrieved his cut of the money from the trunk, and Jenkins never mentioned it. Ward's wife was a vice cop, and he wouldn't be able to explain where that kind of money had come from. And he had a son in his teens, the age when kids start snooping around the house, getting into everything.

He often thought about asking to get out of Jenkins's unit. If theft was supposed to breed trust, it wasn't working that way with Jenkins. Balancing a life as a cop and a robber was stressful. Belvedere Towers kept Ward paranoid. He imagined the guys they robbed were undercover or that it was all caught on camera somehow.

Ward would have to accept whatever money they took from Stevenson when Jenkins returned with a warrant. There was no way he could just leave it in the trunk. He would be blackballed.

Maybe he already was. Maybe they'd stopped trusting him after Belvedere Towers where he'd forgotten his part of the cash. Maybe this was all a setup to ambush him. The three entrances to Stevenson's house promised some kind of retribution for everything he'd ever done wrong. Time was an interminable terror.

Then the thing he feared happened—a car, a couple of voices, someone pounding at the door.

It wasn't gangsters with guns ablaze but the sister of Stevenson's wife and her girlfriend. Ward wouldn't let them in, and the girlfriend was raising hell, acting all aggressive.

He called Jenkins, who told him he was working on the warrant with Hendrix. Taylor was submitting the evidence and would be back as soon as he could. Ward called to get a cop in uniform to help him watch the house. Hours earlier, Jenkins said he'd called a sergeant to watch the location in the first place. You never could trust what Jenkins said.

A patrol officer arrived and helped Ward drive the two women away, and then Ward stood there with a uniform waiting for his squad to return to rob the place.

When Taylor finally arrived, they sent the uniform away.

Then Stevenson's wife, Keona Holloway, and Stevenson's mother walked in the door.

The women asked the cops what they were doing there.

"Oreese sent us here," Taylor said.

He showed Holloway a paper that said they had found drugs and money in Stevenson's van. That would be enough for a warrant on this house. The cops kept both women in the living room like prisoners. The room was dim, lit by lamps that cast long, ominous shadows. Holloway sat in a chair against the wall, her phone casting dead blue glow across her face. Ward and Taylor stood back across from the couch and took turns looking around the house.

Taylor couldn't help trying to be Jenkins, trying to spin out the story further, starting a conversation with Holloway and with Stevenson's mother and recording it.

"I don't know why your son ran," Taylor said.

If the women agreed with him and acknowledged on camera that the kid had run, it would be more evidence to show the police had been justified in entering the house.

"I said, 'Come here, man,' and he just took off running," Taylor said.

"Mmm-hmm," both women said at once.

"I don't know why he was scared. We had our vests. Said, 'Police,'" Taylor said.

"He probably scared," Stevenson's mother said.

"There's been a couple times police was at my house growing up. I never ran," Taylor said.

Stevenson's mother left to go help with the kids, and Holloway sat there with the two cops. Sometime after midnight, Jenkins and Hendrix finally came back with a warrant.

They had worked hard on the affidavit. The trip to Stevenson's Presstman home was omitted from the narrative entirely, and the whole confusing saga of the fleeing kid was condensed into a plausible and brief explanation for entering the house. It claimed Stevenson had told them everything, that he had hung his head and begun breathing heavily and had asked how he could get out of it; that Stevenson had told them to open his phone and find his sources; that when Jenkins started to get out of the van, Stevenson had said, "Wait, you won't arrest my child's mother." Then, the affidavit said, Stevenson told them he had "seven, maybe eight" kilos and guns and a safe full of money in the house.

Jenkins waved the paper in Holloway's face as he entered. Then he went back out the front door, and Taylor recorded video of him using the key, to show that it fit and enabling them to make a connection between the drugs in the car and the drugs in the house. Jenkins read Holloway her Miranda rights, and Taylor recorded that too.

"Ma'am, do you understand your rights?" Jenkins asked.

"Mmm-hmm," Holloway said.

"Yes or no, ma'am," Jenkins snapped.

"Yes," she said.

"Okay, what do you do for a living?" he asked.

She told him she was a nursing assistant.

"Do you know, in this house, if there's any firearms, narcotics, or money?" Jenkins asked.

"No, I don't," she said.

She clutched her phone, and Jenkins leaned forward, asking about drugs, guns, and money again.

"No," she answered.

"Okay, ma'am, what you're—" Jenkins said and stumbled over his words, trying to talk too fast. "We're about to search your residence."

Taylor turned off his camera. They told Holloway she had to leave.

JENKINS AND HIS squad eased the bar into the creases between the door and body of Stevenson's safe in the basement and pounded the back of the bar with the ram.

There is a sense of wild satisfaction when a safe pops open. Especially when it is full.

"How much did he say was in there? Was it a hundred?" Jenkins asked Hendrix, looking at the stacks of hundred-dollar bills.

Hendrix said Stevenson told them $100,000.

Jenkins pulled out the stacks and started to count each bundle of $10,000. Well over ten bundles. He left $100,000 in the safe and put the rest of the money in a black duffel bag and shut the safe.

He had an idea: Close the safe, break into it again, and capture the whole thing on video like they were cracking it for the first time. Jenkins took the bag of money, told Taylor to start recording the re-creation on his phone, walked upstairs, and waited to be called just before they got it open.

Ward and Hendrix attacked the safe, grunting for the second time, now for the camera.

"Hey, Sarge?" Taylor yelled. "Come downstairs right quick. They about to get it open."

"You ain't got it yet?" Jenkins asked as he walked down the steps.

"They almost got it," Taylor said.

"Oh, shit," Ward said when the safe snapped, nearly open now.

"Oh, there it is," Hendrix said.

The safe was open.

"Stop right fucking there," Jenkins said. "Take a picture of it, Taylor. Or record it. Do not, nobody touch it, you understand me?"

A flashlight illuminated the stacks of hundred-dollar bills nestled in the upturned safe.

"Keep your fucking camera on that," Jenkins said.

Taylor stopped recording. It was a convincing act.

In the police report, Hendrix claimed they had found $100,000 and eight kilograms of cocaine—more than $100,000 and two kilos erased.

It was not a bad day. They had spotted Brown with a backpack at 3:30 P.M.—half an hour before the end of their usual 8:00 A.M. to 4:00 P.M. shift—and now, it was getting close to dawn and they had clocked up an entire shift worth of overtime.

A heist on time and a half.

TAYLOR WAS THE only one who was single, so they met at his new town house in the suburbs twenty minutes from Baltimore to split up Stevenson's money.

They sat around a table in Taylor's basement den like they were playing cards, except everyone walked away a winner. Jenkins hoisted up the black bag onto a table and zipped it open.

Tall stacks of cash.

Hendrix, Taylor, and Ward each got $20,000, and Jenkins kept the rest. He warned them not to spend the money conspicuously. Don't buy a car or a boat or anything flashy, and whatever you do, don't deposit it in a bank.

Hendrix was gonna hide his loot in the basement and use it to feed and clothe his five children. Taylor was all about spending the cash on home improvements, as his sergeant suggested. Jenkins even had a guy who would cook the books for them and issue false receipts.

Ward looked at the money. All that dirty green paper that had been passed around the upper echelons of the streets was his, and he didn't know what to do with it. He pondered the problem as he drove home. He rented his townhome—he couldn't build a deck. Just bringing the money into the house would put his wife's career in jeopardy. He couldn't keep the money. It was an unnecessary risk. They were all getting plenty of overtime. Every gun recovered brought a "G day" or a "slash day," a quasi-official police policy that rewarded cops with a paid day off for each gun seizure. Jenkins added to that, by giving extra overtime for guns too.

Ward couldn't keep the money.

He parked his car in front of his town house, one of a few dozen identical ones. He popped the trunk of his car. The money was still in bundles wrapped in rubber bands inside a duffel bag.

There was no one around.

As Ward later remembered it, he lifted the bag, heavy with the cash, and walked across the parking lot, past a wooden fence hiding a dumpster, toward a wooded area with a small dirt path connecting his complex to another one through the trees. He slipped into the strip of woods. A small stream of water nearby gurgled.

Ward opened the bag and heaved it, chunking stacks into the woods, the bundles of bills hitting the tangled brush, others landing in the dirt. He went inside, knowing, even if the money was gone, this was not over.

TWO

DEFENSE ATTORNEY IVAN Bates saw the city stretched out before him through his nineteenth-floor windows, historic church steeples high in the sky and glass buildings reflecting off one another, as he waited in his downtown office for Keona Holloway.

Conversations with the distressed loved one of a man sitting in a cell, hoping for some kind of magic from him, were a major part of Bates's job. He knew how the system worked, and, as a black man in twenty-first-century America, and worse, in hyper-segregated Baltimore, he knew how hopeless it was for many of his clients and how hard it was for their families.

On the wall across from his desk, Bates hung a racist advertisement for Bull Durham tobacco that showed stereotypes of African Americans sitting on a cabin porch eating watermelon. People always noticed it when they came in, but no one ever asked him about it. He bought the vile print at a thrift store one day to force himself to face the racism inherent in the legal system every time he sat at his desk.

Bates grew up on military bases where his father was deployed. He spent a large part of his childhood in Germany where he never really thought about race at all. Then they moved to Virginia, where he attended Jefferson Davis Junior High. He never forgot the shock—as a black man, he was never allowed to forget it.

There was another picture, less prominent, on the wall off to the side—a portrait of Supreme Court justice Thurgood Marshall. In black and white, the great man looked old and worn down and dignified and wise. Marshall was Bates's hero, and he kept the picture there to remind himself that however bad it was for him, it was worse for Marshall.

He overcame it, and so can you, Bates told himself. He was thinking about that a lot these days.

"Keona Holloway is here to see you," an administrative assistant said.

He walked out of his office and into the lobby of his firm, Bates & Garcia, where Holloway waited on one of the leather couches.

Holloway had called earlier and said her husband, Oreese Stevenson, who had just been arrested, was demanding to see Ivan Bates. Stevenson's arrest was the kind of case Bates had built his career on—a high-profile drug arrest involving a lot of weight and, likely, some Fourth Amendment violations.

Bates asked Holloway why her husband wanted to see him specifically, and she dropped the name of one of Bates's earliest clients, an old head who'd bet on Bates when he'd first started his own firm. The old head beat the charges, and it helped Bates build a clientele among people involved in very big and expensive drug cases—people like Oreese Stevenson.

That name Holloway dropped was enough for Bates to set up an appointment and meet with her, even though he was sure he would end up passing the case on to another lawyer.

Sometimes, clients got mad when he had another attorney take the case—but they were even more pissed when he did take it and they felt he didn't devote enough time to them. And the truth was, he just didn't have the time for another client. He was dealing with a federal gang case, and he was representing Alicia White, one of the six cops charged in Freddie Gray's death. White's case had just started moving forward again after being stalled in the state's high court for months. It was the most stressful case he'd ever worked, but he was gaining a more nuanced picture of how both prosecutors and police function.

More important than his clients, though, was his wife, Lana, who was about to have a baby in May. He needed to be there for her. Lana, who was consulting on cultural competency in public schools, was not particularly impressed that her husband was a big-time lawyer. She just needed him to be a big-time dad. She had Brielle, a daughter from her first marriage, and had been suspicious of Bates's career at first because she worried the kind of people he represented might somehow harm her family. Right before one of their earliest dates, he had just been paid by a client in cash bunched in a takeout container, and it popped open when he set it on her counter. Lana was almost done with him right then and there.

She'd stuck it out, and now, nearly a decade later, after a long struggle to get pregnant, she was just over a month away from giving birth, and he wanted to be there for every minute of it with a goofy grin on his face. He'd even rented a boat to take a hundred people out into the Inner Harbor for her baby shower. The love he felt for his wife was part of why he felt such empathy for black women like Keona Holloway, who were desperate to help their husbands.

Holloway sat, the Bull Durham advertisement behind her, old Thurgood Marshall to her right, as Bates listened to her story. She didn't say much; she just wanted to know how much it would cost for Bates to go and see her husband. Stevenson would give Bates the details.

"He must see Bates," Holloway said. "That's what he told me."

Bates told her he normally charged $250 to go visit a client in jail, but out of respect for his old client that Stevenson knew, he'd waive that fee.

He would get over to Central Booking sometime that weekend,

even if he was sure he would pass the case on to someone else in the firm.

JENKINS WAS JUGGLING several other large investigations, and his crew kept up with near-nightly prowls around Baltimore grabbing guns and drugs, but he was obsessed with the calls Oreese Stevenson made from jail.

Jail calls are all recorded and logged. Cops and prosecutors can sign into a computer program that lets them listen to inmates awaiting trial, trying to gain evidence to use against them. Jenkins was both a connoisseur of crime and a practitioner, logging long hours monitoring the "private" conversations of monsters.

On one call, Jenkins heard Holloway tell Stevenson how the house looked the morning after the robbery. There was white powder everywhere, covering the floor with a fine dust. The motion detectors for their alarm had been ripped off the walls and destroyed. Downstairs in the basement where she did laundry, a safe was busted open, on its side. Stevenson told Holloway that he had $300,000 in the safe. He did not mention the ten kilograms of cocaine. She said bags with the new leather jackets they bought were gone and asked if he had been wearing his expensive Breitling watch. No, he said, it was in the house. So that was gone too.

On another call, Stevenson told Holloway to call Ivan Bates, this smooth, Obama-eared defense attorney who had gone up against Jenkins in the past.

Jenkins had a certain respect for Bates. For one thing, Bates was representing Alicia White, the police sergeant from the Northeast District where he used to work who was charged in the death of Freddie Gray. She was one of "the Six," as cops regularly referred to the defendants, as if they were political prisoners like the Catonsville Nine or the Central Park Five.

Bates and Jenkins moved along parallel career paths. Sons of servicemen, Jenkins served in the marines after high school, and Bates was a Howard University graduate who'd joined the U.S. Army in the late 1980s. Bates began his legal career as a prosecutor, working his way up to homicide cases, and then in 2003, the same year Jenkins joined the Baltimore Police Department, Bates became a defense attorney, often working for people busted by cops like Jenkins.

Both thrived in that extreme environment. Bates was a fighter, and Jenkins could appreciate that, even in a defense attorney.

It also meant he did not want Ivan Bates representing Oreese Stevenson. Bates knew about sneak and peeks. He knew Jenkins took money. And if Stevenson told him how much money was missing, Bates might listen.

WAYNE JENKINS WAS a hardscrabble county boy and the pudgy-cheeked baby of his large family. He had a stutter as a kid and got called "Rudy" after the movie because he always showed up for football practice even though he rarely got to play. In high school, he met a girl named Kristy, who was too pretty for him by adolescent standards, but they started dating. In their senior year, Kristy was diagnosed with lupus. Jenkins took care of her and, around that time, began talking a lot about honor. His father was a marine, and after high school, Jenkins found meaning in the Corps. Though he would brag later about the fight club he started at Camp Lejeune, his career as a transport operator in the USMC was lackluster, and he left the marines just before September 11, 2001.

He kicked around for a couple of years, laying tile and then working in a factory that made caulk. He had married Kristy and needed something better, especially if they were having kids.

In 2003, Jenkins joined the Baltimore Police Department, then involved in one of the most ambitious programs of mass incarceration America had ever seen, and he took orders well—especially when they were to arrest anybody and everybody—and he rose uninterrupted through the ranks. For years, he worked the night shift, living a nocturnal life on edges of the underworld, where people knew him as Jenks. He used an extensive network of snitches to control the streets.

A lot of other tough guys who bent the rules—"hard-chargers," they called them—took him under their wings. Sergeant Keith Gladstone, especially, always had Jenkins's back in a tight spot, downplaying missteps and covering up crimes.

Then came the cameras, which complicated things even for Jenkins, a master liar who could talk himself out of anything—except maybe incriminating video evidence. In 2008, he was going after a guy named Antonio Lee, who hung out at Smithee's, a West Baltimore liquor store and lounge. Jenkins and Gladstone and a few other cops went into the bar and locked everyone inside and took the keys out of the bar patrons' pockets. One guy tried to make a call, and they hit him and took his phone. They had no warrant, but they searched the bar and then went out and searched all the cars in the parking lot. They said they found nine ounces of coke in Lee's car and arrested him. Then Jenkins told the owner of the bar that he'd seen a lot of faulty wiring in the basement and that if they said anything about this, the inspector would show up and shut the place down.

The owner talked. It turned out he had a hidden camera in the place, and it showed the bust didn't happen the way Jenkins had written it up. All six of the guys in the bar hired Richard Woods, another one of these defense attorneys like Bates, who went hard after Jenkins and other crooked cops back in those days.

Before the case ever made it to court, Antonio Lee was murdered. He was sitting at a stoplight when a white van pulled up and several guns opened fire on him. The van made a right turn and disappeared. In court, the lawyer for Jenkins and his codefendants described it as a "gangland-style hit."

A jury ruled that Jenkins had deprived one patron of his rights and only awarded the plaintiff a dollar.

The video from the bar followed Jenkins, though, and kept causing trouble. In another 2008 case, he took down a guy named Mickey Oakley, who said he was sitting in his car when Jenkins slammed into it from behind, shattered the car window with a gun and pulled Oakley out through it, took his keys out of his pocket, and broke into his house.

The case went federal, and Richard Woods defended Oakley and called for a Franks hearing, a procedure where defendants can dispute the honesty of an officer's statements before the case ever comes before a jury. During the hearing, there were a number of witnesses, including Oakley himself, who testified that nothing happened the way Jenkins said it did. And then, to show that Jenkins had a history of such discrepancies, Woods played the video from Smithee's—proof Jenkins had lied in the past.

Jenkins won those motions, but every day, there seemed to be more and more cameras waiting to ensnare him. Mayor Martin O'Malley launched the Citiwatch program in 2005, shortly after Jenkins joined the force, with fifty interlocking cameras surveilling the city twenty-four hours a day. There were ten times that many a few years later. For a good cop, it was like a totalitarian fantasy that would eventually allow you to see everything. For a dirty cop, that kind of surveillance was a dystopian field of unseen eyeballs, always watching, ready to take you down.

In 2014, the Citiwatch surveillance program expanded again, looping in an extensive network of private security cameras, which could also be monitored by police, with the seven hundred cameras they already operated around the city. That year, Citiwatch caught Jenkins and almost brought him down.

Jenkins's partner at the time, Ben Frieman, busted a dude and flipped him, and the guy gave up the name of a coke dealer: Walter Price.

The next day, they were watching Price's house when they had their new snitch order a half ounce of coke from Price, and sure enough, Price came out and got in his van. He must have seen Jenkins and Frieman, because he turned around and drove back to the house, went inside for about thirty seconds, and came out again, getting in the van, and pulling off.

Jenkins made up a pretext to stop Price, and when Jenkins and Frieman searched Price and the van, they found nothing. Suddenly, after more than an hour of fruitless searching, Jenkins pulled a bag of coke out of the van. Frieman wrote it up on charging documents like they had located the coke after just a few minutes.

Molly Webb, the prosecutor in the case, started asking all kinds of questions after Price's defense attorney provided her with video that showed that Frieman had blatantly lied. Price was there for more than an hour. Price's wife showed up to the scene, and they detained her.

Because of the video, Webb dropped the charges against Price and filed a complaint against Jenkins and Frieman.

Jenkins sent Webb a long text message, trying to get her to back off: "States attorneys are informing me that you believe I'm a dirty cop that should be fired. BPD members are advising me that you said I lie on everything I write and again a dirty cop," Jenkins wrote. "So unlike what has been said about me from your voice to other credible adults I would request if it's true that you attempt to remember that we are professionals and it's slander and hurtful to me what is being said. This is not a promise nor is it a threat to you in anyway shape or form."

The text didn't work. The State's Attorney's Office gave Walter Price immunity to tell them what happened, and Price admitted he'd had the coke and that he'd gone back in the house and stashed it in the arm of the couch when he saw cops following him. It was the same coke they'd said they'd found in the van. During the time they kept Price and his wife, Sakinah DeGross, confined there, it seemed someone went and broke into their house and took the coke he had stashed there and brought it to Jenkins to "find" in the van.

"Have we raised the possibility of a wire?" the chief of staff to the state's attorney asked at one point in the Jenkins investigation. They couldn't get any cops to cooperate. The State's Attorney's Office brought the matter before a grand jury, but they decided not to bring criminal charges against Jenkins. The Internal Affairs Department (IAD) investigation found Jenkins "Guilty of Misconduct, General Neglect of Duty, and Failure to Supervise." The head of IAD let it be known that he had recommended serious repercussions, but ultimately, the penalty was only a warning. Jenkins told Ward, who was in his unit by the time the investigation was completed, that Darryl De Sousa, a powerful Baltimore Police commander, had intervened on his behalf.

Webb, meanwhile, was fired and criminally charged for signing off on overtime for a drug cop. She was later found not guilty.

It had all worked out for Jenkins in the end, but surveillance, intended to make his legitimate job easier, would soon render his criminal enterprise impossible.

The rollout of body-worn cameras would begin in May 2016, which was only a month away. By 2018, all 2,500 cops working in the city were going to have to wear them all the time, and that would be the end of the criminal activities in which he'd been engaging under the color of law for nearly a decade. There was a small window of time before that life ended, and Jenkins was going to try to enjoy it and secure his future. He was already working with Stepp, utilizing his law enforcement intelligence to commit off-the-books robberies, cutting the legitimate policing out of the equation altogether. If he had simply robbed Stevenson and not bothered with an arrest, there wouldn't be any of these problems.

He had to solve this Oreese Stevenson problem.

. . .

WHEN IVAN BATES arrived at Central Booking, he got a printout of Oreese Stevenson's charging documents, saw the name *Wayne Jenkins,* and was suddenly much more interested in the case.

Stevenson was sitting there in the interview room, on the other side of the glass window, hard and stoic, a very serious man with two serious cases against him—one for drugs in a car and another for drugs and guns in his house.

Among his charging documents was a piece of paper stamped WAR ROOM, which recommended Stevenson be held without bail because of the guns and his prior convictions.

Bates, light-skinned and tall with broad shoulders, sat down on the wooden bench, across from the bulkier Stevenson. Both men picked up telephones that allowed them to talk through the glass. No sound. The phones were broken—as usual. Nothing in the Baltimore justice system worked, not even the phones. There were guys at other windows on either side of Stevenson. Bates looked for another empty slot. Both Bates and Stevenson got up and walked to another spot. Again, no luck.

Finally, on their third try, sound crackled through the lines. Bates tried making a joke about the broken phones and the broken criminal justice system. Stevenson just stared. He was not paying Bates for comedy.

Bates asked Stevenson who had recommended him. He mentioned the old client's name again but didn't have much else to say about him. His silence did more than anything he could have said to prove that Stevenson was of the same cloth as Bates's old friend.

That's how these old heads roll.

Bates looked at the paperwork again: "8 wrapped kilo-grams of suspected cocaine, a money counter, trashbag containing empty kilo-gram wrappers, 2 clear plastic bags of large amounts of suspected cocaine in igloo container; plastic bag containing a handgun with numerous magazines/ammo, 2 black firearms with 3 magazines (2 glock .40 cal/ 1 glock 9mm), large amount of US currency seized by HIDTA, door keys taken off Oreese Stevenson's person."

Serious stuff. It also had Jenkins written all over it. Bates asked Stevenson to tell him about the case.

"It's bullshit," Stevenson said. "They boxed me in the wrong way. Those motherfuckers robbed me."

It fit Jenkins's pattern.

In 2010, Bates had a case involving Jenkins and Jenkins's mentor, Keith Gladstone. They stopped a man named Jamal Walker, who was on his way to watch football with friends. "Don't worry about nothing," Jenkins told him. "I'm not cruddy." Then Jenkins pulled him out of the car, put him in plastic zip-tie handcuffs, searched the car, and found money. Gladstone dangled a half-gram bag of weed in front of Walker, said he found it in Walker's car, and arrested Walker. They submitted $20,000 to evidence control. Walker told Bates he had $40,000.

Then Jenkins and Gladstone went to Walker's house without a warrant, and when Walker's wife, Jovonne, an educator and part-time party planner, saw a stranger outside her door, she hit her silent alarm. Jenkins and Gladstone searched the house, charged Jovonne with an old shotgun they found in the basement, and took her to jail.

When the case went to court, Bates was able to use the alarm company's log to prove that Jenkins and Gladstone had lied about how they entered the house and what time they entered. Bates won the case for the Walkers—and ever since then, he'd been looking for people Jenkins had done dirty in the same way.

Bates listened to Stevenson tell him the details of his case—they were remarkably similar to the Walkers' arrest six years earlier.

"It is what it is," Stevenson said. "But it's bullshit."

Stevenson said he would pay up front. He just wanted Bates to fight.

Bates took the case.

NOW THAT BATES was involved with Stevenson, Jenkins had to think fast, deflect, improvise, and neutralize this whole situation.

Earlier in his career, older cops had helped him out of these kinds of jams. In 2010, when Jenkins chased a guy named Umar Burley, who crashed into another car, killing the driver, Jenkins called a sergeant to bring an ounce of heroin to plant on Burley. And in 2014, a man named Demetric Simon was fleeing from Frieman on foot and Jenkins ran him over. While the car was still on top of Simon, Jenkins called Gladstone, who brought a BB gun and planted it under a nearby truck for other officers to find. Then Jenkins wrote up the incident report in Frieman's name and claimed that it looked like Simon was about to shoot Frieman, forcing Jenkins to run him over to save his partner.

The lies caught on camera, the slipups, and moments where he lost control no longer mattered after 2015, when everything changed for Jenkins. There was Freddie Gray when, in cops' eyes, the city had declared war on police, and that made a supercop like Jenkins indispensable.

Then, much worse, he and his wife, who already had two boys, lost a child.

Jenkins had been working that day, November 6, 2015, when Kristy thought she was going into labor and drove herself to St. Joseph's Medical Center. Doctors and nurses prepared her for delivery and then discovered the baby had no heartbeat.

The Jenkinses buried Lucas Colton Jenkins on November 10. Hundreds of police officers showed up to the somber service. Bagpipes stretched out choked and lonesome notes. Below the Marine Corps emblem in the upper-right corner of the stone marking the tiny grave, the epitaph read: "We'll see you someday in the future not so near. Until then, baby boy, we'll love you from here."

Jenkins started asking his sister about God and why bad things happen. In court one day, when he saw the wife of a man he had arrested, she told Jenkins he should pray to God for what he had done to her husband. Jenkins told her he didn't believe in God anymore. "He took my son," she recalled him saying.

Now, almost six months after Lucas Colton was buried, Kristy was pregnant again, due in November. There was so much at stake. Jenkins's family was counting on him. Policing was changing, his crimes with Stepp were escalating, and there was no Gladstone to save him. Jenkins was left to clean up his latest mess, this Stevenson bust, alone.

Taylor was fast, which helped with chasing people down, but he couldn't keep his mouth shut and sucked at lying. Hendrix was loyal and he could write a report, and that's about all you could say about him. Ward was loyal too, but he got freaked out when the stakes got high. Besides, Ward had been on the force as long as Jenkins, and he still hadn't made sergeant. No ambition.

Then, on one of the jail calls, Jenkins said he heard Stevenson talking to another woman. If he could make Holloway aware of this other woman and cast her as a side chick, maybe she'd stop helping her husband and Stevenson wouldn't be able to hire Bates.

He took the plan to his squad. That way they were implicated.

"Jenkins came up with the idea that he was going to write a note and put it in his wife's door to make it seem like it was from the other female and leave her phone number to call her and say that she's pregnant by Mr. Stevenson," Ward recalled.

Jenkins got the crew in the car and drove back out to Stevenson's house.

He got Hendrix to write the note, saying his own handwriting was too sloppy to look like a woman's. Then he turned to Taylor.

The fast guy was going to put the note on the door and then haul ass back to the car.

Ward watched Taylor get out of the car. A moment later, Taylor returned, still clutching the note.

"There was a light on," Taylor said as he climbed back into the front seat.

Fuck it, then, Jenkins would do it himself.

WAYNE JENKINS REALLY needed a better crew.

When he'd stop by Stepp's house to drop off drugs, pick up money, or plan heists, Jenkins regaled his bald, burglarizing bondsman buddy with crazy stories of the mishaps and close calls that made up the life of a corrupt cop. When Stepp was trying to become a bail bondsman, despite his felonies, Jenkins wrote a long letter commending Stepp's impeccable character. They laughed when the logo of Double D Bail Bonds, which featured a buxom woman whose breasts hung down over handcuff chains, pissed people off, and Stepp plastered the design across his truck.

Stepp felt legitimate and powerful working with Jenkins. Drugs, hookers, dirt bikes, chop shops, guns—Jenkins was plugged into everything underground and illegal in the city while climbing steadily to the top of the legit world of police. Sometimes the commissioner called Jenkins when he was with Stepp, and they would put the call on speaker and laugh.

The top cop "was cuddling Wayne's balls," Stepp said.

It was exhilarating and intimidating. Jenkins, who had fought a few short, victorious mixed martial arts matches under the name Silverback and now carried brass knuckles, had a short temper. At the high-stakes card games they attended, Stepp had seen Jenkins turn on other cops, ready to take them into the yard and fight over the smallest slight.

But it was all part of the package. And Stepp, like the Baltimore Police Department, thought the gamble on Wayne Jenkins was well worth it.

Jenkins had been talking a lot about taking over a particular squad, the Gun Trace Task Force (GTTF), an investigative unit targeting "bad guys with guns," as then commissioner Frederick Bealefeld, who created GTTF in 2007, said, and literally tracing the weapons back to their dealers.

It was the kind of pill-to-pusher-to-plug work Jenkins had made a name for himself doing—only with guns. A war on guns, like the war on drugs—Jenkins could get with that.

GTTF also had citywide jurisdiction, which meant that he was no longer confined to a single police district. The entire city would be his if he ran GTTF. He almost took over the unit a few years earlier, but another cop, Thomas Allers, got it instead.

In 2016, with the homicide spike and Commissioner Davis's renewed focus on Bealefeld's "bad guys with guns," Jenkins was getting hundreds of firearms off the streets a year. The whole department knew that—because Jenkins would send emails to everybody in the department telling them every time he got a gun.

As the murder rate steadily rose, command needed GTTF to do more. The unit needed to trace guns, but it also needed to be more aggressive in getting them off the streets. Jenkins, who was seizing hundreds of guns a year, could make it happen.

With GTTF, he would be able to create a sort of supergroup of grimy cops. With a corrupt crew like Danny Hersl, Jemell Rayam, and Momodu Gondo already in the unit, the deck was stacked.

It would be, Jenkins told Stepp, a "front for a criminal enterprise."

THREE

A WEEK AFTER the robbery of Oreese Stevenson, Gun Trace Task Force detective Momodu Gondo, a tall, muscular black man with a tight fade and street scholar's beard, was spending his day off in Philadelphia when he got a call from Antonio "Brill" Shropshire.

Gondo answered. Shropshire was from Gondo's old neighborhood. They'd grown up on opposite sides of the Alameda, one of the main arteries that connected the black middle-class neighborhoods near Morgan State University in Northeast Baltimore with the nearby county. They had gotten to know each other over the past few years through Kyle Wells, Gondo's closest friend. They shared a sense of fashion and both liked casinos and clubs. Shropshire was smart but erratic and sometimes careless. Like Gondo, he had been shot.

"What's up, brother?" Gondo asked.

"I got a question for you," said Shropshire, a bulky street dude with a thin beard and a big smile, who sold heroin from the gas station beside the Alameda Shopping Center, a couple of blocks from where Gondo's parents still lived.

"I'm listening," Gondo said.

"I took the car to the shop and, um, the thing was, what I heard, the thing was lit," Shropshire said.

Gondo knew what that meant—someone had placed a GPS tracker on Shropshire's car.

"What time the shop close?" Gondo asked, briefly considering an early return to Baltimore to advise.

It closed at 8:00. Not enough time to get back down to Baltimore, really.

"Just FaceTime me, yo," Gondo said.

He could get a good look at the tracker that way.

Over FaceTime, Gondo saw a small black box attached to the undercarriage of the 2016 Acura, wrapped in tinfoil. It was something he had seen many times before.

Gondo and the rest of GTTF used GPS trackers as one of the central tools of their trade.

The trackers had been in the news recently after two bandits had used one to follow a man from the downtown Baltimore casino back to the county, where they tied up the man and his wife and stole $6,000.

Shropshire didn't know whether to worry more about cops or robbers, and it wasn't like he could call 911. So he called Gondo.

Gondo was stuck in the middle, bridging two worlds—it was where he had been for much of his life, long before he became a drug-dealing cop with drug-dealing friends.

"Yeah, basically, when something like that happens, yo is basically, you know what I mean, on the other side," Gondo said to Shropshire. "You know, it's just a loss. You feel me?"

"Right," Shropshire said.

"Definitely somebody been tracking you," Gondo said. "Get rid of—"

"Ain't no question, I'm-a pop it on somebody else's car," Shropshire said. "Like a working-people car."

"Just be mindful of that, brother," Gondo said. "You definitely got to get rid of it, all right?"

. . .

SIX MONTHS EARLIER, in November 2015, Gondo and his GTTF partner, Jemell Rayam, had stuck a similar tracker up under the car of a guy they knew as "Black." Wells and Gondo, best friends for most of their lives—except for a brief period when Gondo first became a cop—were hanging out, and Wells told Gondo that this guy Black had $100,000 in his apartment. The money was there, all bundled up. They could go in and take it—easy cash that would slow down Black's crew—which, like Shropshire and Wells, catered to an ever-growing cast of white people in the county now venturing into Baltimore to score. Gondo was interested.

Wells knew that Gondo's partner, Rayam, had experience breaking into houses and suggested to Gondo that they all work together.

Wells was right about Rayam. He was a master of home invasions with a repertoire of slick moves. Rayam used to fuck with this girl who also hung out with drug dealers, and she'd leave the window open and tell him when they were out so he could slip in and take their cash. One time, he put a tracker on someone's car and then dressed like a mailman to sneak into the guy's place in the middle of the day and rob it when he knew the guy was gone. He may have been addicted to the thrill, but he also always needed the money. A thin, light-skinned black man with eyes set low and deep beneath a towering bald forehead anchored on either side by big, awkward ears, Rayam was a gambler with a bunch of kids.

When they got to Black's apartment, Rayam said they should just do a fake search warrant and be done with it.

"That way, you know, it wouldn't be any violence or anything involved, and we can just confiscate the money," Rayam said.

He'd done that a couple of months earlier when he'd robbed the owners of a bird supply store with his cousin, David Rahim, and a friend named Tom Finnegan. Rayam gave Rahim and Finnegan police vests, and they pounded on the door and the people let them in while Rayam played lookout. The two fake cops took all the cash and walked out, and that was that.

Wells didn't like Rayam's fake warrant idea.

"We just going to run up in there," Wells said.

That could mean they'd have to kill whoever was in there, and Gondo and Rayam really didn't need that kind of headache. They went back to the GTTF office, found John Clewell, a white cop in their squad who looked kind of like a grown-up Bob's Big Boy with a buzz cut, and hit him up about borrowing a tracker.

Clewell, a former marine who had served in Iraq, had off-the-books GPS trackers which could be used to get around a Supreme Court ruling that said police needed a warrant to track a car.

"Can we just use it real quick?" said Gondo, who had already lost a couple of Clewell's trackers. "We're just looking into something."

Clewell gave them the tracker, Gondo and Rayam drove back out there, and Rayam stuck the magnetic box under Black's Jeep.

For a few days, Rayam watched the tracker with an app called LiveViewGPS to get a sense of Black's routine, and then, one day when Gondo and Rayam saw that Black was out in the county, it seemed like the time was right.

Wells and Rayam would go in while Gondo stayed in the car, watching LiveViewGPS and listening to the police scanner, acting as lookout for what seemed like forever.

Finally, Wells and Rayam came running out the door and jumped into their separate cars and drove out to Gondo's house in Owings Mills, where they split up the loot.

Black hadn't been home, but some girl had been in there sleeping. Rayam stuck a gun in her face, and she told them where the cash was. There was a lot less cash than they'd thought—only $12,000—but when they broke out the scales, they had almost a kilo of heroin. Wells had someone who would buy a chunk of that right now, so he and Gondo would deal with that. Rayam could move the rest, he said.

They never retrieved Clewell's tracker off Black's car.

IF GONDO WAS worried about either of the trackers, it wasn't because of anyone in BPD. His sergeant, Thomas Allers, a white guy with a mullet and a Fu Manchu mustache who did a goofy gun dance every time GTTF seized a weapon, had been in charge of the GTTF since 2013 and had stolen enough money with Gondo and Rayam that he couldn't say much.

And then there was Danny Hersl, a tall white cop with a bony bald head, the erratic eyes of a teenage bully, and the breath of a heavy drinker. Hersl had been a terror in East Baltimore, where he allegedly planted drugs, stole cash, and bashed people's heads for years. As he racked up Internal Affairs complaints, Hersl's reputation on the streets only grew. It was almost mythical. People called him "Put It on 'Em" and said he planted guns and drugs on people he didn't like.

Hersl became even more notorious when a rapper named Young Moose started recording diss tracks about him: "Detective Hersl, he a bitch, I swear to god he ain't right/ Heard about my rap career, he trying to fuck up my life," Moose rapped on the song "Tired" from 2015.

The word on Hersl had spread and suddenly, after a career in the Eastern District, Hersl was transferred out of his beloved district and into the GTTF at the end of 2015.

Gondo didn't fully trust Hersl. He wasn't really worried about him either.

And Rayam—Gondo trusted him with his life. They told each other everything.

"Fuck it, I just didn't want to chase him," Gondo recalled Rayam saying about a man he shot and killed in 2009.

"You know you murdered that dude?" Gondo replied.

As Gondo heard it, Colonel Dean Palmere had come on the scene and coached Rayam and the other cops there about what to say: Sean Cannady, the victim, was going to run over Rayam's partner, and Rayam had no choice but to shoot him. It was one of three shootings Rayam was involved in that year.

Rayam was not punished for the Cannady shooting. He was awarded the Silver Star.

Early in his career, a couple of guys shot Gondo out in front of his parents' house. The department turned it into part of a war on cops. Rayam understood it as a drug beef. The streets were way harder. Gondo wasn't worried about no police.

He was police.

WAYNE JENKINS LOOKED bloated, bored, and above it all as he watched Commissioner Kevin Davis from the audience at BPD's Meritorious Conduct Awards Ceremony on April 21, 2016.

Jenkins's Class A dress uniform was a little too big on him, stiff and awkward, so different from the Henleys and T-shirts on top of long-sleeved tees he usually wore to work. He was out of place. If he was going to get promoted, he'd have to get used to it. It was better than the khakis and polos they'd tried to make plainclothes wear. Just another part of what Jenkins called the "gay training" ushered in by the previous commissioner, Anthony Batts.

Jenkins saw his mentors up there on the stage. Sean Miller, a bald and severe ops commander who watched out for Jenkins and ran the War Room. Beside him, Darryl De Sousa, who'd helped Jenkins with his IAD issues in 2014. And Deputy Commissioner Dean Palmere, slumped back in his seat, manspreading.

Palmere was a dour-faced and cold-eyed white man who oversaw units like SES and GTTF and ran them like a counterinsurgency. He had survived a number of administrations, and after

Commissioner Davis took over the department from Anthony Batts in July 2015, Davis gave Palmere more power. On Davis's first day, there was a meeting of all plainclothes squads, and Palmere stood before all the squads and told them the gloves were off.

"The days of Batts are over," Palmere said that day. "It's time to go out there and do what you know how to do."

Today, Davis, who had empowered the godfather of plainclothes Palmere, stood up on the stage dipping his toes in change-agent language that came out of what some called the "Baltimore Uprising," and most referred to as the "Baltimore Riots."

"So after last April and May, after the unrest, I think you look at every aspect of the city," Davis said as the ceremony began. "After we endured that very unique time in our city's history, we wanted to make sure that their voice was still heard and their contributions were still recognized."

A unique time in our city's history. The unrest. To the cops in the room, they had been attacked on April 27, 2015, turned upon by the citizens, and betrayed by Batts, an arrogant academic from Oakland, who told them to "stand down," and by the mayor, Stephanie Rawlings-Blake, who said she would give Baltimore "space to destroy."

Fuck all that. Now at least they knew who their friends were. Batts was fired. Rawlings-Blake wasn't even running for reelection. Yet here in front of a bunch of cops and their families and supporters, Davis was still not able to say *riot*. He sounded like a liberal. They knew Davis had to sound like that. The DOJ was watching everything they did. Nobody knew whom to trust. Jenkins's mentor Gladstone was being sued for grabbing a protester wearing a FUCK THE POLICE shirt and slamming him to the pavement by his dreadlocks.

A lot of people in the room thought that if someone like Trump got in, all this cop-hating and political correctness and gay training bullshit might go away.

"We're simply just taking a moment to recognize your contributions and just say, 'Thank you,'" Davis said.

Around 150 cops were injured on April 27, 2015, including GTTF's sergeant, Allers. Jenkins and a couple of other cops had rushed right into the chaos to rescue some of them. They would hand him a Bronze Star for it today.

"They were confronted with gridlocked traffic, scared motorists, and violent and aggressive protesters," a captain handing out awards said. "They then commandeered a then unused city van, solicited volunteers to assist in the recovery and aid of the injured officers, and made their way through the chaos as they were being bombarded with bricks, rocks, and other flying debris."

Jenkins was being rewarded for acting rashly and taking a city van, because it had been a time of crisis. He walked across the stage in his stiff uniform, eyes covered by his hat, took the award, grinned quickly, then froze for a photo with Davis, who smiled, while Jenkins turned blank and opened his eyes more, an actor's approximation of kindness. After the flash, Jenkins turned to Davis, grinned again, shook the commissioner's hand, nodded, thanked him, and walked off the stage.

The Baltimore Police Department knew only half the story. Donny Stepp knew the rest.

The fires were still burning on the night of the riot when Jenkins called Stepp.

Stepp knew this must be serious. Jenkins had been dropping off dope at Stepp's house on a nearly nightly basis since back in 2012, when they celebrated their new partnership with a trip to New Orleans to watch their beloved Ravens win the Super Bowl. Jenkins usually just dropped stuff off, locked the door, and left, without waking Stepp. He didn't call unless it was serious.

Jenkins, still smelling of acrid riot smoke, pulled his unmarked police car into Stepp's shed and took two trash bags from the trunk.

"I just got people coming out of these pharmacies," Jenkins told Stepp. "I've got an entire pharmacy. I don't even know what it is."

Jenkins and Stepp began digging through the bags of stolen pills, googling the name or the numbers stamped on the side of each pill. A lot of it turned out to be junk—only worth something if you have the ailment it was intended to treat. They threw all that away and kept what Stepp could move. Viagra and Cialis were the biggest sellers. For some of Stepp's county customers, they went nicely with coke.

Commissioner Batts later blamed the stolen pharmaceuticals for the steep uptick in murders right after the riot. He said the influx of pilfered pills was enough "to keep [Baltimore] intoxicated for a year."

Stepp knew, if anything, the stolen pills kept the county hard for a few weeks.

WITH EVERY REPLAY of the most dramatic footage of the city burning and all the "one year later" commentary, panels, and think pieces, everyone in Baltimore was reliving their own personal version of 2015's trauma, including Ivan Bates. The cases against the Six were set to start moving forward again.

Bates had always rooted for the underdog. It was why he'd become a defense attorney. He was a prosecutor, until a judge, noting how he humanized defendants, suggested that Bates switch sides. Practicing law as a defense attorney could be a kind of protest. Defending the Fourth Amendment during the course of Baltimore's vicious drug war felt, at times, especially radical.

Bates knew Baltimore's rage against police well, but he didn't expect to see the city in flames. He had just flown into San Francisco where he was defending a former Baltimore DEA agent who had been accused of stealing millions of dollars in Bitcoin cryptocurrency in the Silk Road online drug market case. He was checking into his hotel on the day of Freddie Gray's funeral, and the woman at the desk asked him where he was from.

"Baltimore," he said.

"Oh my God, your city is on fire," she said and pointed to the television playing CNN's footage of the CVS burning at the corner of North and Pennsylvania Avenues and the skirmishes between high school students and lines of riot police outside of Mondawmin Mall. It was strange to see it like that. He knew that corner. The news made it seem like the entire city was on fire.

A couple of days later, he was back in Baltimore, being interviewed live on CNN by Don Lemon during the curfew that had been imposed on the citizens after the riot. Bates said that many neighborhoods were like "military zones," in the sense that the police are always there.

"They're asking you questions. They want to stop you. They want to detain you. They want you to give ID in your own neighborhood," Bates said. "If we did that in other neighborhoods in this country, there would be an uproar."

The next morning, Bates sat in his office and watched a livestream of Marilyn Mosby on the steps of the city's War Memorial building announcing charges against six officers for the death of Gray.

Mosby began to read the statement of probable cause, detailing the way that two bike cops saw Freddie Carlos Gray Jr. and chased him when he started running, even though there was no legal reason to do so. She detailed several different stops the van made on its way to Central Booking, multiple times where officers could have called for help and did not.

"Sergeant White, who is responsible for investigating two citizen complaints pertaining to Mr. Gray's illegal arrest, spoke to the back of Mr. Gray's head," Mosby said, working her way through the charges. "When he did not respond, she did nothing further despite the fact that she was advised that he needed a medic. She made no effort to look or assess or determine his condition."

Mosby was still speaking when Bates's phone rang. On the other end, a woman, weeping, and almost screaming as she gasped for breath, "That's not true! That's not true. I tried to help him."

It was Alicia White. Mosby had just charged her with manslaughter on live television.

Bates knew of White from back when he represented the Vanguard Association, an association of black officers, which sued the department for its policy that prohibited black officers from wearing their hair in locks. He told White to come to his office immediately.

White was a community liaison. She didn't even make arrests. She was there that day only to investigate the complaints citizens immediately made against the officers for their handling of Gray as they pulled him into the police van, screaming. She saw Gray only at the very last stop, while other white cops, who were far more involved, were not charged at all.

As the small, black woman with short hair sat across from him in the conference room, explaining what had happened, it was hard for Bates to understand exactly why White had been charged. He asked her questions in the way he would ask them on the stand, tough and seeking contradictions. She told the same story again and again.

Bates came out of the conference room and went into his office, where he looked at the racist tobacco ad hanging on his wall and then looked at the black-and-white Thurgood Marshall photograph. He'd been waiting all his life for what he thought of as his "Thurgood Marshall case," which would change everything. He'd imagined he would be defending a poor black kid who had been framed by crooked cops and had no other options. Instead, it looked like he would be defending a cop who had been charged with killing a poor black kid who didn't have any other options.

He would take the case. Not because White was a police officer but because she was black. In his mind, she was like all the other black women who had walked into his office knowing that the system was stacked against them.

The rest of the world did not see it that way.

His old Howard University friends started saying that he was a sellout and asked him why he was representing the cops.

"I'm not representing cops. I'm representing the people, like I always have," he said.

"No, you're not. She's representing the people," they would say.

She was Marilyn Mosby, of course, a prosecutor whose job was putting people in jail—the people Bates defended. She was in charge of the State's Attorney's Office, which Bates believed was regularly looking the other way at misconduct from cops like Wayne Jenkins.

Old friends called him an Uncle Tom. Online it was worse. One night, on the couch, he broke down, manic and distraught. He just couldn't understand. His wife, Lana, calmed him down, and he went back to work the next day and kept up the fight.

While Bates defended one cop, he began preparing to go up against another one. Alicia White was a case. Wayne Jenkins was a cause.

ON APRIL 27, the one-year anniversary of the riot, a Baltimore cop shot a fourteen-year-old kid who was carrying what turned out to be a BB gun. The timing could not have been worse and the optics were terrible, but Commissioner Davis twisted a situation where a teen was shot by cops on the anniversary of the riots into a story about how BB guns that looked real needed to be banned. Then he blamed the shooting on the teen's mother, who let him outside in the first place.

"This has nothing to do with police-community relations,"

Davis said. "This is a police response to a person seen in broad daylight with a gun in his hand in the middle of the street."

The next morning, April 28, GTTF was out early, ready to get some guns. Gondo, Rayam, Allers, Clewell, and Hersl waited in the damp fog, watching the front door of the townhome.

Rayam had gotten a tip that Davon Robinson, the guy who lived there, had guns. Rayam ran a background check and saw that Robinson's license was suspended, so the minute Robinson got in his car, they could stop him and arrest him for driving with a suspended license. Then they could try to get into his house and find the guns and see what else was lying around.

Around 9:30 A.M., Robinson got into his car. GTTF followed him out of the neighborhood so no one would see that he'd been stopped and get rid of any guns, cash, or drugs he had inside the house.

Allers flashed his lights and pulled Robinson over. Robinson didn't have a license on him, so they identified him through a database, ticketed him for driving on a suspended license, and detained him.

Then GTTF drove back to Robinson's house. They didn't have a warrant, and they weren't going to try to get one. They knew what he had and figured they could lean on his girlfriend to let them inside.

They pounded on the townhome's door. Robinson's girlfriend answered. Hersl asked for permission to search the house. Robinson's girlfriend agreed.

Hersl handed her a consent form for the search and stuck his phone in her face as she signed it and they entered. He didn't need to record video—the signature was enough—but it helped everything look extra legitimate. If everyone else was filming police, they'd start filming too.

In the upstairs bedroom, Rayam found the guns—two 9mms, including one with the serial number removed, and a bunch of ammo. He also spotted $10,000 in cash in a drawer. After the crew arrested Robinson for the handguns and ammunition, Rayam re-entered the house, took the $10,000, and split it up with Gondo and Allers.

They didn't share the money with Clewell—because they never shared with Clewell—or Hersl.

Allers didn't trust Hersl yet, he told Rayam.

It was less ambitious than Jenkins's Oreese Stevenson heist, but the MO was not all that different—pull someone over, gain access to their home, use video, seize evidence, steal money, charge them for the guns, and move right along, knowing full well that a drug dealer facing gun charges wouldn't report the missing cash.

Allers was on his way out of GTTF. At the end of May, an opportunity to join a DEA task force opened up, and Allers took it. There, he would listen to wiretaps, off the streets and safe.

Command decided Jenkins would take over the squad. Jenkins's SES crew would be absorbed into a new and improved GTTF, and Jenkins would have a supergroup of dirty cops at his disposal. To his current team of corrupt and mutable followers, Jenkins would add notorious bruiser Hersl, habitual thief Rayam, and, perhaps most interesting of all, Gondo, whom Jenkins considered the biggest drug dealer in the department.

With a little guidance from Jenkins, the Gun Trace Task Force could do great things.

FOUR

JENKINS BROUGHT HIS old SES crew together with the Gun Trace Task Force for their first meeting. It was June 13, and SES was in the process of moving its stuff from "the barn," a satellite building by the police training academy where they had their offices, to the GTTF office on the seventh floor of police headquarters.

"He wanted to lay down the rules and how he wants to run the unit. He expected everyone to work, be honest, if you have a family or emergency to let him know, if you're going to be late to let him know, things along that effect," recalled Taylor, who looked down on the guys who were already in the GTTF, since they didn't risk their lives chasing down armed suspects in dark alleys every night like he did.

Gondo made a show of not listening to Jenkins during the meeting. Because he was a young black man with money, people like Jenkins assumed that he must be a drug dealer. It was ridiculous because Jenkins, who was the kind of hyped-up white cop convinced he was close enough to the streets to throw the word *nigga* around, was way cruddier than Gondo anyway. Jenkins and Gondo had even robbed together—they'd stolen $1,800 from a guy they'd chased back in 2011. And now Jenkins was his boss.

After the meeting, Jenkins approached Gondo.

"Yo, Gondo, you ain't even come over to listen, man," Jenkins said.

Gondo thought Jenkins had been talking shit.

Jenkins told Gondo he didn't say nothing.

When Gondo didn't believe him, Jenkins said his words had been misconstrued.

Gondo still wasn't having it. But they shook hands—Gondo had no other choice.

The next morning, Gondo was still stewing over the conversation with Jenkins and called Ward. They'd known each other for a few years, and, as youngish, hip-ish black men who were also cops at a time when those two identities were especially hard to reconcile, Gondo and Ward hung out together and confided in each other. Ward knew that Gondo and Jenkins had robbed together before, and Ward had told Gondo about the Oreese Stevenson heist. He did not tell Gondo that he threw $20,000 into the woods.

"Yo, old boy, he definitely know how to lie to a nigga, huh?" Gondo said.

"I told you he was going to try to smooth it out," Ward said.

"Jesus Christ, yo. Come in there, yo, the way he thought I really was going to walk over there, Ward, and listen to what he had to say, yo," Gondo said.

Ward told Gondo how Jenkins characterized it: "'We squashed it. We shook hands at the end, so we all good,'" Ward said.

"We'll see how that shit goes, man," Gondo said. "But that dude looked at me, lied to my face, man."

"Yo, that's just, that's the type of nigga he is," Ward said. "That's how he did me when me and him got into it."

Gondo emitted a deep belly laugh. "Yo, that nigga something else," Gondo said. "If he kept it in the office, but yo. Nigga's gonna talk again. He want everything to be smoothed out at once. Come on, it don't work like that."

"Especially when it's all because of him," Ward said. "It's his fault."

"Right, talking about 'words got misconstrued,'" Gondo said. "Nigga, please."

"First it went from him not saying nothing to, 'It got misconstrued,'" Ward said. "Get the fuck outta here."

"Yo, he's funny as shit, yo," Gondo said. "Wayne is something else."

Ward told Gondo how he had been softened up by the overtime money he was bringing home regularly under Jenkins's command.

"He don't like to come in on time, yo. He'll come in late every day, yo," Ward said.

The way it worked was, Jenkins would send a group text to the squad, saying break off your investigation and meet me at headquarters at whatever time, and that's when they'd come to work.

Ward explained to Gondo that today was a good example.

"His wife's got a doctor's appointment, so he probably gonna try to come in that bitch until like 2:00, 3:00, and be like, 'Anyone want to work overtime or you can go ahead home,' or some shit like that," Ward said.

Gondo laughed. Ward explained that Jenkins met with GTTF's Lieutenant Christopher O'Ree the night before and the overtime budget had opened back up thanks to Commissioner Davis, who was desperately trying to motivate the cops.

"Bangin' our overtime shit," Ward said.

When they hung up, Gondo called Rayam to tell him what he'd learned.

"He always want to come in late and make shit on the back end," Gondo said.

"I can rock with that," Rayam said.

"That nigga say, 'Y'all can work whenever y'all want to work,'" Gondo said.

"That's what's up, then," Rayam said.

"Just passing the word, brother," Gondo said. "Get that check, man."

GONDO DIDN'T SHOW up for the new GTTF's first raid on June 15. Rayam, Hersl, and Clewell got the guy dirty in his car, and Hersl and Rayam waited on the porch while Clewell went for a warrant to search his house.

"Hey, if there's any money, you know, we'll split it," Rayam said. Hersl agreed. It was no big deal for either of them.

Clewell returned with Jenkins, Hendrix, Ward, and Taylor to execute the warrant. Ransacking the house together, GTTF found weed, coke, heroin, two pistols, and a massive rifle with banana clips.

"I figured, you know, it should be money in there," Rayam said. "But I didn't find any."

There was always the possibility that one of the new guys had found the cash first and not cut them in. Even if they didn't get any money, Jenkins's new unit gained glory in the form of news coverage.

"Guns and Drugs Seized in Southwest Baltimore Raid," the local CBS affiliate declared the next morning with a photo of all the dope and guns laid out on a table.

The new GTTF was already making BPD look good.

AT AN IN-SERVICE training, Jenkins ran into Ryan Guinn, his old partner, who told him to watch out for Gondo and Rayam. Guinn had worked with both of them in GTTF back in 2013.

In December 2015, the FBI had come to ask Guinn about Rayam and Gondo. When Guinn heard that Jenkins took over the squad, he figured he ought to say something to his former partner.

That warning didn't stop Jenkins from stealing with Gondo

and Rayam a week into his new post as their sergeant. On June 24, Jenkins, Gondo, Rayam, Hendrix, and Ward entered Milton Miller's row house in East Baltimore and forced him to show them where he kept his money. In Miller's bedroom, they found a shoebox with $10,000 stuffed in it. They sent him downstairs and stole $2,000. They also found $15,000 in a boot along with fifty grams of heroin. They took the money and left the heroin.

A few days later, Jenkins called Gondo, who was with Rayam at an auto shop in South Baltimore. The two were trying to get some additional police lights put on an unmarked car. Jenkins mentioned "some fuckin' ballers" he was up on and suggested getting together to do "some street ripping" later on.

"We over here right across from the Ravens' stadium now trying to get these lights in," Gondo said.

"Oh, you found somebody to do it?" Jenkins asked.

"Yeah, we did, man, but I mean, we strikin' out," Gondo said.

"How much they want?" Jenkins asked.

"They talkin' like four or five hundred," Gondo said.

"Man, tell them bitches three hundred cash, it's for the police," Jenkins said. "And they get a get-out-of-jail-free card with my boss's phone number."

Gondo laughed hard.

"Right. This is a legitimate business, though. They saying, I think they can't even do it, though, they talking to Rayam now, they saying they can't do it," Gondo said.

"Man, there ain't no legitimate business anywhere," Jenkins said.

"Right," Gondo said dutifully.

"Lazy motherfuckers," Jenkins said. "Tell them we about to drop a case on 'em."

THAT NIGHT, THE new GTTF got together for a series of door pops.

A little after midnight, two GTTF cars—Jenkins, Clewell, and

Hersl in one, Gondo and Rayam in another—rolled down Baltimore's historic Pennsylvania Avenue not far from where Freddie Gray was grabbed, looking for groups to roll up on and grab anybody who ran.

"A couple of nights a week, we would just go out to hot areas, we would drive around," Hersl recalled. "There are certain hot spots in certain areas where they're pretty well known for drug activity and violence is pretty high, so we drive around them areas— kind of go hunting, see what we can get into."

A group of black men were hanging out near a corner store, some against the wall and one sitting on a bus stop bench emblazoned with *Baltimore: The Greatest City in America*.

Jenkins whipped a manic turn and pulled up to the curb. Clewell popped the door, scattering the group, moving targets running in all directions.

Someone in a white T-shirt rushed around the corner, and Clewell went after him, but he was too fast and Clewell lost him. Clewell was no Taylor. From the back seat of the car, Hersl saw another man dart the other way, holding his waistband like he was trying to stop a gun from slipping through his pants.

Clewell went after the man, and Jenkins and Hersl followed in the car. This was the whole door-pop concept—one guy jumps out and runs, the car follows behind, always ready to speed up or send a second runner into the chase.

Hersl hopped out and ran with Clewell. When the suspect leaped off a retaining wall, a gun fell out on the ground and Clewell grabbed it.

The door pop was a new strategy for the GTTF, which had been an investigative unit that didn't waste time running around the streets. They served warrants, and this was beneath them. And it was unconstitutional. But numbers were numbers. They got three more guns that night with door pops.

Under Jenkins, GTTF became a hybrid of SES hard-charging,

street-level enforcement and GTTF intelligence-gathering investigation.

An informant Allers had used noticed the shift in the unit. Jenkins sounded more like a dealer than a cop, even throwing the word *nigga* around in front of him. Before an undercover gun buy, the informant, a heroin user, told Jenkins he had to "get right," and asked to be driven somewhere with a bathroom where he could shoot up.

He said Jenkins told him he could do it right there in front of him in the car.

DAVON ROBINSON WAS posted up in the very back of a Baltimore City courtroom at 11:05 in the morning on July 1, his arms stretched across an old wooden bench, waiting for his arraignment.

The fact that the cops stole from him that April morning had already caused plenty of problems. Being $10,000 short slowed just about all his moves down. He had to pay money back to some people, including his plug, who'd heard he had gotten locked up, though that excuse never went too far, especially because in Robinson's case, the police report didn't say anything about seized money.

"Pull your pants all the way up too, please," the judge said to Robinson.

"They is," Robinson said back.

"I don't want to see your underwear," the judge said.

"I apologize," Robinson said.

Robinson sighed and sat down. All the defendants were called to the front of the courtroom. Robinson was the youngest and the most underdressed. All the men were black, except for one man in a pointy-collared dress shirt and jeans who didn't speak any English.

Robinson stepped forward first. He held his baseball cap in his hand and listened to his charges read aloud, six counts in total: Gun possession was a maximum sentence of fifteen years and a mandatory minimum sentence of five years. Because he was a felon, that added more years. The ammo could add another year. Scraping the serial number off the gun could add another year.

"And how do you plead, sir?" the judge asked.

"Not guilty," Robinson said.

"Not guilty on all charges. And do you wish to have a jury trial?" the judge asked.

"Yeah," Robinson said.

Robinson got his court date, signed the court summons, and left. It was all over by 11:20 A.M.

AROUND NOON THAT same day, Rayam called Gondo, geeked up about overtime. It was a Friday, payday.

"A nigga's check was over four grand," Rayam said.

"Who, yours? Damn!" Gondo said.

"I mean, like, it's damn near forty-two, forty-three hundred, yo."

"So you damn near almost doubled the shit you did this go-around," Gondo said, calculating.

"I'm gonna at least get $13,000 this month," Rayam said.

"Listen, man, these niggas been doing this shit, yo, just imagine," Gondo said.

"I don't think I'm ever going to be a sergeant, yo, as long as this nigga Wayne here," Rayam said. "I can't be a sergeant and make this much money, fuck this. I'm chilling."

"I mean they said one time they had a hundred hours and Wayne's check was like eight or nine thousand and their checks was like six or seven, something like that," Gondo said.

"Imagine bringing out that—we could have made $6,000 or $7,000 and all your problems go away," Rayam said.

"I mean, yo, I mean he, he got a method to his madness, he off the chain, but them niggas stay because of that money, yo," Gondo said.

"Yeah, like I'm saying, let's enjoy it now, get it hard now because all good things come to an end. That nigga's off the chain, yo," Rayam said.

"He's off the fuckin' chain, B," Gondo said. "It's like, it's like, it's like giving your daughter the keys to the car, yo, and saying, 'Drive that bitch right now,' that's how bad he is."

"Like giving my eight-year-old the keys to the car, like, 'Hey, you drive,'" Rayam said. "'I'm drunk, get me home.'"

Gondo and Rayam laughed for too long, and then Rayam got to business. The Southwest District put him on a snitch who said that Ronald Hamilton, a major cocaine dealer back in the '90s, was still at it and had dope and guns. They planned to put a GPS tracker on his truck.

"That shit ready to go, brother," Gondo said.

AROUND 3:00 P.M., Davon Robinson sat in his car on the West side when a man drove up, pulled a hood over his face, and fired at Robinson, hitting him in the head and the chest. Robinson's girlfriend and their four-year-old daughter saw the whole thing.

Robinson was pronounced dead at the scene at 3:19 P.M. It was homicide number 139 of 2016—a year that ended with 319 homicides. Robinson's obituary provided a loving portrait of the father of three, nicknamed "Wooda," and along the way, a portrait of a whole generation of Baltimoreans—young men brashly riding dirt bikes through the city, passing the transgressive tradition on to others, and blasting the music of yelping, diaristic Baton Rouge rapper Lil Boosie, a hero in a city where joy and pain are never too far from each other and often intersect. In photos, Robinson flashes a smile, giving up a glimpse of his gold fronts.

"Wooda had a smile like no other and a tight pocket that a mouse couldn't get in, but Wooda had a heart of gold," the obituary reads.

FIVE

SHORTLY AFTER HE took over GTTF, Wayne Jenkins started to target Gondo's friend Kyle Wells. Wells had been telling Gondo about Jenkins's antics for a while.

Jenkins was running wild, out of control. Gondo heard the same kind of things from Ward.

"We had several high-speed chases every day," Ward said. "When he chased cars, he always had tunnel vision, and we would have to physically shake or hit him to make him come out of it."

Now that Gondo was working with Jenkins, he saw for himself and saw that his boss was targeting his best friend.

"He normally targeted people for money in, like, robberies. So I didn't want him to target my childhood friend and rob him, or, you know, I'll be stuck in between, because I was working for him. He was my supervisor," Gondo said. "So I just tried to alleviate it by letting Kyle know what was going on."

When Gondo cruised around with Rayam, he called Jenkins to try to figure out where he was and passed that information to Wells. He also called and texted Ward, who would drop a pin on the iPhone map that signaled the precise location of Jenkins's car.

"That is some straight, like, off-the-wall-type shit," Gondo said when Wells described Jenkins's tactics.

"Yeah, he's on a different wave," Wells said.

"A whole different wave," Gondo said.

They joked and called Jenkins "Stew Love," a cheesy soul singer–like nickname they'd given him, comparing him to someone who is horny, out of control.

"Like a Rottweiler with the pink thing hanging out," Wells said. "Must be working. Crashes and all that shit. Give you what you looking for."

Jenkins was texting Wells, pretending to be someone looking for dope.

"Bitch put me on you," Jenkins's first text read.

The awkward *bitch,* the inconsistent use of the catchall Baltimore pronoun *yo,* and a fast-and-loose approach to emoji skin tone made Wells suspicious. And the number Jenkins texted from wouldn't let him call it back.

"Man, look, do you know who you are talkin' to?" Wells asked.

"Yo like, man yeah yo, I'm talking to yo with the dreads," Jenkins wrote back. "I met you at the gas station, you told me to hit the phone. I'm trying to get straight."

Wells sent a screenshot of the texts to Gondo. "That sounds like Stew Love, yo," Gondo texted.

"The language, the black emojis, just being around him, you know, how he talks, just trying to talk slang, you know," Gondo said. "That's just something I picked up on and believed it was him."

Gondo and Wells had never talked about Jenkins being racist. "We didn't need to," Wells recalled. "There's not a clear delineation between racist and cop doing his job."

Gondo knew this. He was disgusted with the department's response to Freddie Gray and talked to Wells about how he didn't "sign up to be an enemy of his own people."

Wells and Gondo kept their distance after Gondo joined BPD, saying little more than "hi" and "bye" until 2006, when Gondo got shot. Wells came to visit him in the hospital, and the two reconnected.

Wells's connection with Gondo didn't really protect him from other cops—and it might have made things worse. In 2012, Wells had just dropped off his daughter at school one morning when a car pulled up and tried to block him in. He thought it was a robbery. Then he saw Jenkins behind the wheel and fled. Jenkins chased him without ever turning on his lights or his sirens, and Wells escaped.

When Jenkins cornered Wells again later that year, another cop recognized Wells from a party at Gondo's and quietly asked Wells if he should call Gondo. Wells had a small amount of coke on him and about $4,000 in cash. He said Jenkins took it all and didn't arrest him, at the other cop's request. Jenkins seemed pissed about it. Before letting Wells go, Jenkins asked what he'd missed that day Wells outran him.

In 2014, Jenkins and two other cops rolled up on Wells for nothing. They came the wrong way up a one-way street as he sat in the car. They said they smelled Wells's small bag of unburned weed even though his windows were rolled up. When they searched the car, they said they found a gun hidden in the mechanism that allowed the seat to slide back. Wells was denied bail. He had recently been shot, and he had a colostomy bag and did seven months on that charge with the bag and all, only to be found not guilty when it went to court.

And now, Jenkins was coming after him again. Gondo told Wells that he thought Jenkins knew they were friends and was using Wells to get to Gondo.

"I was to be collateral damage," Wells recalled.

Gondo promised Wells he would confront Jenkins and get him to back off.

He also sent Rayam the screenshot of the texts, just to make sure.

Rayam was shocked that Jenkins's hunt for Wells had progressed so far. Gondo was going to deal with Jenkins directly. He had to say something to Ward first.

"You basically know that Wayne's not right," Gondo told Ward. "You shouldn't be a part of that."

WARD GOT DAILY reminders that Jenkins was not right. Recently, they boxed in a man in front of a sub shop, charged him with a gun and took $550 and his cell phone. Jenkins used the phone to text the man's girl, pretending to be the man, first hoping to get her to say something incriminating, and then, when that went nowhere, he asked her to send naked pictures.

That's how Jenkins was with his old SES—small stuff, played for stats and thrills.

While the old squad was doing door pops and car stops and Jenkins was doing his digital blackface routine, Gondo and Rayam had been prepping to take down Ronald Hamilton, a target they had been working for weeks.

Hamilton was a big name with a history from way back. Federal agents said he was "the person who controlled most of the drug trafficking in West and Southwest Baltimore City and county" in the late '90s, and he did almost a decade in federal prison after state police intercepted a four-pound pack of blow sent in a refrigerator from California to Baltimore. They found more cocaine inside his house, along with almost a half million dollars in a gym bag.

In prison, Hamilton demanded the government return the $496,000 they had seized from him, filing the paperwork himself and suing the DEA, though to no avail. When federal sentencing guidelines for drugs changed, he also filed his own motion to reduce his sentence and won. He got out early in 2009 and was soon back in it, caught with someone else's ID at the airport and connected to fifteen kilograms of coke coming his way. He pleaded guilty to conspiracy and was locked up until 2013.

"He at this big-ass mansion with a pool in the backyard," Rayam told Gondo.

"I'm down for it, but I would wait, especially to see where he takes his profit," Gondo said.

They sent Clewell to watch some properties Hamilton co-owned in Southwest Baltimore, a few ragged row houses on Fairmount Avenue that they thought might be a "dope strip," and Rayam sneaked a GPS tracker on Hamilton's truck.

"I used that as my eyes and not me physically being there," Rayam recalled. "I was actually using a tracker that I didn't have a warrant for, basically using—it was illegal—to track Mr. Hamilton's whereabouts and to get a pattern for where he was at."

A lean, wiry man in his forties with kind eyes and a menacing swagger, Hamilton darted around Baltimore and the surrounding counties, sewing up used car sales and, Rayam speculated, making coke deals.

Hamilton often ended his evenings at the Maryland Live! Casino about twelve miles outside of Baltimore on the way to D.C. They also stopped his truck one night but found a friend at the wheel, driving the truck back from an auction where Hamilton had bought a car. Hamilton was either smart enough to know he was being watched, or he really wasn't doing anything illegal.

That's when Jenkins stepped in.

Jenkins told Rayam that he saw Hamilton get out of his car with a bag and hand it to a man in a black Honda with New York plates late one night on a side street in Baltimore.

"Man, I know it was money in there or something big in there," Jenkins told Rayam. "I felt like just hitting him and taking the bag."

Rayam finally wrote up the warrant, based mostly on GPS locations. The whole warrant was mostly fiction. Based on what was presented to him, a judge signed the warrant for Hamilton's properties in Baltimore and a seven-bedroom, six-bathroom home Hamilton and his wife, Nancy, had just purchased in Westminster, wide-open cow country in Carroll County, forty-five minutes from Baltimore.

. . .

THE HAMILTONS HAD closed on the half-million-dollar house in late June, putting $17,000 down on the $535,800 mortgage. It had been in foreclosure and it needed some work, and the couple were going to meet a contractor at Home Depot on July 8 in the afternoon to talk repairs, discuss interior decorating, and buy some blinds.

When the Hamiltons arrived at the store, Rayam, who had been watching the app as Hamilton drove around that morning, was ready to make the takedown.

Rayam, Gondo, Hersl, and Clewell drove out to the store with instructions to call Jenkins once they'd pulled Hamilton over.

The Hamiltons strolled through the DIY superstore, the smell of cut wood in the air, shopping-friendly pop whispering from speakers up above. In a long labyrinthine aisle full of kitchen and bathroom fixtures, Hamilton noticed a man staring at him. The man was tall and his arms were strong and his bald head and dead eyes were hard to miss.

When the Hamiltons moved over to the blinds, a maze of eye-level displays showing off wood shades, solar shades, roller shades, and jalousies, the bald man was behind them again.

"Man, that guy is staring at, like, a product for about twenty minutes, just looking," Hamilton said to Nancy.

Hamilton got nervous and decided to split.

"We pull them over, bring them back to the academy, that's per Sergeant Jenkins," Rayam said over the radio to Hersl and Clewell when he got back in the car.

"All right, I got you," Clewell said, following as Hamilton's truck pulled out of Home Depot.

When the Hamiltons pulled into a neighboring shopping center, the two unmarked GTTF cars sped up and blocked Hamilton's truck in.

"Get out the car," Rayam told Hamilton. "Where your money at?"

Rayam dragged Hamilton out of his truck, shoved him up against a car, pulled $3,400 out of Hamilton's pocket, and stuffed it in his tactical vest.

Nancy was hauled out of the truck, handcuffed, and put in Clewell's car. She believed they were crooks impersonating cops.

She was only half-wrong.

"WHAT'S GOING ON?" Hamilton, handcuffed, asked Gondo from the back seat.

"Oh, that's not my investigation. I don't know what's going on," Gondo said calmly from the driver's seat.

"What's going on?" Hamilton said again.

"I don't know," Gondo said.

They all drove off.

Gondo called Jenkins.

"We got, um, we got the package," Gondo said.

"Is he in the car with you?" Jenkins said.

"Yeah, I got the male, they got the female," Gondo said.

"Did you tell him anything at all?" Jenkins said.

"No," Gondo said.

"Then tell him you gotta wait for the U.S. Attorney," Jenkins said.

"Yeah, we wanna meet up with you, and we wanna talk before anything," Gondo said.

"And when I get there, treat me like I'm the fuckin' U.S. Attorney. Like 'Hey, sir, how are you, we got a, our target in pocket,'" Jenkins said.

"Got you," Gondo said.

"And then introduce me as the U.S. Attorney," Jenkins said.

"I got you," Gondo said.

"All right, dog," Jenkins said.

They drove the Hamiltons to the police training facility in the Park Heights neighborhood, a blighted black part of town bumping into a Jewish suburb and ignored by much of the city for most of the year except for when the Preakness horse race comes through.

The training building used to be an elementary and middle school until it closed after the 2007 school year due to low enrollment, and Baltimore did what it often does—it transferred resources from schools to police. Now police used it to train cops, plainclothes units used it as a satellite office, and a gray trailer near the building that cops called "the barn" was something like a black site, right there in plain sight, where they sometimes did interrogations.

They took Hamilton inside the barn and left Nancy Hamilton with Clewell.

"I'm Detective Jenkins with the U.S. Attorney's Office," Jenkins said. "I'm a federal agent."

Jenkins told Hamilton they had enough evidence to convict him on federal charges.

"Okay, well, just take me down to the federal courthouse," Hamilton said.

"You don't tell me what the hell to do," Jenkins said, before pushing the fabrication further. "We got you under three controlled buys."

"Man, that's a lie," Hamilton said.

Hamilton thought he would probably get the shit beat out of him if he resisted, so he hardened up, contained his rage, and didn't say much.

Jenkins asked Hamilton if he had any guns or drugs at his house. Hamilton said he didn't. He did have money, entirely legitimate money, he insisted.

"We got you," Jenkins said.

He hit Hamilton up for the names of dealers.

"I ain't doing nothing," Hamilton insisted.

Gondo and Rayam took Hamilton outside and put him into their car with Nancy while Jenkins and Hersl got in Hamilton's truck.

Rayam and Jenkins devised a plan to get Clewell out of the way.

"Wayne had made a decision for Clewell to go and do a search warrant on the other house," Rayam recalled. "Clewell just wasn't, you could just basically say he wasn't part of the team, I guess. We knew that he wouldn't take any money."

GONDO RACED THROUGH traffic with the confidence of a cop who can't get pulled over. From the back seat, Hamilton searched for some clear sense of what was next for him and his wife.

They left Park Heights. The sky grew bigger. Trees lined the road. They were driving away from Baltimore, not toward it.

"Take me down to the federal courthouse," Hamilton said.

If they were federal agents like they said they were, they would take him downtown to the Edward A. Garmatz United States Courthouse to a magistrate judge where he would hear his charges, since he was still on federal probation.

"Where are we going?" Hamilton asked.

"We're going to your house," Rayam said.

Gondo bobbed through traffic honking his horn, speeding, driving on the shoulder to get around traffic and into quiet Carroll County, where he curled through roundabouts that connected tiny, almost-nothing towns, gliding along twisted, two-lane thoroughfares, a rural blur of corn, soybeans, and cows on both sides and as far forward as they could see.

They turned onto the street where the Hamiltons lived on a couple of acres on the edge of a huge, high-end horse farm. Seething green grass and fluffy cloud bushes hovered in front of the Hamiltons' brick manse, a gingerbread prickly with wildly pitched roofs—five different points jutting boastfully into the country air.

"Just don't say nothing," Hamilton told Nancy. "They're trying to rob me."

Nancy had to say something about the kids. She told Gondo and Rayam that their children—ages eight, nine, and eighteen—were all in the house. She asked if the cops could let them leave to avoid seeing whatever was going to happen. They said she could make a call.

In handcuffs, Nancy maneuvered her cell phone and called her eighteen-year-old son, telling him to help the younger kids pack and get them out of there. She couldn't tell him anything else. They just had to leave. The police were going to check their bags on the way out.

Hersl stood there bald and monumental against the wooded backdrop of the Hamiltons' new home, watching the couple still in the back seat. He was getting ready to buy a house himself, in the county, north of Baltimore. His new house was not as nice as the Hamiltons' house.

THE FLOORS OF the Hamiltons' house were gleaming hardwood and patterned marble and white carpet. Everything about the place screamed coke dealer or suburban supermom whose kids are finally off to college and out of the house.

Gondo went upstairs and into Hamilton's bedroom. That's where he found the money—a block of cash in a heat-sealed bag and $20,000 in loose hundreds under a towel in the closet.

Gondo counted out the money—$5,000, $10,000, $15,000, finally $20,000—and then put it back in the closet under the towel just like he'd found it. He took some pride in his ability to count cash right. It could be a matter of life and death. Rayam was with him. Then Hersl came in.

Rayam went and found Jenkins, who was calling Carroll County Drug Task Force to come in and assist since they were well out of Baltimore Police jurisdiction. Rayam told his sergeant about the loose bills. Jenkins said to take it.

There was still the heat-sealed $50,000 to put into evidence.

And there had to be more. They interrogated the Hamiltons until Carroll County arrived, moving them around the house, questioning them, never allowing them to talk to each other.

"There's no drugs in here, man. I don't sell drugs," Hamilton said.

"Listen, ain't nobody telling," Gondo assured Hamilton.

"Man, I'm not doing anything, man. I don't know what you're talking about," Hamilton said.

"I'm letting you know, none of your friends—" Gondo said.

"I don't be with no one. I be with my wife and my kids. Take me back upstairs," Hamilton said.

"They playing a good cop, bad cop," he told Nancy when he passed by her as they brought her into the basement to be interrogated.

In the basement, all the questions from Rayam made Nancy cry. She didn't have any information they wanted.

Rayam worked Hamilton next.

"Listen, if it's some drugs in here, just give it, just tell us. We'll put it up for you," Rayam said.

"There's nothing in here," Hamilton said.

The Carroll County cops arrived with drug dogs, going through the house and putting everyone on edge, especially Nancy. Her husband's temper was tipping, she could tell, her kids were elsewhere, worried, and one cop stalked around handling a drug dog—it was all too much, a nightmare.

Jenkins handed Hamilton a piece of paper confirming that money was seized in the house and said he had to sign it. Hamilton demanded they write an amount on the form.

"We can't put an amount on it," said Jenkins, who did not mention that he had stolen an expensive watch while searching the house.

"I'm telling you what I had in here," Hamilton said, mentioning his $70,000.

Hamilton stood up, angry. He wanted to talk to the Carroll County cops. Jenkins pushed him back down into his seat.

"Just sign the paper," Jenkins said.

"Man, put the amount," Hamilton said. "I want to see what's the amount."

Reluctantly, Hamilton signed the paper. The dogs hadn't discovered any drugs in the house, and the squad hadn't located any firearms, so the Hamiltons weren't arrested and they weren't charged with anything. Civil forfeiture laws allowed the Carroll County cops to seize Hamilton's sealed $50,000 anyway.

When the real cops were gone, Rayam walked outside and stuffed the $20,000 under one of the seats in Gondo's car.

Gondo asked him what he was doing with the money.

"Yo, G, I'm taking it," Rayam said.

"Why would you take it?" Gondo said. "There's nothing in the house."

Back inside, Jenkins took Hamilton's cuffs off.

"Clap," Jenkins said.

"For what?" Hamilton said.

"Because we don't usually miss," Jenkins said.

"Man," Hamilton said.

"Just be honest, man. If you know. If you can help us, we can help you," Jenkins said.

He asked Hamilton who was "big-time as far as drugs."

"Man, I'm not in the streets," Hamilton said.

"Who would you rob?" Jenkins asked.

"What?" Hamilton asked.

Jenkins repeated the question.

"I'd rob President Obama," Hamilton said.

"You want to be a smart-ass," Jenkins said.

He hinted that he could get drugs for Hamilton if he played along.

Hamilton still said nothing.

Before they left, Rayam handed Hamilton a business card.

"Man, if you change your mind, here go my card," Rayam said.

When Hamilton looked at it, there was no name, just the letter *J* beside a phone number.

THE SUN WAS setting and the midsummer landscape rose up in washed-out color beyond the road and all that corn and all those cows as GTTF drove off. They stopped at a bar about fifteen minutes from the house they had just robbed together.

Rayam was his side partner and all, but Gondo was not always cool with the way he operated.

"With me, if you're going to skim money or take money off the top, it's better to have some type of evidence," Gondo said. "That's just my personal feel. You know, it's just basically a better cover-up than just taking the money boldly and there's no drugs; there's no guns, nothing at all."

Jenkins acknowledged the sensitive situation. They had taken over $20,000 and a watch.

"We can do this three times a year," Jenkins told his new crew. "But don't be greedy."

Gondo saw that they were now entering into what he thought of as "a pact."

AS GTTF DINED on Hamilton's dime and crammed into their car for the long drive back into the city, a few hundred people surrounded police headquarters in Baltimore as part of the "Justice for Alton Sterling, Philando Castile, & All Victims of Police Terror" march.

On July 5, a police officer named Blane Salamoni killed Alton Sterling, a thirty-seven-year-old Baton Rouge man selling rap mixtapes in front of a convenience store. The next day, July 6, near Saint Paul, Minnesota, Officer Jeronimo Yanez shot and killed Philando Castile, after the thirty-two-year-old informed Yanez he had a licensed gun on him and reached for his driver's license. Castile died in front of his girlfriend, Diamond Reynolds, and her four-year-old daughter as Reynolds Facebook Live'd her boyfriend's death. Then in Dallas on July 7, after a protest, Micah Xavier Johnson ambushed police and killed four Dallas Police Department officers and one Dallas Area Rapid Transit officer. Baltimore Police put snipers on buildings in Baltimore during the protest, worried about a copycat attack against police.

Protesters bunched around BPD headquarters and chanted, "Fuck the police." And then it got more specific as a few East side teens who had joined the protest shouted out, "Fuck Hersl!"

Hersl's name was a symbol. All bad cops were Hersls. The name was also a verb. Even cops used it sometimes. An Eastern District commander once asked a detective who'd made a bust in his district if it was a good arrest or if he had "Hersl'd" the suspect caught with a gun.

Rapper Young Moose had really put it all out there for years, spreading word about Hersl through his songs. Hersl had been out of the East side for eight months, but the East side would never forget his petty brutality and imperious pocket-surfing.

"Fuck Hersl, man! He a snake!" a teen screamed at the protest, his voice rising above hundreds of others, trying to be loud enough that somebody inside police headquarters might hear him.

. . .

RAYAM SAT IN his car in the police headquarters' parking lot, counting Hamilton's money.

The plan was to split up the $20,000 and celebrate at Looney's Pub, one of many bars in the Canton neighborhood. Jenkins was big on celebrating after a serious bust—or a robbery—and the formerly industrial waterfront of Canton was one of the new-money party spots in the city for white folks. It was a cop-friendly neighborhood too.

Rayam counted only $17,000. Gondo either miscounted the $20,000 back at the house or stole $3,000. Or Hersl lifted a little bit for himself.

Rayam called Gondo, who insisted there had been $20,000.

Gondo had other things on his mind. He was supposed to go visit a woman named Lee in New York, but the Hamilton robbery, which began around 3:00 P.M., with all its back and forth—from Home Depot to the dry cleaners to the barn to the Hamiltons' and then back to Baltimore—had taken all night, and he hadn't called her.

It was 10:35 P.M. when Gondo called her, his car stereo blasting Migos' springy summer hit "Pipe It Up."

"You in bed?" Gondo asked.

"I mean, I'm laying down," Lee said.

"Oh," Gondo said. "What's up, what's your problem with me, man?"

"I don't have a problem with you," Lee said.

Rayam called back.

"Hey, listen, don't hang up, this is a two-second conversation, hold on," Gondo said to Lee.

"Real talk, I'm counting and counting and counting," Rayam said when Gondo switched over.

"No! Negative. I would never, come on, man, I would never lie to you," Gondo said.

"I'm-a count it again," Rayam said.

Gondo switched back to Lee. Her television was loud now; a black man spoke stridently about money and power and police brutality. She told him what the man on BET—it was Atlanta rapper Killer Mike—was saying about recent police shootings and black economic empowerment, and Gondo got distracted again.

"This nigga saying I'm three grand short, though, I'm just so mad about that," Gondo said.

"Well, I don't know what you're talking about, but you called me, so I would, I would think you ought to be talking to me and not counting money or whatever you're doing," Lee said.

"Hey, listen, let me, let me, let me—I'm-a call you right back, baby," Gondo said. "This is business. Let me handle this business real quick."

"Oh my God," Lee said, laughing at Gondo.

GONDO AND RAYAM met at a 7-Eleven parking lot and recounted the money together.

There was $17,000. Had to be Hersl who'd taken it.

Rayam snagged his share, and Gondo took his along with the rest to give to Jenkins and Hersl and headed into Canton's Friday-night parade of loud, barhopping drunks.

In front of Looney's, Gondo handed Jenkins a stack of bills and told him about the missing $3,000 and suggested Hersl took it.

"Don't say anything to him. Just leave it alone," Jenkins said. "Just give me his half."

The $3,400 Rayam took from Hamilton when he'd pulled him out of his truck never even came up. When it came to money, no one in the GTTF trusted anyone else, not really.

Inside the bar, the squad spent more of Hamilton's money on booze, buying rounds, feeling flush, flashing cash in this bar

bouncing with goofs from the county: white boys who still popped the collars of their polos, college kids, and obnoxious urban professionals now occupying the once working-class, white
neighborhood.

Loud rock and roll played, and the eighteen flat-screen tele-
visions fired sports and news across the dimly lit room full of
drunks struggling to be louder than the music. Gondo simmered.
Hersl, here drinking amid the drunken throngs, had snatched the
cash, and Jenkins was watching out for him. The fact that they'd
robbed Hamilton together, that there was a pact now, that Gondo
had agreed not to say anything to Hersl, all made it the right moment to mention Wells to Jenkins.

"I was already feeling some type of way," Gondo recalled.
"With alcohol involved, I just confronted him."

He needed to lay off Wells, Gondo told Jenkins, a drunken
combination of confrontation and confession—and a flex.

"You know, there's plenty of other people out here you can target," Gondo told Jenkins.

Jenkins agreed to ease off Wells. He would find a way to hold
this over Gondo. Since he was so tight with Wells, maybe they
could work out an arrangement that would move the heroin Stepp
refused to sell.

After Looney's, Gondo got on the phone with Wells.

"I got up Stew Love's butt for you tonight," Gondo said to
Wells.

He told him Jenkins had agreed to back off.

For a moment, Gondo's two criminal worlds were at peace
with one another.

The next day, Rayam got a text message from Ronald Hamilton.

"You robbed me," Hamilton's text read.

Rayam didn't respond.

. . .

BEFORE HE LEFT for vacation, Jenkins talked to his old crew about overtime.

"He asked me, Taylor, and Hendrix to take care of him on the overtime tip," Ward said. "Whatever we got, if we were able to get overtime, to actually fill him out an overtime slip also and get it signed."

As Jenkins drove past garish billboards and golden palmetto trees rippling in the warped, humid atmosphere, his wife, Kristy, sat in the front seat instead of Taylor, and his two boys replaced Ward and Hendrix in the back.

The first boy was born in 2005, the second a few years later, and Wayne and Kristy brought them up in a midsize house just blocks away from his parents, where the family would gather on holidays and Wayne would hook a trailer full of kids to the back of his dad's golf cart and careen around the yard as the kids whooped and hollered with delight. At the very least, Jenkins was dedicated to looking like a good dad. He didn't ever miss parent-teacher conferences or baseball games. Whatever else he did, he would protect his family, first and foremost and above anything else. That was especially true now that his family, like his squad, was getting bigger.

Kristy was pregnant again, five months now. She was due in November 2016, exactly a year after their son Lucas had died. The death truly "devastated our family," Kristy said.

She praised Wayne as her "rock through this nightmare."

They visited the grave every Sunday. Jenkins struggled to comfort his wife. He confided in his sister.

"How can I move on? What can I do to help Kristy?" Jenkins asked her. "I feel helpless."

Now the Jenkinses had reason to hope they were coming to the other side of that despair, with a new child on the way in the fall. If Jenkins ever needed to cool down, or duck out on the body cameras, he could take leave when the baby was born. Everyone knew what had happened before. There would be no questions.

While Jenkins was in Myrtle Beach, Commissioner Davis announced a reorganization of the department that promoted Sean Miller and made him a chief in charge of investigative operations. It was a very good thing for Jenkins's new crew. Miller was one of Jenkins's biggest supporters.

Jenkins told Stepp that he was still managing the criminal operations of other crews, via phone, and earning overtime as he hung out with his family and sipped a cold drink, his jarhead haircut shining in the sun above his cunning, clear blue eyes.

Wayne Jenkins was on vacation. He had a lot of cash to throw around. His wife was having a new baby. And he had the GTTF at his disposal when he got back.

Momodu Gondo now owed him. Soon Jemell Rayam would too.

ON THE MORNING of July 15, Ivan Bates leaned back against the headboard of the bed in the room he was using at his father's house, his newborn daughter lying on his chest.

Ivan and his wife, Lana, had Brielle, Lana's daughter from a previous marriage, and Bates doted on her, but the couple had been trying to have a baby since they'd first gotten married in 2011. Finally, in May, she had given birth to London, a beautiful baby girl.

Bates placed London's head against his bare chest, her dark eyes bulged in wonder at the world. It was 8:21. He had to be in federal court at 11:00, and it would take him an hour to get there. He took a selfie with her, laid her back in the bassinet, checked on Lana, checked on London once more, and got in his Lexus SUV and drove up I-95 into the city.

He turned onto Charles Street, where he had his office, pulled into the garage, eased his SUV into its slot. He walked to Café Poupon, a French café next door to his office, and scanned the morning crowd perched at small tables, looking for lawyers he knew.

He considered grabbing something to eat. Then his phone rang. It was the U.S. Attorney's Office. They told Bates that they were likely going to bring a federal case against Oreese Stevenson, and they wanted Stevenson to make a deal.

Jenkins's ruse with Keona Holloway had not worked. Stevenson paid Bates up front and told him to fight, so the letter hadn't interrupted Stevenson's cash flow at all. Bates knew Jenkins had been listening to Stevenson's calls. He figured the feds had been listening too. He'd expected this call.

Bates told the federal prosecutor he didn't think his client would cooperate.

"Oreese ain't built that way," Bates said.

He also told the prosecutor that they ought to look closely at the details of the Stevenson car stop. He was preparing a couple of motions that would question the veracity of the information that the police used to get the warrant.

It was a bad stop, and whatever Jenkins had found in Stevenson's house would be thrown out.

GONDO HAD INDEBTED himself to Jenkins when he'd told his sergeant to lay off his friend Wells. And confronting Jenkins may not have even been necessary. Wells was going away on a six-month DUI bid any day now. Importantly, Gondo had demonstrated his loyalty to his friend.

Wells called Gondo around midnight the night before he was going away, and the two friends talked on the phone as they'd been doing since they were kids. Wells griped about Shropshire's reluctance to throw around money in the club, which didn't really make him seem like a boss. Worse, he wasn't earning his share.

"That's why I'm not fuckin' with him," Wells said. "There's no reason I should keep lappin' you, yo. If I keep lappin' you, then you end up bringing me down one way or another."

He told Gondo he didn't think Shropshire would help him out and pay him for what he lost while he did his time.

"You can't really worry about that," Gondo said.

He reminded Wells that Shropshire had set him up with cash last time he returned.

"At the end of the day, I'm the enforcer," Wells said.

Gondo said he found it hard to enforce because Shropshire was "all over the place."

Neither Gondo nor Wells looked particularly like an enforcer. Both men retained something boyish about them. Wells, in particular, with his mass of braided hair lumped up on the back of his head and his huge and soft almond eyes looked more like a rapper or a model than a tough guy.

The two lifelong friends reaffirmed their loyalty to each other and acknowledged the ineluctable rhythms of the game they played together, on ostensibly opposing sides.

"Look, when I be talking to other people, right, I be like, 'Man, my best friend went right, I went left, man, but we still here,'" Wells said.

"No question. We through thick and thin," Gondo said. "It's always gonna be like that."

"We still here," Wells repeated.

"Still here," Gondo said. "Both getting money."

"I'm-a go ahead and knock this little six months out," Wells said.

"Oh yeah," Gondo said. "That's what you supposed to do."

. . .

BATES WENT TO see Stevenson in the jail, an old, medieval tower twisted and hunched behind Interstate 83.

"Yo," Stevenson said to Bates with the narrowest of nods, barely raising his eyes.

Bates told him about the offer from the feds.

"Eight kilos, two guns, and a hundred-some thousand? And you have a prior manslaughter and you did time for a felony?" Bates said. "Dude, you're a poster child for the feds—I mean, this case ain't that hard."

Stevenson said he wouldn't make a deal. The bust was bullshit. It was Bates's job to prove it, feds coming at him or not.

These dirty cops had really fucked his life up.

BOOK
TWO

– – – – – – – – –

"IT'S NO PABLO ESCOBAR.
IT'S POLICE."

SIX

"THERE'S BLOOD EVERYWHERE!" Wayne Jenkins yelled into his radio. Flashing lights reflected off black blood pouring out of Rodney Thomas, pooling on the street in front of Pop's Liquors.

It was right where Wilkens runs into Bentalou. West side. There had been a crowd there around Pop's—hanging around, getting high, doing hand-to-hands—before five shots sent everybody scattering.

Jenkins's more ambitious busts involved monsters in nearly suburban communities that were more Anne Tyler than David Simon, while he used the poorer, blown-out neighborhoods of East and West Baltimore for street rips, door pops, random stops—what the officials called "street-level enforcement."

These parts of the city were often described as *war zones,* and it looked that way to a cruising plainclothes squad, seeking out an enemy, creeping by dope corners and liquor stores, looking past the ordinary lives of workaday residents, searching for their own strange kind of fix as Baltimore slowly went mad in the blurred lights outside the window.

It was July 21. Twenty-four people dead in the last twenty days. The nonfatal shootings were worse. One guy was murdered, four more shot in the past twenty-four hours. The more people shot, the more people felt the need to carry. Now there was Rodney Thomas stumbling out of the alley, falling to the pavement, likely about to die.

Hendrix saw the crowd emerging from the dark after the five shots. Charles Smith ran off like he'd had something to do with it. Hendrix chased after him. Taylor followed. Gondo skidded ahead in the car. Smith tried to get up and over a fence behind Pop's. Hendrix, out of breath, grabbed him, slammed him down.

"Gun!" Hendrix yelled.

Gondo's car pulled up out back by the fence behind Pop's. Hendrix walked through the crime scene, sloppy. A few residents stomped through the crime scene too.

Jenkins plopped down on the concrete, his head in his hands. "There's blood everywhere!"

Charles Smith was under arrest.

TWO DAYS LATER, it was just the two of them in the car, Jenkins at the wheel, Gondo forced into the runner's seat, ready to jump out into the wild night.

Jenkins had something to prove. He had gone on vacation after the Hamilton robbery, so the mutant trust established that night in Looney's, a pact that promised new opportunities, was still being worked out.

He would show Gondo, who didn't like to run, who was in charge.

"With Taylor, you know, he's just like my little pit bull," Jenkins told Gondo. "I just tell him to get them and he goes and gets them."

They drove around and kicked off four foot chases. Gondo sprinted on three of them, losing a guy in Northwest who bolted like a straight-up athlete. He didn't really try to go after another, who ran with his hands out in front of him, not holding on to his jeans—free hands were a clear sign there wasn't a gun lodged in elastic compression shorts, a pistol held secure right near a perp's junk.

Jenkins gave Gondo a break and jumped out himself one time and came back to the car empty-handed. They still hadn't gotten a gun.

At 1:00 A.M., near the intersection of North and Pennsylvania Avenues, where the CVS had burned and cops could always find someone to fuck with, they found some young black men posted up on the corner.

Gondo popped the door. The two men ran. One escaped easily, but by the way the other moved, reaching down, hobbling a little, Gondo figured he had a gun.

The guy turned in to an alley, and Gondo was right there on his ass, and then an arm extended and something flew through the dark and then landed, what sounded like steel smacking the pavement, ringing out between the sound of sneaker soles slapping the street.

Gondo grabbed the runner, and, jacked up on adrenaline, he was unafraid to be the boss for a hot minute.

"Go up there and look for that fuckin' gun because I heard it hit the ground," Gondo told Jenkins.

Jenkins said he found the gun. As they made the arrest, a crowd gathered to hassle the cops who had chased yet another man near where Freddie Gray was grabbed. Time to get out of there.

At headquarters around 3:00 A.M., Gondo wrote up the report. He invented a "reliable source" who, he wrote, informed him that "a black male wearing white T-shirt/black w/ barber shop clippers on the same, black sweatpants and white shoes had a firearm in his right pants pocket."

Computer screwups slowed them down. They didn't wrap up until almost 5:00 in the morning.

All that for one gun.

. . .

"WHAT'S UP, WAYNE?" Gondo answered his phone at 8:38 P.M., still weary after his long night running in the dark chasing men with guns down their pants.

"Dude. Listen to what I'm telling you," Jenkins said. "I'm gonna be hitting a condo on Boston Street. The guy's got a G-Wagon, 2016, and a 2015 Twin Turbo CLK."

Gondo knew cars. The 2016 "G-Wagon" was a Mercedes-Benz truck that goes for at least $150,000, and the twin turbo was a smaller Mercedes that cost about $50,000.

"I just saw him take work from one trunk to the other, and then he went into apartment 201," Jenkins told Gondo. "I'm fly-ing home because I'm in flip-flops and shorts, and I already called the judge. The judge told me to write it and come see him and I'm good with it. I already called Danny."

"Okay," Gondo said, easing his way into another late night with Jenkins.

Jenkins had found a monster: Damon Hardrick, "a fucking baller," according to Jenkins.

Gondo listened to Jenkins go on about Hardrick. He lived with his girlfriend, April Sims. She was often at the club, showing off on Instagram. She was a motivational speaker, talking money man-agement and selling beauty products, and she ran a salon.

"It's a search warrant in a condo downtown. It's gonna be legit," Jenkins said.

They lived in the Beacon Condominiums, fourteen floors of half-million-dollar condos on the waterfront in Canton, a spot to work surveillance for Jenkins, a block from Looney's.

"You, Rayam, and Danny. That's it," Jenkins said.

The Hamilton crew was about to get into it again. When the time came, Rayam was a no-show. That just meant one less person to split the loot with.

. . .

ON THE WAY to the condo, Jenkins pulled over and told Gondo and Hersl to get out. He was careful, worried the car might be bugged.

Jenkins told them the condo should have at least forty to fifty thousand dollars in it. Hersl told Gondo he could use the money. A few days earlier, he had settled on a house.

At 2:30 A.M., Jenkins strutted into the Beacon's lobby. No police vest on or anything else identified him as a cop. He looked a little too sloppy to be a renter there, though. He walked by the security desk toward a locked door, didn't introduce himself, and avoided eye contact with Tim, the security guard that night. He pulled the handle. It didn't open. He paused, turned around, and asked to get into the building's garage. Tim let him in. Jenkins wandered around the garage, returned to the lobby, and left.

"The next thing you know, he walks back with a bulletproof vest on with the label, labeling him as a police officer, and he brought two more colleagues," Tim recalled.

Hersl, in a bright orange Baltimore Orioles shirt and no police vest, followed Jenkins in, shaking a packet of papers at Tim, holding them up, implying it was a warrant, never saying what it was or letting Tim get a good look at it. Gondo, hat on backward, wearing his police vest, stood back.

"Do you have the keys to apartment 201?" Jenkins said. "We need to get there."

They crowded around Tim. Jenkins and Hersl crossed their arms, rested them on the desk. Owens gave Jenkins the keys and walked them up to the second floor. Jenkins stuffed the keys in the door and burst through all in one motion. Two small dogs were yapping. Somebody sprinted to the back of the unit. Hardrick. Jenkins and Hersl grabbed him and pulled a pair of house keys from the pocket of his board shorts.

While Jenkins and Hersl dealt with Hardrick, Gondo searched

the condo, shining his flashlight through the three-bedroom, three-bathroom condo, with a large balcony that spread across one whole side of the building.

"Get up and go in the living room," Gondo said when he found Sims's fifteen-year-old daughter in one of the bedrooms.

The girl took her time, stalling as she FaceTime'd her mom and showed her what was happening. She saw two big white cops digging around her mom's spot and yelled at them. Hersl yelled back and called her "stupid." She called Hersl a "racist." Hersl argued with the fifteen-year-old. He wasn't racist, he told her.

"My wife is black," Hersl said.

Jenkins asked her if she knew what was going on in the house. She didn't answer.

They found a strainer full of light tan dope, heroin in baggies, a digital scale, a larger ziplock bag full of dope, gel caps, and a spoon. There was no cash. Hersl grabbed a pink Chanel bag.

Then Sims burst into the apartment ready to throw down in her club-casual clothes—a white T-shirt, tight pink sweatpants, and a brown baseball cap that read, in all caps, RELEVANT, the name of a clothing line she was about to launch.

Jenkins questioned Sims about the heroin. She didn't know whose drugs these were and she didn't know why they were here in her condo either, and where the fuck was their warrant?

"You up in here like it's the hood," Sims said. "You niggas don't know, you in Canton now."

Hardrick and Sims were placed under arrest, zip-tie handcuffs strapped tightly around their wrists, and charged with possession and distribution of drugs and related charges. Cops in uniform came and took the couple away, and an aunt came to pick up Sims's daughter.

Jenkins, Gondo, and Hersl walked by the front desk, carrying boxes.

Outside, Hersl gave Gondo the Chanel bag.

"Hey, you can just give this to your girl," Hersl said.

IVAN BATES WAS back in a courtroom with Sergeant Alicia White.

Another one of the Six, Garrett Miller, the white bike cop who actually arrested Freddie Gray, was supposed to begin his trial that day.

White had been suspended since Gray's arrest. She told Bates that she had seen Wayne Jenkins at a fund-raiser for the Six.

"He said to tell you hello," White said. "And he said you should run."

Cops were often telling Bates to run for state's attorney against top prosecutor Marilyn Mosby, who was up for reelection the following year. Bates had to laugh at an endorsement from Wayne Jenkins.

Mosby, the youngest state's attorney in the country, had captured the imagination of the nation when she announced the charges against the six officers involved in Freddie Gray's arrest and death. It was a beautiful bit of theater that Bates and other defense attorneys saw right through. Mosby's prosecutors overlooked illegal search and seizures and every other Fourth Amendment violation committed by police like Jenkins and Hersl and then capitalized on a national conversation about police brutality by charging the Freddie Gray cops.

Bates had gone to Mosby's office with complaints about Fabien Laronde, a Jenkins associate, and heard nothing back from her. Time and time again, prosecutors overlooked officer misdeeds and lies and went forward with dirty cases. No one saw that part of the picture when Mosby was onstage with Prince or being photographed for *Vogue*.

"All rise," the clerk said, and Judge Barry Williams, shining bald head and long black robe, walked out.

Bates studied Williams's face for a hint of what was coming.

Deputy State's Attorney Michael Schatzow said the SAO would not be prosecuting Miller.

They would not prosecute any of the remaining officers either.

It was all over.

The Six were free.

While Bates prepared some remarks for a press conference of his own, he watched Mosby's on television. She was outside Gilmor Homes, on the block where Gray was arrested, a mural of Gray painted during the Baltimore Uprising positioned behind her.

"Baltimore finds itself at the epicenter of a national conflict between urban and rural populations of color and the law enforcement agencies that are sworn to protect and serve them," Mosby said. "However fitting it is for observers to use the untimely death of Freddie Carlos Gray Jr. as a barometer of our nation's progress on police brutality, my professional role in this matter is plain. To seek justice on behalf of an innocent twenty-five-year-old man who was unreasonably taken into custody after fleeing in his neighborhood, which just happens to be a high-crime neighborhood, and had his spine partially severed in the back of a Baltimore police wagon."

Gray's mother—who had attempted suicide the previous fall—and stepfather were by her side. The city had awarded them $6 million.

"We love you!" people in the crowd shouted.

"For those that believe I'm anti-police, it's simply not the case. I'm anti–police brutality," Mosby continued. "I need not remind you that the only loss and the greatest loss in all of this was that of Freddie Gray's life."

Bates had to give it to Mosby. She made a loss look like a victory. Her failure to successfully prosecute the case, she claimed, was the police's fault.

"We're with you," the crowd chanted.

An hour later, Bates stood at a podium in front of cameras, the six cops and their lawyers and the Fraternal Order of Police president standing behind him in the FOP lodge in Hampden, a historically white, working-class neighborhood that was once the home of Baltimore's KKK faction and now a haven of Baltimore kitsch, hipster bars, and high-end restaurants.

Mosby clearly had the better backdrop.

Bates did his best.

"It is the Baltimore City State's Attorney's Office that has denied justice to the Gray family," he said.

Mosby's office refused to accept the police investigation—and failed to do an adequate investigation on their own, he explained. Mosby and her team were ready to twist the facts. The police said the knife that had been found on Gray when he was stopped was illegal, making the arrest valid. Mosby said it was a legal knife.

"During the discovery process, we were able to find out that the current state's attorney for Baltimore City was prosecuting thirty young black men for having the same exact knife in the same exact time period," Bates said. "Why would you tell the community that that knife is in fact legal when you're prosecuting others and telling them that it is illegal?"

Then he threw in a little nod to Jenkins, a gesture his FOP audience might not have appreciated.

"As a defense attorney, I've seen good officers. I've seen bad officers," he said and called on God to bless both Freddie Gray's family and the police. "It's time to heal."

JENKINS STOOD IN front of a gas pump talking fast to Albert Brown. Hersl turned his body camera on.

"At any time when questioned by myself or any other officer, you have the right to answer questions or refuse to answer questions," Jenkins said.

He waved the hand that wasn't gripping Brown's handcuffed wrists all around and pressed his forefinger to his thumb, punctuating certain lines during Mirandization.

"Sir, do you understand your rights?" Jenkins asked.

"Yes, sir," Brown, in a wifebeater, looking weary, said.

"Is there a reason you have a gun in the car and cocaine?" Jenkins finally asked.

"No reason," Brown said.

"How come you have that?" Jenkins asked.

Brown didn't answer.

"Is there a reason you don't have your seat belt on today?" Jenkins asked.

"I just got in my car," Brown said.

"We are on camera. You are lying," Jenkins said, pointing at the body camera strapped to Hersl's wide chest. BPD had started rolling out its Body-Worn Camera program in May. Hersl was the only member of GTTF unlucky enough to be issued one so far.

"The car pulled out, we pulled to your bumper because you don't have a seat belt on and a white shirt, and it's on camera, and we also got it on the body camera and we also got it on the video pole," Jenkins said. "Are you going to continue to lie to me? You moved the car, and then we went to your bumper. You have a white shirt on."

Hersl's body camera didn't record any of that. The beginning of the stop relied on Jenkins's word and the security cameras at this BP gas station across from Druid Hill Park next to HipHop Fish & Chicken.

"You have a gun and cocaine—probably, I would say probably two and a quarter just by looking at it, I didn't touch it yet—up in the visor. And a gun," Jenkins said. "You work for Safe Streets?

Because this is like the third time we got a guy on Safe Streets with a gun."

Brown did work for Safe Streets, a violence-interruption program that employed people who had the respect of the streets to interrupt the cycle of violence by targeting those likely to retaliate and helping to quash the beef.

The program was effective. Zones where Safe Streets operated showed a sharp decrease in homicides, despite the general increase in violence citywide.

Cops didn't buy it. Safe Streets seemed like a scam. In December 2013, Jenkins, Hendrix, and Ben Frieman stopped a Safe Streets worker named Levar Mullen in the Harlem Park neighborhood because they said he wasn't wearing a seat belt. They pushed him for information about a shooting in the city, and when he didn't give them anything, they searched his truck and said they found a Glock. Mullen said the gun was planted. He was now serving federal time. In 2015, cops raided the Safe Streets office over on East Monument Street, Hersl's turf, and found guns and drugs in the office.

"So you work for Safe Streets?" Jenkins asked.

Brown didn't answer.

Jenkins altered his approach, lowered his voice, stopped waving his arms all around.

"You wanna go somewhere and talk this out? Wanna make it look like we're arresting you, get out of here so people don't see it?" Jenkins whispered. "I don't care about the gun or the drugs. You wanna go somewhere and talk and keep it a hundred or not? Last chance. If you do it, we gotta go now. Wanna go to jail?"

"You might as well take me to jail," Brown said.

"Very good," Jenkins said and smacked Brown's chest. "Sit him down."

Jenkins and Gondo placed Brown next to a pump.

"Danny, keep that on," Jenkins said. "I want you to go up and pull the visor down, and you're gonna see everything."

Hersl walked toward Brown's minivan with Rayam. "You can see the cocaine up in the visor, and right after that, you can see a little, you can see the handgun right there too. Right there is the handgun," Hersl said.

Gondo called for a wagon to come and transport Brown. It was a Monday during rush hour. There was a car accident nearby, someone told him on the radio. They'd be there as soon as they could.

"We'll go to the Western. We're only right down the street," Jenkins said, shaking his head, aggrieved and muttering. "We get fuckin' kilos and nobody notices."

Jenkins lifted Brown and shoved him in the direction of Gondo's car.

Two women walked out of the BP and hollered at Brown, asking if he was all right. Hersl began screaming, trying to drown out Brown's response as he tried to tell the women his phone number. Jenkins slammed Brown into the side of the car.

"Record them, record them!" one of the women yelled as her friend pulled her phone out.

Brown yelled his phone number out again to the women. Hersl got between Jenkins and Brown and the women.

"We're recording as well," Rayam said. "Everybody's recorded."

They got Brown in the car and drove down the street, where they reconvened to come up with a plan.

"It's off," Hersl said, approaching Gondo.

His body camera was not off.

"I was gonna hurt that dude," Gondo said.

"It's too many cameras, they got cameras all over," Hersl said, laughing.

Jenkins and Rayam went through Brown's wallet and saw that he lived right across from the Western District police station on Mount Street, which officers in riot gear had defended from protesters in the days following Freddie Gray's death.

Fifteen months later, the streets were quiet as Gondo, Jenkins, and Rayam drove to Brown's house and broke in.

Hersl sat in the car with their captive.

"Is anything else in there we need to know about you? You might as well be straight, man. You should've been straight before. He would've worked with you, you know what I'm saying?" Hersl said. "Then you wanna act like that. Don't act like that."

"Y'all pulled me over for nothing, though," Brown said.

"You had no seat belt!" Hersl yelled. "It's on camera. I told you when I approached the car, and you apologized for not having it on. Don't you remember? It's all on camera."

"So y'all just go in somebody's house without no warrant," Brown said.

"It's called *exigent circumstances*," Hersl said.

Hersl fielded a phone call. He discussed the details of a beach trip and then returned to Brown.

"Safe Streets, boy, I tell you, all them guys are cruddy," Hersl said. "The whole program's got to be shut down. That whole program's got to go."

Brown started to respond.

"Dude, we lock everyone up from Safe Streets for drugs and guns," Hersl interrupted. "They ain't out here trying to help kids."

Jenkins lowered himself into the car, emitting a pained, unhealthy grunt. Hersl got out and ambled off.

"You can't go up in somebody's house like that," Brown told Jenkins.

"You need a warrant to search, not to clear," Jenkins said. "Don't pick a legal fight because you're gonna lose."

Gondo and Hersl stood outside the car.

"He's a straight bitch, man—I don't like him," Gondo said. "That's why I ain't wanna touch him: I know I would hurt that dude, man."

"Everyone we get from Safe Streets—dirty," Hersl said. "Every one. That whole program."

Gondo yawned and wiped his eyes.

"So, you can actually see the video?" Gondo asked, nodding at the camera on Hersl's chest.

"Let me see if I can pull it up," Hersl said. He giggled as he grabbed it and then stopped short.

"Oh?" Hersl said to himself. "Still recording."

JENKINS CALLED STEPP and told him he was coming over to grab $5,000 that Stepp owed him for some coke and weed. When he got there, though, he started asking about the heroin Stepp had that was piling up.

"He told me that there was an officer that was retiring, that he was going to do a onetime deal and he was going to unload all the heroin and that he was going to get rid of it," Stepp recalled.

Stepp's daughter was a user, so he wouldn't consider selling smack, so it just sat there in a massive safe stuffed with drugs.

Collected over a period of years, the dope was a mess. Some of it was raw. Some was packed in gel caps. Some was scramble, heroin cut with quinine or smashed-up Benadryl or even bits of drywall. Stepp was glad to see it gone.

When he left with the dope, Jenkins forgot to take the $5,000, the whole reason he had stopped by. They lived only a few miles from each other, so Stepp called Jenkins and jumped in his truck and drove over to Bay Country, Jenkins's little suburban neighborhood near the Gunpowder River. The Jenkinses' house on Cunning Circle had a porch on the front and a deck on the back—the kind of home improvements he recommended to his squad.

"When I turned onto his block, it wasn't the cop that he mentioned to me that was taking the heroin," Stepp recalled.

It was Rayam. Shortly after the Hamilton robbery, Jenkins

had approached Rayam and Gondo about selling drugs for him. Rayam wasn't sure about it at the time, but by August, Rayam, thirsty—and dangerous—said yes to Jenkins.

Having Rayam and Stepp at his house at the same time made Jenkins nervous, Stepp noticed. It was bad timing, two formerly isolated coconspirators bumping into one another, both wrapped up in Jenkins's complex scheming.

Rayam sat in the car while Stepp handed Jenkins the money. Then the two cops went down into the basement, where Jenkins had quickly stashed the two boxes of heroin, putting a half key aside as a test package for Rayam. The wild mix, accumulated from different sources over the years, was hard to accurately price. Whatever shape the five hundred grams were in, it added up to a lot of money, and if Rayam could get rid of it, it would be a fast come-up. Rayam wasn't plugged in like Gondo, though, and when he thought about people who understood dope, he mainly thought of users like his burglar buddy Tom Finnegan or a cousin in Newark, Kyle Harris.

Rayam left Jenkins's house with the heroin, hit Interstate 95, and headed straight to New Jersey. Rayam negotiated a price—$20,000. Then Harris pushed it down to $17,000. Rayam didn't have much of a choice. He had to pay $14,000 to Jenkins. Still, getting rid of this dope would bring an easy three Gs.

SEVEN

DENNIS ARMSTRONG SAT in his van at a red light in East Baltimore with a whole bunch of cocaine next to him, $8,000 in his glove compartment, and a black Impala full of white plainclothes cops one lane over.

One of them motioned for Armstrong to roll his window down and then shouted, "Where you coming from?"

"The post office," Armstrong said.

The thirty-five-year-old maintenance worker for the Baltimore City Housing Authority had just left Extra Space Storage across the street from a post office, where he grabbed some blow out of his closet-size unit.

Another shout from the Impala. "Pull over!"

Armstrong floored it.

The van's frame wobbled and its steering wheel vibrated as Armstrong whirled around the winding roads that surrounded Herring Run Park and fed off into a messy tangle of residential streets.

He was going 70 mph in a 25 mph zone, sailing over wide, alignment-wrecking speed humps. He had to get away. In 2011, Armstrong got ten years suspended on a drug charge. If he went back now, it would be for a long time.

Armstrong reached down and grabbed the coke he had on him and threw it out the van's window, costly baggies of white smacking the street, leaving behind powder smears on the pavement.

He turned onto Belair Road, a four-lane street full of car dealerships, liquor stores, small mom-and-pops, and row houses. He could still see the Impala in his coke-caked rearview. He turned in to another neighborhood, a maze of alleys and circles and little lanes and coves that might make it easier to lose the cops. He honked his horn. He had to warn people to get out of the road. Kids played in these streets, Monday evening in the summer, around dinnertime.

The tiny residential road rose up in front of him, and he saw it end at the bottom of the hill, a dead end.

He slammed on the brakes, flung open the door, covered in white, and fled.

Clewell was breathing heavy, running behind him. The sun was setting. The two beefy silhouettes collided in the alley.

He walked the handcuffed Armstrong to Jenkins's Impala. Hersl and Clewell got in Armstrong's van and retraced the path of the pathetic chase and, keeping an eye out for any unexploded bags of coke, headed back to Extra Space Storage.

Gondo and Rayam joined them there.

Jenkins searched Armstrong's van. He didn't mention the $8,000 in the glove box. He sent Gondo and Clewell off to go write the warrant for Armstrong's storage unit and called Stepp.

"I need you here now," Jenkins said. "I got a storage locker."

Extra Space Storage was nicely situated for Stepp to hit and get out without being seen. Jenkins told him to cut through the woods and climb a fence.

"There's no cameras, there's no nothing," Jenkins said.

He told Stepp there was $220,000 and eight kilograms of cocaine inside the unit.

"I'm on my way," Stepp said.

This would be easy. Stepp grabbed his gear.

When he arrived, Stepp saw that it wasn't going to be nearly as easy as Jenkins had let on. There was no way he could climb the fence in the woods. And there were security cameras. He would just have to cover his face as best he could and heave himself over the fence right in front.

Stepp ran from his truck and pulled himself up over the fence, fell onto the other side, and rolled his ankle when he landed. It hurt like hell, broken maybe.

"For like $220,000 and eight kilos, I was going to rough it out even if I had a broken leg," Stepp recalled. "I went ahead and sucked it up and started heading in to get into this storage unit."

He dragged his busted ankle behind him and found Armstrong's small unit. He pried the door up with his crowbar just enough to get inside.

There wasn't much in the unit. Construction tools, mostly. No money. He kept digging and found a bag that had empty kilo wrappers in it and another with about three quarters of a kilogram in it. Hardly the score Jenkins had promised.

Stepp took everything out of the unit and went back through it a second time. His ankle hurt, and he wasn't thinking straight. He was scared he'd blown it and was already reverse engineering the break-in too, worried he was sent there as a decoy.

He took stock of the situation.

"I'm looking at the tools in the small storage thing. And I'm thinking that the product, or the money and stuff, is hid behind the walls," Stepp recalled. "So I start systematically taking the roof and the walls and the stuff down, and, and looking in those various places."

Still nothing. He took the three-quarters of a kilo and returned to his truck and called Jenkins.

"There's empty kilo wrappers there, but there's not no eight kilos there," Stepp said, worried Jenkins might think he took the money.

"Taylor blew the whole thing," Jenkins said.

Jenkins told Stepp he had sent Taylor to watch Armstrong's house and make sure no one left with anything.

"Taylor had called and said that there was a lady that left that house with two large trash bags and that he didn't pull them over," Jenkins said. "Taylor blew it."

Taylor wasn't even in the country. He had been in the Dominican Republic, on vacation with Hendrix and Ward since August 5, and he would not be back until the next day.

While Jenkins talked to Stepp, Hersl and Rayam divided up Armstrong's $8,000. When Jenkins got off the phone, they gave him his share and put the rest of the cash back in the minivan.

Gondo and Clewell returned with a warrant and seized the cash that was left—just $2,800.

Armstrong was charged with driving with a minor in the car without a seat belt—a totally made-up charge—and simple possession. They made almost all the cocaine disappear.

Later that evening, Jenkins came to Stepp's house to get the money for the coke he had found. The money was for Hersl, Jenkins explained.

"It was Danny's score," Jenkins said.

Stepp gave Jenkins a few thousand dollars. He figured he'd grabbed about 750 grams from the unit and that was three-quarters of a kilo, and if it was $15,000 for a kilo, that meant about $15 a gram.

Jenkins told Stepp that Armstrong was the brother-in-law of Thomas Wilson, a sergeant who was one of Jenkins's closest friends. The two provided security for a coke connect that Stepp brought into town a year earlier. They'd gone to a high-end strip club. Taylor worked security with them that night. It was wild with Stepp's source, a Dominican, throwing around thousands of one-dollar bills.

Stepp didn't get it. If Armstrong was Wilson's brother-in-law, how did he fit into this? And if he did, how was it Hersl's score?

It was impossible to tell what was true with Jenkins. For "insurance," Stepp took a photo of his rolled ankle, now swollen, the pale white skin puffed up and irritated, the red turning purple ugly—it still hurt like hell.

BATES SAT IN his office studying the evidence the prosecution would use against Stevenson.

First thing he noticed was the photo of Stevenson's van. No way they could have seen drugs through those tinted windows. And the narrow one-way street. Jenkins blocked the van in with his car. If Bates's argument about the stop was strong enough, he wouldn't have to deal with the cocaine they allegedly found in the house at all because it would be "fruit of the poisonous tree," and those charges would have to be thrown out. If his motion to suppress that evidence failed, he might be able to win a Franks hearing against Jenkins, showing that the search warrant contained knowing lies.

The affidavit for the search warrant claimed that Stevenson confessed and told them the drugs were in the house, but the material Bates had from the state said that no statement was given. There was also a video showing them finding the money in the safe. And another video showing the next-door neighbor that Stevenson mentioned talking to Jenkins and Taylor.

Bates sent a private investigator out to talk to the neighbor, a former schoolteacher—someone a judge and jury would believe. His report said the woman who lived next door to the Stevensons had been working from home when she saw men approaching her door. When she got down there, she said, one was trying to put a key in her lock.

The investigator learned that Jenkins then entered Stevenson's house with Stevenson's key. This was all early in the afternoon. It was daylight. Holloway had told Bates they didn't have a warrant until after midnight.

When Bates got home that night, the Department of Justice's patterns and practice report on the Baltimore Police Department had leaked online, a day early.

COMMISSIONER KEVIN DAVIS, his face redder than usual, his lip pursed out, waited for his turn to talk—after Mayor Stephanie Rawlings-Blake and Vanita Gupta, head of the Department of Justice's Civil Rights Division.

It was August 10, and the DOJ released its report based on a fourteen-month investigation into BPD. The 164-page compilation of federally documented corruption detailed excessive force, retaliation against whistle-blowers and residents who spoke out or made complaints, racial disparity, abuse and exploitation of sex workers and transphobia, and endless Fourth and Fourteenth Amendment violations.

In every major category of complaint, the department disproportionately targeted black Baltimoreans, making "520 stops for every 1,000 black residents, but only 180 stops for every 1,000 Caucasian residents." The report mentioned one supervisor who sent out a template to use when making a trespassing arrest. Officers needed to fill in the name, time, and address—the race of the suspect was already included in the paperwork.

The report read almost like a résumé of GTTF activities.

A 2013 police shooting stemmed from a foot chase where cops claimed a man threw a gun moments before they shot him. When the shooting was investigated, the report explained, "Four officers involved in the case were interviewed for only 5, 8, and 14 minutes."

A cop illegally searched a man's car and, when he found nothing, strip-searched the driver on the side of the road and discovered weed and cash. The cop told the driver he could keep it all if he gave up some information about serious crimes. When the man refused to give anybody up, he was arrested, and the cop kept some of the man's money. "Despite the serious charges in the complaint and the officer's lengthy record of alleged misconduct," the report said, "[Internal Affairs] deemed it 'administratively closed' without interviewing the complainant."

A sergeant, who was supposed to investigate excessive force, came to the scene of a drug arrest and ended up choking the suspect for an extended period to keep him from swallowing a little weed and blow.

The report included a photo of a poster that hung inside a plainclothes unit's office showing two cops walking two handcuffed men toward a police van and under it the words *Striking fear into loiters City-Wide.*

Headlines in news outlets around the world used words like "incredibly damning," "stunning," "blistering," and, a favorite, "scathing" to characterize the report. The complaints that black Baltimore had been making for decades had been validated by the federal government: BPD was not only corrupt but racist in its corruption.

When Commissioner Davis stepped up to the podium to speak about the report, he declared, "Change is painful, growth is painful, but nothing is as painful as being stuck in a place that we do not belong."

It was a quote cribbed from inspirational Pinterest and Facebook posts, widely attributed to Mandy Hale, author of *The Single Woman: Life, Love, and a Dash of Sass.*

Then he deflected.

"It is critically important for me to say in my opening remarks that this report is not an indictment of every man and woman that has the privilege of wearing this uniform, this patch, and this

badge. This report is, however, an indictment of those bad be-
haviors by a relatively small number of police officers over many,
many years," Davis said. "There are officers right now that are
just as offended as we are to see the details that are laid out in this
report. Why? Because they wear this uniform proudly, and they
serve the citizens of Baltimore honorably each and every day."

The DOJ report was a setback for the BPD's public image, but
there was no whiff of the worst crimes committed by Jenkins and
his crew. The DOJ's investigation almost seemed like a superficial
project—its investigators unequipped to deal with cops primarily
operating as a criminal enterprise.

The Justice Department's office inside police headquarters was
on the seventh floor, the same floor as GTTF. They shared a wall.
And those federal investigators couldn't interact with police while
they were investigating them, so it wasn't uncommon to see mys-
terious faces around headquarters. This gave Stepp cover when he
came by the GTTF office to work with Jenkins.

"They think that you're a fed," Jenkins told Stepp. "So just
don't say nothing, just keep cruising."

AROUND THE TIME the DOJ released its report, Clewell transferred out
of the unit, further freeing Jenkins to go wild out on the street.
Whatever the DOJ report said, a gun was still a gun, and Jenkins
could do what he wanted as long as he kept bringing them in.

About a week later, Jenkins, Hersl, Rayam, and Taylor stopped
a man named William James and his wife, Tiffany Coby, on Hil-
len Road in Northeast, near Morgan State, cutting the couple off
and forcing them off the road.

James rode dirt bikes—which Jenkins sometimes stole and sold
on Craigslist—and had a history with the law. But he was working
for Amazon now and he and Coby were on the way to the mall to
buy some clothes for a trip to Atlanta the next day.

Taylor pulled James from his car and told him they'd let him go if he could give them the name of somebody who had guns or drugs. James didn't know anybody dirty like that, he said.

Rayam tried Coby. He told her that her husband was going to go to jail for a gun if one of them didn't speak up.

"A gun? What gun?" Coby said.

She asked the cops where they had found the gun. She hadn't even seen them go into the car. It was sticking up out of the center console, they told her.

There was no gun there she tried to tell them.

"Give him a kiss and tell him goodbye," one of them said to Coby.

The four cops walked off a few feet and huddled up, scheming. When Jenkins broke the huddle, he approached James holding a gun.

"This is your gun right here," Jenkins said.

They charged James, who was prohibited from possessing a firearm, with six felonies related to the gun.

IVAN BATES SUBPOENAED Oreese Stevenson's neighbor to testify in the suppression hearing about Jenkins coming to her door. "The defendant is filing a motion to suppress all evidence gathered from Mr. Stevenson's vehicle and house on the grounds that the initial search of his car violated Mr. Stevenson's Fourth Amendment right against unreasonable searches and seizures," Bates wrote.

He laid out the facts of the Stevenson case again: "The officers then proceeded to search the car, without a warrant, without permission, only based on the money apparently seen in an open box, in an open backpack, belonging to the passenger who just got in the car and the nervousness of two individuals who had just been surrounded by police."

Bates filed another motion requesting Jenkins's Internal Affairs files. He knew there was a lengthy file based on the Walter Price case alone, and with it, he could show that Jenkins had, at best, failed to supervise officers who were writing up false statements of probable cause.

Even if Jenkins beat all that, Bates had the testimony of the neighbor.

RIDING AROUND WITH Hersl and Rayam, Gondo was griping about an old case that had come back.

It was a big one from 2015 out in Anne Arundel County—multiple defendants, a huge haul of guns and drugs, news coverage. Gondo and Rayam's guy was Zachary Newsome, and they'd investigated him for months. They saw him leaving the casino downtown, suspected he had guns and drugs in the car, so Gondo lied and said he smelled weed coming from the car so there was a reason to pull him over.

When it went to trial, Newsome's lawyer, Justin Brown—also a lawyer for Adnan Syed of *Serial* podcast fame—ridiculed Gondo on the stand and showed the jury that it was impossible to smell packaged weed from across the highway with all the windows in Newsome's car rolled up. It led to a mistrial. Now a year later, Newsome was back on trial and Gondo would have to testify again.

Gondo couldn't go through with it. His father was sick with pancreatic cancer. He was dying, Gondo told the prosecutor, and that was no lie. The prosecutor said the trial could not be put off. And Rayam wasn't a credible witness anymore since he had lost a Franks Hearing where Judge Barry Williams had ruled that Rayam had lied to enter the house of a man named Gary Clayton. So Gondo was the only one who could testify.

"She gotta ask for a postponement," Gondo said to Hersl and Rayam about the assistant state's attorney who had the case. "No way I'm going in there."

Hersl made a suggestion.

"If you lock this guy up today, transfer him to Central Booking, they will not take him to court tomorrow," Hersl said.

They called around. There was an old outstanding warrant out on Newsome. The three went to Newsome's house and arrested him, delaying the trial. Gondo wouldn't have to worry about Newsome—or Justin Brown clowning him on the stand again.

Later that night, during a car stop, Gondo, Hersl, and Rayam got a man's keys, entered his house, and stole $1,500 from him. Then they linked up with Jenkins and Hendrix at another car stop and stole some more.

JENKINS HIT THE gas, cutting out of the Exxon parking lot where Taylor had spotted a guy in a Chevrolet with a big pile of weed in his lap. The guy gunned it, and Jenkins raced toward downtown after the Chevy.

Gondo followed and tried to keep up. The roads were slick, city lights reflected off them, shining, making it hard to see.

"No lights, no lights," Rayam said from the passenger seat.

They entered the Inner Harbor area, glowing glass and steel buildings slurred in the rainy sky.

The Chevy ran a red light. A Hyundai sailed across the intersection at the same time.

The driver had no time to react and T-boned the Chevy.

A loud, crashing crunch and then the defeated hiss of two totaled cars flung up onto the sidewalk.

"Shit," Gondo said.

"Keep going, yo," Rayam said.

A horrible quiet.

"I don't know," Rayam said. "Like go around, we may have to help out."

"Yo," Gondo said.

"I don't know, yo, call Wayne on your personal," Rayam said.

From the back seat, Hersl got on the radio and asked Jenkins to call them.

"I wanna know what's in that car," Rayam said.

"I think Wayne's disappeared too," Hersl said.

"I think Wayne gonna wanna see what's in that car," Rayam said. "There's something in that car, though, yo."

"A hundred percent in that car," Hersl said.

"Let me walk up to that bitch, yo, step in that car," Rayam said.

Gondo drove by the crashed cars. Jenkins finally called Hersl on his cell.

"Wayne says go back," Hersl said.

"I could get on the air and make a report of an accident," Rayam said.

Rayam clicked the radio to engage it. Hersl stopped him.

"Wayne just wants to stay in the area close by, until he gets there to see how it comes out," Hersl said.

"How about we just go and see and just act like, 'Oh, is everything okay?'" Rayam said. "You get what I'm saying?"

"He wants to sit here and see how they handle it in case they get on the air saying they pull Citiwatch up," Hersl told Gondo and Rayam. "He's saying we gotta stay in the immediate area."

They had started this chase at the gas station, where there were certainly security cameras. And there was no way at least some of the chase hadn't been caught by Citiwatch, Baltimore's vast network of interlinking and real-time monitored surveillance cameras that could show that they had instigated the chase that caused the crash.

Jenkins had gotten away with plenty of crashes before. He'd dinged, dented, and destroyed cars for more than a decade, and nobody from BPD asked too much about it. His hard-charging policing career was a loop sometimes, the same out-of-control scenarios playing out again, months or years apart.

A THOUSAND RAINDROPS on Jenkins's windshield captured and distorted the downtown light. He sat in the car, scheming, haunted by ghosts.

Back in the spring of 2010, Jenkins believed he was onto something big in the Grove Park neighborhood. He had been busting people over there, not far from Park Heights and Pimlico, with distribution-level weight, and then he flipped them for monsters.

He was out with Ryan Guinn and Sean Suiter, his crew back then in the Organized Crime Division, watching Umar Burley, a guy he suspected of being a dealer who had a gun case that went federal the year before.

On the morning of April 28, Burley pulled his black Acura to the side of Parkview Avenue in front of an apartment complex to take a phone call, his cousin Brent Matthews in the passenger seat.

Jenkins pulled up in front of Burley's car, and another car pulled up behind Burley, hit Burley's rear bumper, and someone jumped out gripping a gun and wearing a black mask.

Burley maneuvered his way out between the two cop cars and sped off. Jenkins, Guinn, and Suiter chased him through the neighborhood. All three cars blew through five straight stop signs until Burley crashed into a Monte Carlo with an elderly couple, Elbert Davis and his longtime partner, Phosa Cain, inside. The impact forced their car into the front of a house. Davis suffered a heart attack when the two cars collided.

Jenkins ignored Davis and Cain and the crashed Monte Carlo. He searched Burley's Acura. There weren't any drugs in the car. No money either. Jenkins told Guinn to call a sergeant who had "the shit."

While they waited on the sergeant, Jenkins called medics, who arrived and extracted Davis and Cain from the car and took them to R. Adams Cowley Shock Trauma Center.

When the sergeant arrived, he slipped thirty-two gel caps of heroin, amounting to just over an ounce, into the front seat of Burley's car.

Elbert Davis died that afternoon. Phosa Cain was in critical condition. Their children, including a son who was a Baltimore Police officer, and grandchildren gathered in the hospital, mourning Davis and holding vigil with Cain, praying for her, clasping her hand. Crying. Davis had been driving back from a visit with their daughter Dolores when Burley crashed into him.

"I'll see you later tonight," were her last words to him.

When Cain finally came to, she discovered that Davis had died. She had no idea how it had happened. She was told that police had come upon a drug deal and the dealers fled. When the police, who said they had not chased the dealers but had driven in their general direction, came to the intersection, they saw the accident and immediately tried to help the couple stranded in the smashed Monte Carlo.

Jenkins found Burley in the hospital and waited for him to get out of a CT scan.

"You're definitely going to jail for the rest of your life now," Jenkins told Burley.

"What? Why?" Burley said.

"Mr. Davis just passed," Jenkins said.

The state charged Burley with Davis's death, and the U.S. Attorney's Office charged both men with the planted heroin.

Jenkins listened to Burley's and Matthews's jail calls and heard them talking about how the heroin was planted. If it went to court, Jenkins would find a way to avoid testifying. The system took care of this one for Jenkins. Burley and Matthews both protested their innocence to their lawyers, who insisted that a guilty plea was the only way they'd ever see the outside of a prison again.

Six years later, Burley was still in prison and Jenkins stared at two more busted heaps of metal and plastic in front of him with injured people inside.

And again, he would render no aid.

"HEY, YO, WAYNE, Wayne, Wayne!" a voice shouted from Gondo's car.

The crash had still not come over the radio.

Hersl had a plan.

"Sarge!" Hersl hollered. "We could go and stop the slips at 10:30 before that happened."

"Sounds good to me," Jenkins said. "You all down?"

"'Hey, I was in the car just driving home,'" Hersl said, laughing at the excuse he cooked up.

"How much longer we gotta wait?" Gondo said.

Jenkins would not let them leave until somebody else reported the crash.

The windshield wipers clicked.

The rain softly tapped the car.

Finally, the dispatcher's voice crackled: "Signal 31 at Light and Lombard."

"Hey, I wonder what was in that car," Hersl, mirthful, called out across the rain.

"I don't care," Jenkins said.

"I know, but I'm curious," Hersl said.

"Signal 31 at Light and Lombard," dispatch said again.

"Go back to HQ," Jenkins commanded.

EIGHT

AS THE MOST erratic and criminally ambitious members of the squad, Jenkins and Rayam mostly understood each other. Rayam just didn't get the point of street rips.

They had recently rolled up on a homeless guy, who kept his clothes, cash, and drugs in a storage unit. They found a few grand hidden in a dirty sock, kept the cash, and let him go—what was the point?

"What you going and doing in people's pockets," Rayam said. "It's a fucking waste of time."

"I'm tired of putting my name on shit," Jenkins said.

"Give me the motherfucker, I'll put my name on it," said Rayam, who still hadn't sold the heroin Jenkins gave him.

Jenkins gave Rayam the name of a monster.

"This dude's good for at least two hundred," Jenkins said. "We could go get him."

If they did it, Jenkins said, it would just be the two of them.

Rayam asked Jenkins about Hendrix, Taylor, and Ward.

"They cool. Love them to death," Jenkins said.

They weren't earning what he gave them, though. He told Rayam about Oreese Stevenson. They'd all walked away with $20,000 that day.

"Honestly, they shouldn't have got that much," Jenkins said. "I put all that time and work."

Rayam understood. If he put his name on a job, he was going to take more too.

"How long you think it will take?" Rayam said. "Because I need, I need fifty right now."

A couple of weeks, Jenkins told him.

"I'll be hitting him on those slash days you give us," Rayam said.

He needed a big one.

SITTING ON A curb in handcuffs, Andre Crowder wished he had time to call Ivan Bates. The cops had spotted a gun beneath his car.

Crowder was driving through the Cherry Hill neighborhood in extreme South Baltimore when a pair of headlights were coming at him like someone who wanted to play chicken. He tried to back up and then there was another car behind him, boxing him in.

Now the fat white cop was asking him questions while other cops rolled around on the asphalt, trying to retrieve the gun from under his car.

"I know you don't want to hear it," Crowder said. "But I can explain."

"Well, tell me," Jenkins said, sitting beside Crowder on the curb.

Crowder said a guy had just tried to rob him and in the tussle, he got the gun from him.

"And you took it from him?" Jenkins said. "Did you hurt him when you took the gun from him?"

"No, he was scared," Crowder said. "I was walking to the car. He pulled the gun out. My first instinct was to grab it. I grabbed it. He ran."

"Your intention when you had this gun on you," Jenkins said. "Were you gonna hurt anybody or kill anyone?"

"No," Crowder said. "If I was gonna, I would have did it then and there."

"I'll be honest with you: You're going to go to the jail this evening for handgun on person and maybe in vehicle. It is a misdemeanor in the state of Maryland," Jenkins said. "But you're being very respectful. You admitted to the gun. Honestly, it's just because I like for someone like you to be respectful and just be like, 'I got a gun, it is what it is.'"

But, Jenkins pointed out, Crowder had tried to flee.

"Thank God, we didn't have to hit you or anything," Jenkins said. "Because if you would've went toward any traffic or children, I probably would have hit you with my car for legal intervention to save the kids."

"So what happened? Why was y'all pulling me over?" Crowder said.

"You didn't have your seat belt on," Jenkins said.

Crowder asked Jenkins if he could call his mom to pick up the car so it wasn't towed. Jenkins called Crowder's mom. He put it on speaker so Crowder could hear.

Later that night, Crowder called his mom from Central Booking. She told him the police had followed the car back to their house.

"The fat white man put his foot in the door," she said.

HERSL, WHO HAD always loved being a cop, more or less quit coming to work. The crew was out of control. He had to wear a body camera. He wanted a transfer. He got emotional when he complained to his brother about GTTF.

He spent his days working on his house and continued filing hours. The $300,000-plus rancher he'd bought back in July sat off a small dirt road across from a horse farm on nearly an acre and a half. It needed some work. Most days in September, Hersl found himself driving his truck back and forth between home, Home Depot, and Lowe's. He'd buy a few things, end up going back later to make some returns or pick up something he forget about. He had all the time in the world with his new home, and he collected a paycheck doing it.

Working on his house was like a vacation. He took the aluminum canopies off the windows and removed the cutesy ceramic cats that were supposed to look like they were climbing on the front of the house. He painted the walls tasteful earth tones, installed hardwood floors, and added a deck.

At night out there in the yard, tucked off in the county, all he heard were the sounds of bugs, frogs, and cars rolling by, far in the distance. He could almost relax.

IVAN BATES ALWAYS picked up the phone when Andre Crowder's family called. Andre's father had been one of his first big clients when he'd started as a defense attorney in 2003, and Bates had known Andre's aunt since the '90s, when he'd first moved to Baltimore. She worked at his doctor's office and always helped squeeze him in when he needed something, so when he saw her name come up on his phone, he wondered if he had missed an appointment or something.

She told Bates that they needed his help. Andre had been arrested and charged with a gun and had been denied bail. They needed Bates to get him out as quickly as possible. Andre's three-year-old son, Ahmeer, was in intensive care, and Andre needed to be there.

No problem, Bates told her. He would take care of it. Bates didn't even look at the details of the case. He just wanted to help Crowder get out to see his kid.

He was also trying to help Albert Brown, the Safe Streets

worker Jenkins arrested at a gas station with a gun. Brown told Bates the claim he had a gun in the visor of his van was bogus.

"How stupid would I be," Brown said. "I hit the brakes and end up shooting myself in the head."

Brown also told Bates how they'd just gone in his house with no warrant.

Stopping another black man sitting in a van and then breaking into his house—Jenkins was getting predictable.

Brown's arraignment was coming up, and Bates figured it would be an easy case: Jenkins, Hersl, Rayam. He knew all three had thick Internal Affairs files he could request. And he sent his investigator Orrin Henry to try to see if there was footage of the stop at the gas station and canvass the area for witnesses.

That didn't help Brown right now. Because of political pressure, the gun charge meant that Safe Streets had to suspend Brown from his work as a violence interrupter. Brown would likely lose his job. Bates called a college friend who worked for Safe Streets and vouched for Brown.

IT WAS SEPTEMBER 29, Andre Crowder's twenty-eighth birthday, and Ivan Bates had come through for the family once again: Bates won on Crowder's second bail review.

Crowder left Central Booking and went straight to the University of Maryland Medical Center to see Ahmeer, whose right lung had collapsed. The child was unconscious when his father arrived. Doctors told Crowder they feared the left lung was going to collapse too.

The morning of September 30, around 7:00 A.M., Ahmeer Emonte Crowder died in the shock trauma unit.

"The little sting or whatever they was running wasn't really worth me losing the opportunity to spend the last moments with my child," Crowder recalled. "If it was the money they wanted, the conviction they wanted, whatever they wanted, they could have it. I just don't like the fact it cost me those few moments."

WAYNE JENKINS PULLED into a lane of oncoming traffic beside Gregory Harding, yelling for Harding to pull over. Harding hit the gas and sped through West Baltimore, lobbing coke out the window, bags of blow dropping in front of bus stops along the street.

In front of Mondawmin Mall—the main shopping center on the West side, ground zero for the 2015 rioting, and a gathering place for kids after school—Jenkins bumped the back of Harding's car and sent it into another car. Chase over.

Hendrix and Ward went back to try to retrieve the coke from the street.

Gondo and Rayam arrived after the crash. They could never quite keep up with Jenkins. Gondo had a body cam by now. He turned it on.

"Where's my phone, man? I wanna call my lawyer," Harding said. "What are y'all bothering me for?"

"You threw cocaine out the window!" Jenkins yelled.

"I ain't throw no cocaine out no window," Harding responded.

"You have the right to remain silent. Use that, sir," Jenkins, dark bags under his eyes, commanded.

Police lights flashed. A bus drove by with a heaving groan. The sun set behind the mall, spreading magic-hour gold across the sky. "Lotta, lotta coke," a passerby in headphones and a hoodie said as he cut across the crime scene. Cars blew their horns. Rayam searched Harding's car.

"Probably got like half a key, so far," Jenkins said to Gondo and Rayam.

Hendrix, with a half brick of coke in his hand, walked up to Rayam, who took it.

"I got it," Rayam said, and he stashed the coke in the car.

Gondo, whose job it was to call accident investigation, kept stalling, unsure of Jenkins's plan. There were already so many uniformed cops around.

"Just like last time," Jenkins said under his breath. "He's got half a key here, we can get big shit."

Jenkins got closer to Gondo.

"This guy's big money. We got to do the right thing. Do all of our homework and get on him because he's already lying saying he's coming from work," Jenkins said.

Rayam pressed Harding for information. Harding said he had no idea what they were talking about.

"I just got off of work at Jiffy Lube," Harding said to Rayam. "This is my life. Don't lie on me like that."

Rayam walked off. He looked ghoulish in the flashing red lights of the accident investigation car.

It was almost dark now, the sky a fulgent purple. Harding told them he was injured in the crash, and they called a medic.

Gondo submitted 73.37 grams of cocaine to evidence control that night.

That left Rayam with over 400 grams of Harding's coke to sell.

JENKINS CALLED RAYAM the next morning to see if he'd made any progress in finding a buyer for the heroin he had picked up back in August. With the Harding coke, Rayam's debts to Jenkins were mounting.

Rayam's cousin up in Newark wasn't getting it done, and Rayam was still trying to get the money he owed Jenkins. If he could only think of someone to move the blow, maybe they would take the H too.

His old friend Eric Snell, a former Baltimore cop now working for the Philadelphia Police Department, might help out. When Rayam and Snell were in the academy together, Snell said he had family that were serious Philly dealers. Rayam had reached out to him once before, when he and an old partner stole some weed and needed someone to move it. Snell had been down to do it, but his partner found someone first, so he never followed up.

Rayam could depend on Snell. Rayam was best man in Snell's wedding. They had vacationed in Vegas together. Partied in D.C. They were like brothers. Rayam called Snell.

"Yo, I got nine tickets to the home game," Rayam said.

People call the Orioles "the O's," which could stand for an *ounce,* giving a unit to the number indicated by the tickets. Their home uniforms are white, identifying he had cocaine.

"Huh?" Snell, a midsize, light-skinned man with a thin beard and a boyish face, said.

"Nine tickets to the Orioles game. Home team," Rayam repeated.

Snell got it now and said he would talk to his people. Rayam called Jenkins, told him it looked like it was going to be a go.

That was good, but Harding was going to be a problem. Jenkins got a call that day from Bates, who had represented Harding in 2009 when he was strip-searched by police without "reasonable, articulable suspicion." Bates reminded Jenkins of *Maryland v. Harding,* which had gone on to set precedent in other cases. Bates said that Harding was his client now, and he was not going to be cooperating under any circumstances.

Bates did not believe the stop happened as Jenkins had said. He would be requesting any and all footage of the arrest and would be filing motions to suppress.

Jenkins decided to let the case—which he left in a gray area pending cooperation from Harding—go away, and Harding was never formally charged. He still had Rayam hustling to sell Harding's coke.

That evening, Rayam hadn't heard back from Snell.

"Any word?" Rayam texted.

Snell called him two minutes later to clarify. He'd misunderstood the code. The Orioles are the O's or "the birds," and a *bird* is a kilo. Snell's people were interested in moving nine keys. Nine ounces was not worth it. Things were getting worse for Rayam. He owed money to a lot of people, including Jenkins.

DESPITE THE TENSIONS within the unit, BPD, blinded by statistics, continued to heap praise upon Wayne Jenkins's GTTF. On page 3 of the October 2016 edition of BPD's newsletter, GTTF lieutenant Christopher O'Ree celebrated Jenkins's squad and their collaboration with Chief Sean Miller and the War Room.

"I am extremely proud to showcase the work of Sergeant Wayne Jenkins and the Gun Trace Task Force. This team of dedicated detectives has a work ethic that is beyond reproach," O'Ree wrote. "Ten and a half months into the year and Sergeant Jenkins and his team have 110 arrests for handgun violations and seized 132 illegal handguns. This is no small task."

NINE

JENKINS HAD BEEN dodging Assistant State's Attorney Anna Mantegna for months, but she was relentless.

Mantegna had a case from back in February 2016 when Jenkins had tried to stop Jamal Johnson and Maurice Hill and, Jenkins said, they crashed into his car, almost crushing Taylor's legs between the door and its frame when he tried to get out. Then Johnson and Hill fled. Jenkins chased them, and they smashed into the steps of a church. When he got to the car, Jenkins found a gun lying in the console between the two men. Jostled around by the wreck, there would be no way to prove whose gun it was. At the orders of her front office, Mantegna was going to try, and she needed Jenkins to show up to trial if she was going to get a conviction.

Ten months later, Jenkins had given Mantegna all kinds of excuses for why his detectives couldn't make it to trial. Taylor's aunt died. Jenkins's mother-in-law was in the hospital. Jenkins was getting hardwood floors delivered. In September, he simply did not show up. It made her look like an ass in court.

Mantegna, a short, tough, Irish Italian daughter of a cop, was friends with Hersl, though she hadn't seen him as much lately. They'd done a couple of gang busts together. She was also an unabashed fan of New Kids on the Block, and one of the reasons she'd pushed to get the case wrapped up soon was because she was going on a fan cruise with the '90s boy band, her annual vacation.

Unable to evade Mantegna any longer, Jenkins called her back. She told him she really wanted to prep Taylor, who was terrible on the stand, and she couldn't get in touch with him. The first big delay in the case had come when Taylor lost the phone he had filmed evidence on. Eventually, he found that the video had been uploaded to the cloud and was able to retrieve it, but the footage wasn't particularly helpful. In the video, the driver tells Jenkins he didn't stop because they didn't flash their police lights and says, "I thought y'all was going to kill me."

Mantegna couldn't take this case to trial, especially if Taylor was going to testify about the footage, without some serious prep.

Mantegna also needed Ward, who'd found the gun. Jenkins would work it all out, he told her.

She thanked him and asked who else he was working with now. She knew her friend Hersl had been moved into Jenkins's unit. Jenkins told Mantegna his old squad had all moved over to GTTF, and Gondo and Rayam were working with them too.

"They're dirty as shit," she said. "You better watch them like a hawk."

She told him about Rayam's Franks hearing. She didn't have any hard evidence against Gondo, just that ever since he'd gotten shot, people were suspicious.

Gondo was there with Jenkins as he talked to Mantegna, and Jenkins made a show of acting shocked—angry, even—that command put cops of questionable character in his squad.

What Mantegna told Jenkins seemed to confirm what his old partner Ryan Guinn had already said back in June about the two federal agents who had approached him and asked about Gondo and Rayam. Jenkins only told his old SES crew what Guinn said; he had not mentioned it to Gondo.

When he hung up the phone, Jenkins, now paranoid, told Gondo everything he'd heard before, including that Gondo was on a wiretap and that the case may have been going on for five years.

Gondo had been hearing things too. He already knew about Guinn from Ward. Then Allers told Rayam that he'd heard Gondo was the target of a sting. Allers said he'd heard it from someone in Internal Affairs. Even Taylor was hearing from sources that Internal Affairs was investigating GTTF's overtime and had trackers on their cars.

A couple of months back, Gondo spotted someone in a car who seemed to be watching his house. Gondo walked up to the car and confronted the driver, who left. It freaked Gondo out. He told Rayam about it, and then, when he never saw the car again, he blew the whole thing off.

An investigation going back years didn't seem possible.

"What case?" Gondo asked Rayam. "It's no Pablo Escobar. It's police."

A student of the game, Gondo ran through a recent history of drug-dealing cops in Baltimore with Rayam.

"King and Murray, it was like a year or nine months," he said, referencing the investigation that brought down William King and Antonio Murray, two Baltimore plainclothes who were robbing drug dealers in the early to mid-2000s.

"Sylvester, it was months," Gondo said, referring to a sting that brought down former Rayam collaborator, Michael Sylvester.

Jenkins told Hersl about his talk with Mantegna. Hersl, who had backed away from the job and immersed himself in his country home, had the right idea. Jenkins was going to go on leave. His wife was due in a month. Everyone knew what happened last time, so no one would ask any questions. He would take an extended family medical leave, cool down.

During leave, they could work full-time on a heist, he told Stepp.

. . .

WHEN ANDRE CROWDER came by to visit Bates, his eyes were "red as beets," Bates said.

Crowder was grieving, and he still had to deal with this gun charge. He told Bates he didn't have the money to pay him at the moment. The cops had taken the cash he hid in his room.

"We're like family," Bates said. "We can worry about the money later."

Crowder handed Bates his charging documents. Bates scanned them and started tapping the names on the paper: Gondo, Hendrix, Taylor, and Ward.

"I know these guys," Bates said.

Bates showed Crowder a photo of Jenkins and asked if this was the fat white cop.

It was Jenkins, all right.

"U GOT SOMETHING," Rayam texted his Newark cousin, Kyle Harris, who had not been able to sell the heroin.

Two months had passed since Rayam first picked it up from Jenkins and gone up to Jersey.

Harris strung him along again.

"This been a journey. Lol," Rayam wrote.

"This has been ass lol," Harris responded.

"U telling me. Lol," Rayam wrote. "Make a nigga want to re think getting a quick come up."

If Gondo managed to project the glamour of dealing drugs, Rayam experienced only its grind.

"If you don't give me my money, then go to the bank and get a loan out," Jenkins texted.

Rayam was trying to move it through a friend in Allentown,

Pennsylvania, and it was going nowhere. Then Snell called Rayam back. His family had reconsidered. They could middle the nine ounces of blow.

ON A SUNDAY in October, Bates drove his Lexus over to Jonquil Avenue, the one-way street where Jenkins and his crew had arrested Stevenson and Demetrius Brown back in March.

With every case Bates had picked up since then, Jenkins's pattern emerged more clearly. He was on Damon Hardrick's case, where his investigator learned that Jenkins had wormed his way into Hardrick and Sims's Canton condo. What was funny about that one, as far as Bates could tell, was Jenkins had it all wrong. Sims brought in the family's real money, not Hardrick. She was a local celebrity, netting a few hundred thousand dollars a year with her assorted side gigs and her salon. That's why the couple lived in a Canton condo with cameras everywhere and a security guard.

Bates requested the security footage from the property managers of the condo. That kind of evidence had a way of disappearing in a Jenkins case. Bates had sent his investigator out to get the footage from the security camera at the gas station where Albert Brown, the Safe Streets worker, was arrested. He was able to watch the footage, but the BP wouldn't share it without a subpoena. By the time the paperwork for the subpoena was filed, the video was gone. The gas station manager said the police came and took it.

So Bates was being especially careful with the Stevenson case, going to the scene of the crime himself to absorb all the details. The suburban street of boxy, brick, single-family homes set back in tree-filled yards was quiet and pleasant. It was that time in the season where half the trees glowed gold while the other half was an almost anachronistic green in the low-slanting sunlight.

There were cars parked on both sides of the street, all facing in the same direction. If Jenkins came the wrong way up this one-way street, there is no way that he didn't block Stevenson's van. He snapped a photo of a Do Not Enter sign in front of the cars.

The house Demetrius Brown ran out of was a nice place—stone façade, concrete steps going down the terraced yard. He would call the mother of Brown's children to testify. She saw the whole thing.

Bates studied the streets that bounded the block: Manhattan to the Southeast, Trainor to the Northwest. Jonquil cut diagonally in a southeasterly direction. He memorized the streets, how they all ran into one another.

"Wayne was really crafty and slippery. If you don't know North, South, East, West, Wayne will get you really confused," Bates recalled. "And once you're confused, he has you."

Bates had filed motions to suppress all the evidence from the car stop on the street. And if that failed, he'd file a Franks motion to show that the affidavit for the search warrant contained a series of lies. The suppression hearing and the Franks hearing, if it was necessary, were set for Halloween. A perfect day to confront a monster.

WHEN AN EAGER young officer named James Kostoplis first worked with Jenkins in the Northeast years earlier, the sergeant articulated just two rules.

"You don't take money, and you don't put stuff on people," Jenkins told Kostoplis, whom he called "K-Stop" on his first day.

Kostoplis was serious about his work. He would hang out with the ASAs and ask questions, make sure he learned how to do things the right way, the constitutional way, so they would not be thrown out. Then four years in, Kostoplis left BPD right after the 2015 rioting—he had already been planning to move back to New Jersey, where he got a job as railroad police. After working the streets in Baltimore, being a railroad bull was a bore, so he called Jenkins and asked if he could join Jenkins's squad.

Kostoplis returned to the BPD in February 2016 and in late October was transferred into GTTF. It was exciting. He was doing serious, tangible police work.

Jenkins was about to go on a long leave at the beginning of November, and he was more interested in wrapping up old cases than in making new ones.

And Jenkins was still pushing Rayam about the heroin. Snell could sell it along with the coke, and Rayam could at least give Jenkins a little bit of what he owed.

THE MORNING OF the Stevenson suppression hearing, in a court, where lawyers wait to be assigned to a courtroom for trial, Assistant State's Attorney Corey Kropp told Judge Melissa Phinn that Ward would not be able to attend the hearing.

"One of the major issues in this case is about plain view, and the officers that actually physically made the plain view had a death in the family last night," Kropp told Phinn. "So he's unavailable."

Bates didn't really buy it. He suspected they were playing Kropp, a rookie.

"I think the reason we ran into the issue was one of the other officers, Sergeant Jenkins, he goes on family medical leave tomorrow for sixty days, so that's why we're here to do it today," Bates said.

Judge Phinn noted that Stevenson and Brown had already been in jail for 214 days.

Phinn ordered Ward to come in. The case would begin today. It went to Judge Barry Williams, who had heard the Freddie Gray cases.

Every courtroom in the circuit court has a distinctive style—some looked almost like brutalist bunkers while others resembled a sad dentist's office—but Judge Williams's courtroom looked like a court you would see on television: wood-paneled walls, pew-style seating separated from the hefty wooden tables for the defense and prosecution by theater-style velvet ropes. It was dark and moody and filled with plants.

Bates, Kropp, and Breon Johnson, who was Demetrius Brown's lawyer, waited. Then Stevenson and Brown were led into the room in jumpsuits and handcuffs. Jenkins and Ward still were not present.

Williams called the lawyers to the bench. Kropp explained the situation about Ward and said Jenkins could testify instead. Williams read the case file, whistling as he thumbed through the pages.

"You believe they'll testify consistent with the statement of probable cause?" he asked Kropp.

"I would hope so," Kropp said.

"And have they told you anything that's inconsistent with this?" Williams asked.

"Not that I know of," Kropp said.

While they waited for Jenkins to arrive, Bates checked on the Stevenson's neighbor who was waiting in the hall. Even if he didn't need her for the Franks hearing, Bates hoped her presence would throw Jenkins off. Then Bates walked into the gallery and scanned the room for the feds, hoping they weren't going to be there to pick up the case and nab Stevenson. He said hi to Keona Holloway, who sat with Stevenson's mother.

Finally, the heavy wooden doors heaved open, and Jenkins, unshaven and a bit bedraggled, walked in wearing jeans, a gray sweatshirt, and his Baltimore Police tactical vest.

Kropp began to question Jenkins, first leading him through his career in the Baltimore City Police Department.

"I started in standard uniform patrol—that's the officers in the blue-and-white Baltimore City Police vehicles—in the Eastern District," he said, recounting his résumé with fierce focus, which, if he was lucky, would translate to credibility and carry him through this.

Kropp asked how many drug arrests he'd made over the course of his career.

"I can't guesstimate how many, but I've made or participated in hundreds," Jenkins said.

The aw-shucks honesty of the word *guesstimate* worked on the stand. Jenkins came across as a relatively normal cop, unschooled and earnest. He called Stevenson and Bates "Mr. Oreese" and "Mr. Bates" each time he mentioned them. Whenever he finished an answer, though, he leaned back, cocked his head to the side, and his eyes invariably cut right, a quick nervous glance at Williams.

Kropp led Jenkins through the events of March 22.

"Would it be your routine procedure to stop and investigate somebody sitting in a car?" Kropp asked.

"No," Jenkins said. "We would stop and talk to people sitting in a car. We always stop and ask if everything's okay. 'How you doing?' Old or young, and we also never know who's going to provide us with information about current crime that's going on or about past crime that's going on—it could be old, young, black, white, female, male. You never know who's going to speak to the police."

His answers stressed the fact that he was aware of citizen rights and always acted in accordance with the law. He insisted that it was normal to drive the wrong way up a one-way. He did it every day.

"So you saw someone getting in the car with a book bag," Kropp asked. "What, if anything, did you do?"

"The vehicle he was driving was parked curbside on Jonquil. I was coming down the middle of Jonquil," Jenkins said. "I stopped in close proximity—not directly alongside Mr. Oreese's vehicle, but I stopped almost in front of it on the left-hand side so he could have pulled off straight or went in reverse."

An important lie. If Stevenson's van was blocked in, then, legally, it was a car stop, and there had to be reasonable suspicion.

"I'm trying to figure this out too," Williams interjected, reading glasses on, pen in hand, squinting down at notes he had taken. "You're going down the wrong way. So you're going toward the vehicle, correct?"

"No, sir. I am going towards the vehicle, but the vehicle's parked curbside and I'm in the middle of the road," Jenkins said.

When Kropp asked Jenkins why he'd parked his car like he had, Jenkins admitted, after a fashion, to unconstitutional policing in the past.

"I had times where I lost cases in the past where I could pull up to a vehicle prematurely and then coming to trial and I would learn that just based off what you seen you can't stop the vehicle and I would lose in motion-to-suppress hearings," Jenkins said. "So now if I pull next to an individual and it's not per se a traffic stop and I'm just going to speak to that individual, I always give them room to exit freely without stopping them or limiting their movement because I don't want to lose in court."

Jenkins finished his explanation, brought his hands together in front of him, and looked up at Williams just a moment too long, his entire head turned, betraying, for the first time that day, something that looked a lot like fear. Then he described, in great detail, the way he witnessed Stevenson throw a bag to the back of the van seconds after they pulled up—suspicious behavior, Jenkins argued.

"When I pull up, a large portion of individuals do not do any sudden movements or make any throwing motions because of the fear of police," Jenkins said. "And on this day when I stopped in close proximity to the minivan after seeing an individual walk to it with a book bag and then Mr. Oreese made a throwing motion, I believed Mr. Oreese was attempting to hide contraband—CDS, currency, firearms—something to make an individual do that kind of dramatic movement knowing the police were present."

When it was time for Bates's cross-examination of Jenkins, his tone was chipper, arrogant, as if he were really going to enjoy this.

"Good morning, Sergeant," Bates said.

"Hello, sir. How are you?" Jenkins mumbled.

"Good, good. Very briefly," Bates responded. "So it's your testimony that there were no vehicles in front of this minivan parked on the side of the street?" he asked.

Jenkins went into another long explanation again of the angle of his car—"The vehicle could've got out of there, sir," he concluded.

"You're in the vehicle, you stop at the bumper, and there are four officers in your vehicle, correct?" Bates asked.

"Yes, sir," Jenkins said.

"All four officers then get out of the vehicle at the same time, correct?" Bates asked.

"Within close proximity of, seconds, yes, sir," Jenkins said.

"And all four officers walk toward this minivan, correct?" Bates asked.

"They did, yes, sir," Jenkins said.

"You have your police vest on, correct?" Bates asked.

"We do," Jenkins said.

"And you have your handgun on the side of your police vest as well—I mean, on your hip as well. Correct?" Bates asked.

Jenkins was not in control. Stevenson, in his yellow jumpsuit, cocked his shaved head.

"You don't know if there was a bag in the passenger seat and he had just thrown it in the back when you were driving up?" Bates asked.

"I do not," Jenkins said.

Bates threw in a little something to trip Jenkins up.

"Now, when you approached this vehicle, you didn't have a CI tip to say anything was about to happen, correct?" Bates asked.

"No, sir," Jenkins said.

"You didn't know these individuals, had never seen them before, correct?" Bates asked.

"No, sir," Jenkins said.

"So someone throws something in their back seat and someone gets in their minivan, then that was the reason you approached the vehicle?" Bates asked.

"No, sir. Mr. Brown already got in the vehicle. If Mr. Oreese was in the vehicle and I never saw Mr. Brown—" Jenkins said, then he lost track, paused and reset. "When I see an individual sitting in a parked car, I stop and speak to that individual, every day, probably fifteen to twenty times a day when I'm on the street."

Bates asked if it was against the law to sit in a minivan, to get into a minivan. Then he switched back to what Jenkins knew about Stevenson.

"Now," Bates said, letting the word drag, before pushing Jenkins again. "At that point in time when you saw Mr. Brown and Mr. Stevenson, you didn't have any information about anything involving them, correct?"

"No, sir, I did not," Jenkins said.

Bates returned to the simplest, strongest point Brown's lawyer already argued—with cops all around the van, it was inherently blocked in—and came back to the moment Stevenson got out of the car.

"Isn't it true that they were in custody at that moment?" Bates asked.

"They were not, sir," Jenkins said.

"Now—" Bates began.

Jenkins cut him off.

"When we asked them to exit their vehicle, they were free to go," Jenkins said. "They could have pulled off, and they were not blocked or restricted whatsoever from the front."

"Now if he'd have pulled off, you would have charged him with fleeing from the police. Isn't that correct?" Bates said.

"No, sir," Jenkins said.

Bates asked Jenkins how Ward came to see the coke. He showed pictures of the van's tinted windows to Jenkins.

"You cannot see the back seat of that van in either photo, right?" Bates asked.

Jenkins swallowed hard.

"It states in the probable cause, like I told you, once they exited, Ward went in the driver's side and saw the narcotics," Jenkins said.

Bates pounced. "He went into the driver's side of the vehicle?"

"He did," Jenkins said.

"So he went into the vehicle?" Bates said with a gestural flourish of the hands.

The questioning continued, but that was essentially it: Jenkins said Ward went into the van before they had probable cause to search. When Jenkins got off the stand, he waited outside the courtroom. He wasn't going to leave until he knew what happened with Stevenson.

Brown's ex, Lillian Ramirez, who saw the whole thing, testified that Jenkins and Taylor came in and took her phone and searched the house. She confirmed Jenkins's car was at a forty-five-degree angle to the van—there was no way the van could have pulled away.

Judge Williams took his glasses off and rubbed his forehead and eyes the entire time he recounted the facts of the case.

"This court makes the finding that at the point in time that at least three of four officers were surrounding the vehicle where the only movement that led to the stopping of the vehicle was a throwing motion," Williams said. "Everything that happened after that was from the conduct of the police stopping the vehicle and seizing the individuals."

Kropp stood up and tried to do the best he could to make a separate case against Stevenson, resulting from the drugs in the house. Williams seemed annoyed.

"Do you really need me to go forward with my analysis?" Williams asked.

"A neutral and detached magistrate did feel at the time that there was a valid reason to give these officers a search and seizure warrant," Kropp argued.

Williams called Bates and Kropp to the bench.

"I'd be happy to go through the entire motion if that's what you want me to do, but then I'll have to make certain findings beyond that which I've already made, which is absolutely fine by me, but that gets into an assessment of credibility," Williams said of the Franks motion Bates had filed to question the credibility of the search warrant. "Is that what you want this court to do?"

Williams was the judge who, several months back, had deemed Rayam not credible. A similar fate could befall Jenkins if they went forward.

"No," Kropp said.

"I'll also say, it's not just the statement," Bates said. "But they took the key off him and went back to his house and then searched it. They went into it. So they wouldn't even have the key if the stop hadn't been bad."

"It's up to you," Williams said.

Kropp announced that the state would drop all the charges. Stevenson stood up, shook Bates's hand, looked him in the eye, and said, "Thanks."

"You need to call me," Bates quietly told Stevenson. "The feds either gonna pick you up because they're going to charge you or make you testify."

Bates packed up all his papers into his briefcase, picked up his long gray overcoat, swung it over his shoulder, and stepped out into the hallway, semi-triumphant.

Jenkins walked up beside Bates, who waited for the elevator.

The two men—one short and white, wearing a police vest and cargo pants; the other tall, and black, wearing a suit, bright-patterned socks, and shiny shoes—stood waiting on the elevator.

Jenkins joked that Bates had finally beat him in court.

The elevator doors opened. Bates's and Jenkins's reflections pulled apart as they stepped into the small musty elevator together.

"I don't know what you're doing, but everybody says the same thing: You're lying, you're stealing, you're breaking, you're violating people's rights," Bates said. "I don't know if you are, I don't know if you're not, I'm not out there. But what I can tell is that's what my clients are saying, and if you are, you've got to stop it because it's only going to end bad."

Jenkins said none of that was true. Bates's clients were lying on him, angry that they'd been locked up.

"I keep winning cases against you, so something must be wrong," Bates said.

Jenkins went on the offensive. He told Bates he was done with locking people like Stevenson up if Bates was just going to get them off every time. Jenkins said he was going to go on his parental leave, come back, make lieutenant, and quit putting himself on the line.

Bates thought of his own daughter. He told Jenkins that was a good idea.

Wayne Jenkins *(Courtesy US Attorney's Office)*

Ivan Bates *(Courtesy Alpine Labs)*

Marcus Taylor (*Courtesy US Attorney's Office*)

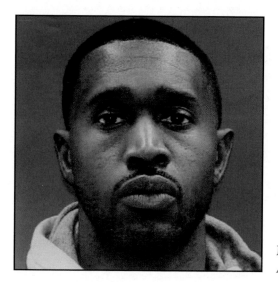

Maurice Ward (*Courtesy US Attorney's Office*)

Evodio Hendrix (*Courtesy US Attorney's Office*)

Donny Stepp (*Courtesy Alpine Labs*)

Stepp and Jenkins at Super Bowl XLVII (*Courtesy US Attorney's Office*)

Police photo of Oreese Stevenson's safe (*Baltimore Police Department file*)

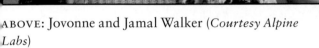

ABOVE: Jovonne and Jamal Walker (*Courtesy Alpine Labs*)

RIGHT: Keith Gladstone (*Courtesy Baltimore Police Department*)

BELOW: BB gun planted on Demetric Simon (*Baltimore Police Department file*)

Jenkins interrogating Walter Price

Jenkins receiving the Bronze Star in 2016
(Screenshot from Baltimore Police Department footage)

Momodu Gondo (*Courtesy US Attorney's Office*)

Jemell Rayam (*Courtesy US Attorney's Office*)

Daniel Hersl (*Courtesy US Attorney's Office*)

Ronald Hamilton (*Courtesy Alpine Labs*)

Charles Smith (*Courtesy Alpine Labs*)

Security camera footage of Jenkins and Hersl leaving April Sims and Damon Hardrick's condo

Albert Brown interrogated by Jenkins, captured on Hersl's body camera

Umar Burley (*Courtesy Alpine Labs*)

Umar Burley's car after the crash (*Baltimore Police Department file*)

Andre Crowder (*Courtesy Alpine Labs*)

Jenkins during the arrest of Gregory Harding, captured on Gondo's body camera (*Courtesy US Attorney's Office*)

Former Assistant State's Attorney Anna Mantegna
(*Courtesy Alpine Labs*)

Eric Snell, Gondo, and Rayam in Las Vegas
(*Courtesy US Attorney's Office*)

Assistant US Attorney Leo Wise
(*Courtesy Alpine Labs*)

Assistant US Attorney Derek Hines
(*Courtesy Alpine Labs*)

Special Agent Erika Jensen (*Courtesy Alpine Labs*)

Defense Attorney Natalie Finegar (*Courtesy Alpine Labs*)

Public Defender Deborah Katz Levi (*Courtesy Alpine Labs*)

Robbery gear found in Jenkins' vehicle (*Courtesy US Attorney's Office*)

TEN

WAYNE AND KRISTY'S new baby boy was born on November 10, one year after Lucas Colton was buried.

The Jenkinses celebrated the baby's birth, still mourning the loss they had suffered the year before. The Jenkins family had taken its hits. Wayne's father, Lloyd, was an orphan who kicked around in the foster system, went into the marines, started a family, and then brought Bobby, his brother's son, into the family, adopting him when his brother died young. While everybody called Bobby Wayne's brother, really they were cousins. Another one of Wayne's brothers had been using drugs for years and was moving along the rocky road of recovery. There was Kristy's lupus, which brought the couple closer together, made them grow up a little faster than most other teens in the county, and always, Wayne's dangerous job out there on the mean streets of Baltimore.

Christmas was coming. Last year, Kristy placed a flower arrangement with poinsettias, holly berries, and pinecones on the grave of Lucas Colton. This year, they would have the new baby to dote on.

RIGHT AFTER HE went on leave, Jenkins texted Rayam, pissed about how long it was taking to get his money.

"Horrible," is all that one text Jenkins sent said.

Rayam ignored it. He hadn't worked much lately. Getting rid of this hodgepodge heroin was a full-time job. He complained to Ayesha Hood, a Baltimore police officer who knew he was moving drugs.

"I think I'm to 'soft' for this or my position doesn't allow me to react the way I want or both," Rayam wrote to Hood. "Either way the tab is 10300 and some of that is what I took out to settle with white boy."

Snell had deposited $2,500 in Rayam's PNC account two days earlier and had some more money for him now. Since they had to meet up anyway, they decided to party at the casino. Rayam texted his wife and said he would be coming home late. This was supposed to be a return to their old, more carefree days of friendship, but the bad feelings from the fucked-up money intruded. A little after midnight, Rayam wrote a series of texts to Ayesha Hood.

"This nigga trying to get shit for even cheaper off me," he wrote. "I took a lot of loses but during this I know who true friends are."

Hood did not respond.

"I know u don't want to hear this but I rather Gondo b in my business. At least $ was never messed up," Rayam wrote.

Next, Rayam texted Gondo. They had drifted apart too.

"Yo my nigga," he wrote. "I got some real <u>100</u> <u>100</u> shit to say."

"What's up," Gondo replied.

"With all the shit I've seen and dealing with 'street' u, meaning 'I' really find out who r really true niggas," Rayam wrote. "I think niggas have to experience the streets to really see how niggers are. Ain't that many <u>100</u> <u>100</u> niggas out here."

"With that being said," he continued when Gondo did not respond. "I never had a problem with u . . . No homo . . . We a dying bried . . ."

The heroin still wasn't selling, so Rayam got it back from Snell and planned to drop it off with his burglary buddy Tom Finnegan.

AS FAR AS Stepp could tell, Jenkins spent all his new free time hatching an ambitious heist with him. They illegally bugged vehicles, listened to conversations, and matched up the intelligence they'd gathered from different sources. The target brought in more cocaine than Stepp had ever imagined possible in a city like Baltimore: 100–250 kilos every 120 days.

Their target had an elaborate setup. Handoffs happened via dumpsters. Drugs would get dropped off in a dumpster, then someone else would grab the coke as the money was retrieved from another nearby dumpster where it had been deposited by another party. The target sat in a high-rise where he watched the whole thing play out with a pair of binoculars—a perch far away from the actual transaction kept him from getting his hands dirty.

They planned to snatch the cocaine and money at the same time, ripping off the dumpsters and then, posing as ATF agents, raid the target's high-rise. They would hide the coke in a car in the police headquarters parking garage until they shuttled it to Stepp's offshore source.

"I had done lined up from out of the country for it to go away," Stepp recalled. "So I was going to wholesale all of it. Quick wholesale and keep some for ourselves."

Stepp thought of it as their "retirement score." Enough cash that he could stop robbing and dealing and weather the changes in the bail bonds industry and go mostly legit. He had done a lot of time in his life, and he realized, at close to fifty, that he didn't have that much left and he didn't want to waste it in prison. He was raising a special-needs child and had a devoted spouse who loved him.

Antsy with more free time, unable to get the daily rhythm of the streets out of his head, Jenkins floated near daily schemes to hit some smaller target somewhere near or in the city for far less, deferring the "retirement score."

Jenkins told Stepp that he should work out a deal with Gondo. There may be something to gain in teaming up, he suggested. Jenkins had always told Stepp that Gondo couldn't be trusted. The change of heart didn't make much sense.

SINCE THE HAMILTONS had been robbed by GTTF in July, Nancy Hamilton had been scared to be in the house alone. When she got off work, she wandered around the Walmart ten minutes away from their house and waited for Ronald to get home. She was taking medication for her nerves.

On November 16, the Hamiltons desperately tried to regain some measure of control over the situation when they walked into the Carroll County Courthouse to get their $50,000 back.

Hamilton had called the Carroll County Sheriff's Office the morning after the robbery and told one of the officers who had come to the house that he was missing $20,000 on top of the $50,000 seized.

"It was only fifty," the cop insisted. Hamilton realized that not only would he likely never see the stolen $20,000, he was going to have to fight like hell if he ever wanted to get the $50,000, even though they'd never charged him with a crime. Civil asset forfeiture laws in Maryland were among the harshest in the country, tipped heavily toward cops, who didn't have to convict, or even charge, someone to take cash and never give it back. The only recourse for Hamilton was to take the state to court and prove that he had earned the money legally.

Hamilton showed up at the old county courthouse, armed with sheaves of receipts from used car sales, Maryland Live! Casino winnings, and rent checks from the buildings he co-owned in

Baltimore—all evidence that he had legally earned the cash that the county had confiscated.

On the other side, the state brought only Rayam and the same Carroll County cop who had not believed Hamilton when he'd called the day after the theft to complain. Hamilton wondered where the other city cops were.

"This is a setup," Hamilton told his lawyer. "If you're gonna sit here and let me go one-on-one against a cop, I'm dead, hands down."

"You're a gambling man," the lawyer said. "You might as well take what you can take."

The prosecutors argued that they had enough evidence to convict Hamilton of crimes. They would not share any evidence because, they said, the indictments were sealed. And so the word of Rayam, who was not generally used in Baltimore City courts because of the Franks hearing he lost, was enough for Carroll County to keep half of Hamilton's cash.

"I produced every document to show my money was legit, but that still wasn't good enough for the courts," Hamilton recalled. "It made me feel like my word wasn't worth shit."

In the hallway outside the courtroom, Rayam took out his phone and started photographing Hamilton.

"We're not finished with you," Rayam told Hamilton.

"He's threatening me," Hamilton said to his lawyer. "He's over there taking pictures of me."

Hamilton took out his own phone and started taking pictures of Rayam taking pictures of him. Rayam turned and started to walk down the marble staircase with the Carroll County cop.

Hamilton kept taking photos.

"Man, he a crooked cop!" Hamilton yelled. "He robbed me!"

ON NOVEMBER 21, the FBI approached Oreese Stevenson. There were two agents—a man and a woman—and they had been listening to the jail calls that had obsessed Jenkins and had a lot of questions about what happened on March 22, 2016.

Stevenson refused to talk to them without a lawyer. Then he called Bates and said he did not want to talk to the FBI at all.

For a while, Bates had felt certain that the feds were looking at Jenkins, but after Trump's shocking November 8 victory, Bates felt like any case they were building might get quashed. It really mattered who the president was in federal cases, he believed. Back under George W. Bush, Bates called the federal courthouse "the Hall of Horrors" because people who went in never came out. Under Barack Obama, all of that started to change. Trump seemed dead set on changing it back, to before the Bush era even, nominating staunchly revanchist, Confederate-sympathizing Jeff Sessions as attorney general.

In those dark fall weeks following the election, Bates wondered what federal prosecutors working under Trump and Sessions would end up doing with information on a dirty cop in a city soon to be under a consent decree.

Stevenson's call confirmed the FBI was investigating Jenkins.

And they were talking to his victims.

ON THE SAME day that the FBI contacted Stevenson, Walter Price and his wife, Sakinah DeGross, met for a Thanksgiving celebration at the Park School, an elite private academy their oldest son attended, just north of the city line.

Since their 2014 encounter with Jenkins, the couple had put their lives back together. Price owned a few properties, was taking care of their house, and took the kids to school in the morning. He was focused on Not Forgotten, the company he'd founded in 2011 and the app it created, Jail Mail.

With Jail Mail, people in Maryland could write letters, upload pictures, whatever they wanted to send to an incarcerated loved one, and he would print it out and send it to the inmate according to prison regulations, which were sometimes hard for the families of prisoners to navigate. Jail Mail had expanded over the past two years; it was now operating all across the country.

Price's case was the closest Jenkins had come to being undone, all because he'd failed to consider the cameras. If it had not been for De Sousa's intervention, the riots, and the new demands of the Davis regime, the case where he'd gotten caught on camera lying might have ended Jenkins's career.

At the Park School that night, Price and DeGross imagined a future for their kid that was much different from Price's past. When the celebration was over and they'd finished shaking hands and wishing happy holidays to teachers, administrators, and other parents, DeGross and their son got in her car. They were going to pick up the youngest child. Price got in his Dodge Ram truck. He told her he would meet her at home.

Sometime that night, men in black masks approached Price, restrained his hands behind his back with zip ties, and abducted him. He was shot and killed, his body left on Random Road, a residential street in a far-off stretch of Southwest Baltimore.

When DeGross got home with the kids to Severna Park, a suburb between Baltimore and Annapolis, she was surprised to find that Price wasn't there. She figured he must have gone out. She went to sleep. She woke up in the middle of the night and called him. Straight to voicemail. The next morning, straight to voicemail again. He was supposed to take the kids to school. He wouldn't forget to do that. She called around to his friends. No one had seen him.

Later that day, a homicide detective knocked on DeGross's door. He told her that Price's body had been found on Random Road. They identified him by his fingerprints. They couldn't find his truck.

The detective asked DeGross if there was any reason Price

would be in the city. He owned property but nowhere close to where they found him, she said. Then he asked her if Price had any enemies. "Anyone who could want to see him hurt?"

DeGross could not think of anyone.

WAYNE JENKINS WAS especially involved in the holiday festivities at his kids' school.

"At Christmas, the Jenkins family sent in toys for the school drive, canned goods for the homeless shelter, and mittens for our mitten tree," Wendy Kraft, who had taught both Jenkins boys in kindergarten, recalled. "They bestowed presents not only upon their child's teacher but also the nurse, secretaries, and administration. This was their way of thanking everyone for all they do for their children and community."

It wasn't only at holidays. The Jenkins family was always active in school life, and Jenkins made sure to go on field trips and speak at Career Day about being a cop.

Kraft became close with the family. She retired from teaching in 2015, and in the fall of 2016, she had an idea: she could watch the kids when Jenkins went back to work in January.

She was hired.

ANTONIO SHROPSHIRE PULLED his car in front of the Rite Aid in the Alameda Shopping Center, parking it alongside the yellow curb. It was November 30, a week after Thanksgiving, a drizzly morning.

He got out of his car and left a package of heroin and cocaine on the seat. No one would mess with him for leaving it there. This was his neighborhood. He'd lived here all his life, except when he was locked up. It was a rental anyway. Always a better move when you've got weight. Insured they couldn't try to keep your car if they busted you.

He walked inside Rite Aid, filled his prescriptions at the pharmacy, bought a drink, and walked back to the car, keys in his hand.

Two cops grabbed him. They weren't city cops. David McDougall was a detective from Harford County, and Scott Kilpatrick came from Baltimore County.

They handcuffed Shropshire and searched him. He had about $5,000 in his pocket and two cell phones—one of which they'd had a wiretap on since fall 2015. In the car, there were several more phones and the package of heroin and cocaine.

McDougall and Kilpatrick had been investigating overdoses in their respective counties, tracing the heroin back to dealers and suppliers, working their way up the food chain, and into the city. The overdose of a young white girl back in 2011—three days after Christmas—went back to a middle-aged guy who had bought the dope from a Shropshire associate, Twan. A lot of other people they'd talked to since then mentioned a city dealer named Brill.

"We've been looking for you for a long time," McDougall said.

Shropshire laughed. As the detectives drove Shropshire in for processing, he tried to keep it light. They discussed sports and music and Christmas.

Shropshire joked to his captors that they should take what they'd found in his car, sell it, and use the cash to buy something nice for their wives for the holidays.

"YO WHAT'S GOOD bro?" Snell texted Rayam on the morning of December 5, checking in on his friend, worried the back-and-forth dealing had created a riff. "You good?"

"Hell nah," Rayam replied an hour later. "I got 2 open IAD complaints. Kind of fucked me up. Been chilling lately . . . Nothing on the level of the streets but a lot of BS."

"Ard. I was seeing what's up. I didn't know if you had an

issue with me or whatever," Snell wrote. "You haven't been hitting me up."

"Yo never going to be an issue with us. U know how I get when a lot on my mind. Big head and all. Lol . . . ," Rayam replied. "I'm about to leave this job."

"I feel you homie. Cool, just making sure. Are they major IAD complaints?" Snell texted.

"Nothing on that level," Rayam wrote of the citizen complaints. "But I did some stupid shit that jus affects me so I've been quiet."

ANNA MANTEGNA REACHED out to Hersl at the end of the year. His girlfriend had left him and taken their son. He had a new house and was in it all alone. It was near the holidays. He wasn't doing well.

On December 21, she texted him about meeting up. He agreed to meet in Canton, at an Irish bar on the same strip as Looney's. They caught up and had a good time. There was also something weird and sad about it.

"Thank you for the drinks and the food and the company!" Mantegna texted later that night. "Sorry, didn't mean to not say thank you!"

"U never have to thank me girl I know where u heart is," Hersl replied.

"Still hun, I appreciate that. I still wanted to say thank you."

"10-4," Hersl wrote, adding emojis of a police officer and a police car.

A couple of days later, she texted him again. "Merry Christmas," along with a Christmas tree emoji.

"Thanxs Anna same too u girl," Hersl wrote.

. . .

LIKE THE JENKINS family, the Bates family spent Christmas with a new baby.

Bates's mother had a difficult time getting around, but when she was with London, she seemed ten years younger. London brightened Ivan's father up too. And Lana's family was all there. Her sister was on leave from the army, and her father was going to start working for Ivan as the office manager in the new year.

Over the holiday, Ivan dropped hints to his family—floated test balloons, as they say in politics—about going up against Marilyn Mosby and running for state's attorney.

Bates was doing exceptionally well for himself. He thought a lot about the phrase he had heard so often at Howard University— "lift as you climb." He worried he wasn't doing his share of lifting. He looked at London sitting there on the floor in a Christmas sweater, the light coming in sideways from the window, and he saw his parents and Lana and her parents all sitting around the tree, and kind of knew in his heart that he would have to try to run for state's attorney.

FOUR DAYS AFTER Christmas, Gondo's father died of pancreatic cancer.

Albert Momodu Samuel Gondo had been part of a wave of young people to travel to the United States from Sierra Leone in the 1970s on student visas. He left his hometown of Gbangbatok and came to the United States, where he met Gondo's mother. They lived in Kansas for a while and ended up in Baltimore. Albert got a master's from Towson University and started teaching. Everyone in the aspirational, tree-lined Alameda, where black families moved their children to escape from the streets, knew and respected him. They called him "Father" at the Lutheran church they attended.

He'd tried to keep his kids on the porch, away from the streets. Gondo's sister had been a track star at Morgan State University, a neighborhood hero, celebrated by the press for her speed and her smarts. This is what the children of first-generation immigrants did: they excelled, became respectable. Momodu seemed to go even one better. As a police detective, he was not only living right but fighting for others, for justice, risking his life. He was an exemplar.

But Gondo was struggling to balance his roles as cop and criminal. Rayam was running around chasing cash. They weren't even really talking. And then there was the tracker on Shropshire's car last March. He was sure he'd seen somebody watching his house. In October, all the talk about an investigation, about wiretaps. Then Shropshire got picked up by county cops in November. That whole crew locked up for dope now—except for Wells.

Wells was there at the funeral, his heavy locks tied back, paying respect, but things were not the same between them.

Momodu Gondo was alone.

DURING JENKINS'S LEAVE, no one did much work. It was a good chance for everyone to clear up some of the complaints they'd amassed under the hard-charging direction of Jenkins.

Kostoplis was frustrated.

"I suggested that we maybe go to the ranges that are around Baltimore and check the shooters' logs to see if maybe any prohibited persons are, you know, shooting a gun there," he recalled. "But, you know, that idea was shot down. They said, 'No, we don't do that here.' And being the new guy, I wasn't sure if there was maybe a reason for that, but I just was like, 'Okay.'"

Kostoplis worked on his own, logging overtime listening to 911 calls where there had been a shooting and going and canvassing the area, asking questions. He did some crime suppression overtime and even went out on patrol looking for action one day.

Kostoplis wasn't the only one eager for Jenkins to return. Command wanted results, and Jenkins usually brought them.

"Get him back to work and focused," command demanded of Jenkins's lieutenant, Christopher O'Ree.

Jenkins had other plans. He told O'Ree that "his family was more important, and he didn't want to continue taking the same chances."

AFTER THE FBI visited Stevenson in November, he changed his phone number and didn't respond to messages people left with Holloway.

The U.S. Attorney's Office really wanted to get in touch with Stevenson, so Assistant U.S. Attorney Leo Wise, who ran the public corruption division, called Bates. He needed Stevenson to show up at the grand jury.

Stevenson's testimony was crucial, Wise told Bates, and they did not want to prosecute Stevenson for any of the drugs. He would receive complete immunity.

Bates told Wise that Stevenson was old-school, but he would see what he could do.

It took Bates a few days to finally get in touch with Stevenson.

"You aren't snitching if it's dirty cops," Bates told him.

Stevenson was not swayed. Then the FBI went to Holloway's workplace and subpoenaed her, and Stevenson relented.

WHEN WAYNE JENKINS returned to work, he went to a supervisor's office and handed her a letter requesting a transfer to the Warrant Apprehension Task Force, where all the burnouts go to finish their time easy. Jenkins was the best gun cop the city had ever seen. Now he was "very disgruntled, and very vocal about getting all these guns for command and being underappreciated," command said.

If Jenkins was not going to make lieutenant, he was going to get away from this squad. At the same time, most of the squad was desperate to escape Jenkins.

"Let's go for a ride," Jenkins said to K-Stop. It was one of the first days Jenkins was back in the office. Hersl, big and lanky, stood beside him.

Kostoplis got off the couch in GTTF's office in headquarters, and the three men walked together to the garage and got into Jenkins's van.

Jenkins drove a couple of blocks, parked. It was dark out. He ordered Hersl and Kostoplis to leave their phones and their radios in the van. They walked around to the back of the van.

"What do you think about this?" Jenkins said to K-Stop. "We conduct an investigation. We start following around a high-level drug dealer, find out where he's keeping all his cash and his money, and we just go take it."

"No," Kostoplis said. "That's a terrible fucking idea."

He thought Jenkins was testing him and took the opportunity to make a little speech.

"You can't have a badge on your chest and do things like that," Kostoplis said. "You know, the fact that law enforcement doesn't do that is what separates law enforcement from criminals."

Jenkins and Hersl told K-Stop they agreed with him.

They got back in the van, and Jenkins drove them over by Eutaw Street, where there was usually a lot of hand-to-hand dealing. Jenkins spotted a drug deal going down and jumped out of the van and started to chase the customer. The guy dropped his dope. Then Jenkins got back in the van and drove a few blocks away, looking for a black Jeep he'd been watching. A patrol car got on their tail, and Jenkins hit the gas to lose it.

The patrol car caught up with the van, and Jenkins rolled down his window and flashed his badge. The uniform drove off. Kostoplis didn't know what was happening.

. . .

BATES WAS LATE to Albert Brown's hearing on January 30. He had another client that same day on another floor of the courthouse and was still wrapping up when Brown's case got called. There was so much to do, the cases were piling up—Sims and Hardrick a few days from now, Crowder's gun charge soon enough, whatever was happening with Stevenson and the grand jury. He spent a lot of time lately thinking about Jenkins and wading through a series of complicit or clueless assistant state's attorneys.

Today, it would be Brian Pritchard on behalf of the state, exhausted and exasperated. Both lawyers approached Judge Charles Peters.

"Have you looked at the body camera footage?" Bates asked Pritchard.

"Yes," Pritchard said.

"Do you recognize your officers have some issues? They went into his house without a warrant," Bates said.

"When do they go in his house?" Pritchard said peevishly.

"When they go to Mount Street, they go in the house without a warrant. They have his driver's license and find out he lives directly in front of Mount Street," Bates said.

"This is a pullover at a gas station," Pritchard said.

"I hear you," Bates said. "But they go in his house."

Pritchard asked if it happened after they'd found the gun and drugs in Brown's van.

"After it," Bates said. "Without a warrant."

"So that has nothing to do with this case," Pritchard said.

"It has everything to do with it," Bates said. "Because they lie about everything."

Pritchard hadn't watched all the footage from Hersl's body camera, which began with Brown mid-Mirandization and goes on for more than twenty minutes after that. Bates told Pritchard and Judge Peters he also had not yet received the Internal Affairs files he'd requested.

"Do you have any idea if there are IAD records?" Judge Peters asked for a case involving, among others, Jenkins, Hersl, and Rayam.

"I know there's some for Wayne Jenkins. I've had a few of his cases," Bates said. "I do know there's one as well."

"Rayam," Pritchard interjected.

Bates took a breath and explained why body camera footage showing them illegally entering Brown's house was an issue, overall, of truthfulness.

"I guess you may have a good lawsuit, potentially," Judge Peters said.

Pritchard said he planned to call only Hersl to the stand anyway.

"As far as I know, he doesn't have any IAD issues," Pritchard said.

Bates mentioned Hersl's "pretty lengthy file." There was also the issue with the gas station footage, which the police took.

Pritchard sighed. His voice went whiny.

"Your Honor, can we please bring this case back in a few weeks?" Pritchard asked.

Bates was pushing cases as far out as he could, anticipating Jenkins going down. Brown's new trial date was March 30.

JENKINS TOLD KOSTOPLIS he was being transferred.

"He said he was on the lieutenant's list and that, you know, he had a lot of complaints. He wanted to get rid of the complaints," Kostoplis recalled. "They weren't going to be going on the street. And he knows I like being on the street."

Then Hersl got transferred. He landed in Citywide Shooting,

out of enforcement and off the street altogether now. After almost two decades of busting heads, Hersl was riding a desk and wearing a suit every day, going out to investigate shootings. It was the end of a very long run. He told his family he was happy to be away from the GTTF squad he had been working with.

When Hersl stopped by the State's Attorney's Office one day shortly after the transfer, his friend Anna Mantegna was shocked by the transformation. Hersl usually wore sweats and T-shirts and sneakers—and when he wasn't out running around, flip-flops— and here he was in a navy-blue suit.

Something about him seemed so sad to Mantegna. She showed him a wall where she had hung pictures of known members of an East side gang she was looking at for a case. Hersl knew the backstory of every one of them and corrected a few mistakes Mantegna had made—one of the guys she had hanging up was actually a member of a rival crew.

He'd looked alive, she noticed, when he was talking about the East side.

ON FEBRUARY 2, Stevenson and Holloway met Bates at his office, and they all walked to Lombard Street and into the federal courthouse where the grand jury was convened.

When Bates knocked on the big, wooden door on the eighth floor, he half expected Stevenson to change his mind and bolt.

Leo Wise and another U.S. attorney, Derek Hines, greeted them. Both young prosecutors had built impressive résumés before coming to Baltimore. Wise had cut his teeth in the government's case against Big Tobacco, moved on to Enron, and, in 2008, was named as the founding director of the Office of Congressional Ethics. Hines, nearly a decade younger than Wise, spent two years in New Orleans rooting out fraud related to the BP Deepwater Horizon oil spill disaster.

The prosecutors led Bates, Holloway, and Stevenson into a small room where they would interview the couple before they entered the grand jury chambers one at a time. Bates was not allowed into the chambers with the witnesses, so Wise and Hines went over everything they planned to ask about while they all sat there together.

They called Holloway first. Bates sat with Stevenson and waited. There was no small talk. Then Wise came in and asked Stevenson if he was ready. He was not ready. He would get it over with.

The whole thing took about an hour and a half. When Stevenson came out of the room to rejoin Bates and Holloway, no one said anything. Bates did not ask what they said. They did not tell him.

Stevenson and Holloway were relieved that it was over.

Before they left, Bates gave Wise a folder full of other cases he might want to look into if he was building a case against Jenkins.

NO ONE COULD find the warrant for April Sims and Damon Hardrick's Canton condo for months.

The State's Attorney's Office finally said they found the warrant on January 23, but it was a copy of a copy of a copy. Then the state dropped Sims's and Hardrick's cases only to immediately reindict them, covering over the confusion.

"There is no original warrant in this case—even now," Sims's lawyer, Thomas Donnelly, told the judge on February 3.

Donnelly added that he and Bates, who represented Hardrick, were considering asking for a Franks hearing for Jenkins.

Bates doubted that the warrant ever existed before January 23.

"It took forever to get this warrant," Bates said. "Now the state is able to find this warrant at the very last day?"

The judge explained that all he could do was give them another date for the trial. Bates wanted this to be on record, and he wanted to be right. He could win later. Today was about being right.

"What they did was wrong, it's just wrong," Bates said.

"I'm not happy about a lot of things I've heard about that have gone on here, but I won't comment upon that," the judge said.

"Yes, Your Honor," Bates said. "And being in the heat of battle, I'm a little more emotional sometimes in this position, so I understand."

Sims and Hardrick would go to trial in May. Jenkins, Bates hoped, would be busted long before then.

IN THE BACK of the van, behind dark tinted windows, Jenkins kept two black duffel bags. He stopped Hendrix, Taylor, and Ward in the garage one day and pulled the bags out of the van.

One bag was full of tools Stepp had bought for Jenkins. Pry bars of varying sizes. Bolt cutters. Binoculars. Ski goggles. A rope with a grappling hook attached. An axe. A sledgehammer. A foot-and-a-half-long machete with a black blade.

"He said he had all that stuff just in case he ran into a monster or a big hit," Hendrix recalled. "He was talking about robbing them."

The second bag was full of black clothing. Climbing shoes. Balaclavas. Gloves. A few heavy-duty black masks with skeleton faces. These masks, made for paintball, had thick gray lenses over the eye sockets that made it impossible to see who was behind them and elastic straps that made them easy to pull on and off quickly.

Jenkins grabbed one of the skulls from the bag.

"He actually put the mask on and was, like, kind of, making like a joke, dancing around with it on," Ward recalled.

In the harshly lit garage at police headquarters, Sarge gamboled about in his monster mask, a banquet of burglary gear laid out in front of him.

Hendrix and Ward discussed the dance and the weapons and the mask later.

They both agreed: "Sergeant Jenkins is crazy."

Both were trying to get out of the unit. Hendrix wanted a transfer. He even had a meeting about it with Jenkins, and it went pretty well. Jenkins was going to let him go. For Ward, becoming a sergeant had been one route out. After a period in charge of GTTF during Jenkins's leave, it didn't seem very likely. Their productivity had declined precipitously under Ward's brief watch, and command had noticed. The game was about the numbers, and as a leader, Ward's numbers were terrible.

No one knew what Taylor was thinking. Half the time, he still seemed to buy into anything Jenkins told him. When Jenkins showed them the bags of burglary gear, Taylor kept quiet.

Soon Jenkins pitched a target. One of his body-shop buddies who also sold blow had been ripped off by his dealer, and Jenkins thought they should take the dude down. It would begin as a typical investigation—stakeout, GPS tracker on his car, listening devices.

Once they had a sense of the dealer's routine, they would go inside his house and clean him out.

"He referred back to the tools and basically said, he has everything, whatever we need," Hendrix said.

Hendrix told Jenkins he wouldn't do it. Ward said the same.

Taylor didn't say much.

Then Jenkins started talking about Oreese Stevenson again.

Neither Hendrix nor Ward were down with the plan. Ward let Taylor know how he felt, and Taylor went and told Jenkins that, since Ward wasn't into it, maybe it wasn't a good idea after all.

Jenkins sent Taylor to pick up Ward for a face-to-face.

Taylor and Ward pulled into the parking lot of an apartment complex near Belvedere Towers, where Jenkins, Taylor, and Ward had robbed a weed dealer two years earlier.

Hersl was in the parking lot with Jenkins, drinking Twisted Tea.

Jenkins asked Ward why he wasn't down with going after Stevenson again and accused Ward of talking Taylor out of the plan.

"We just hit the guy's house before, and we took over $60,000," Ward said. "Why do we chance it, hitting this guy's house again and robbing him again?"

Ward misunderstood what "hitting" Stevenson meant, Jenkins explained. Jenkins didn't want to arrest Stevenson. He wanted to rob him. Track his car, kick in the door, use the gear in the black bags, take the drugs and the money and guns, and go. No warrant. No charges. This would have nothing to do with police.

Ward told Jenkins he wouldn't do it.

IN HIS HUNT for ever-bigger off-the-books heists, Jenkins had become a monster in a minivan.

According to Stepp, his new van was going to play a crucial part of the "retirement score." Jenkins and Stepp figured that a police vehicle parked in the garage at police headquarters was the safest possible place to hide a bunch of money and drugs until they could offshore the coke with Stepp's connection and secure the cash somewhere safe.

They were getting close. Stepp hoped they could move on it soon. Like Ward and Hendrix, he was getting scared, avoiding Jenkins's calls, hesitant to pick up the phone and hear what Jenkins had to say. Stepp's business was risk assessment, and for a long time, Jenkins seemed like a sure thing. Now Stepp wasn't so sure. He was backing away.

One night, Jenkins looked Stepp straight in the eye and asked him what was going on.

"I want to tell him, like, 'I know something's going on with you,'" Stepp recalled.

He didn't. Jenkins was too volatile.

On February 27, Stepp answered a call from Jenkins, who told him he was coming over with some very good news.

Jenkins pulled his van in back by Stepp's garage and started talking about Gondo's wife, who, he said, was selling forty-eight ounces inside the Johns Hopkins Hospital and couldn't re-up fast enough.

Stepp wasn't interested. Just go over to the Alameda Shopping Center, where Gondo was moonlighting as a security guard, and talk to the man, Jenkins told Stepp.

"He's trying to convince me that it's good for me, that I can make $10,000, $20,000 a week by supplying Gondo and Gondo's wife," Stepp recalled.

Stepp had never heard about Gondo even having a wife, and he had no interest in driving onto Gondo's turf to talk.

"I didn't want the exposure with the other members of the Gun Trace Task Force," Stepp recalled. "I'm a person that knows from the streets that the more codefendants, the more risk."

Jenkins was adamant.

"I'll give you the drugs and you go do it," Stepp said.

Jenkins told Stepp that there was going to be a family party that night and he should come.

"I knew that it wasn't going to end good, I could feel that," Stepp recalled. "I kept saying to myself, 'Donny, you don't need this.'"

He still believed in the retirement heist, though. With that, he'd be set for life. He could walk away. They were too close to quit now. They'd seen the drugs delivered, seen the money picked up. Bugged cars and homes. Made spare keys. They had the buyer set up to take it out of the country and the plan to hide it in the van. It was beautiful. He couldn't give it up, the idea of it.

He drove down the road through the dark winter night to the Jenkins party, conflicted.

When he walked in, he was not comforted.

"Jenkins was completely out of character, getting plastered, getting drunk, he's on the dance floor," Stepp recalled. "And you can see how out of it that he is. But you can, I can just feel that something's up."

Stepp took his phone out and recorded Jenkins, who had once seemed untouchable, stumbling and staggering across the dance floor.

"He's dancing," Stepp said. "And he's—it's pitiful."

Drunk that night, Jenkins told his brother that he was either about to get promoted or fired.

The next day, he shared his concerns with his mentor, Chief Sean Miller.

Miller said Jenkins had nothing to worry about.

WAYNE JENKINS PARKED his minivan in the lot of Internal Affairs headquarters, a lonesome old building on a bombed-out postindustrial strip in East Baltimore.

The whole squad had orders to come in at the same time, even Hersl, who was now in Citywide Shooting—9:00 A.M. on Wednesday, March 1, 2017.

Jenkins got out of the van, dressed for the streets: boots, cargo pants, a long-sleeved T-shirt. He left his police vest in the back of the van, draped over the top of the two black duffel bags. His brass knuckles rested in the console. If his promotion went through and he made lieutenant, he would leave this kind of scheming behind, and he'd be wearing starchy white shirts and itchy dress pants from here on out.

He checked in his firearm, and stepped into the elevator. When the doors opened on the second floor, he was surrounded by IAD detectives and FBI agents, who handcuffed him.

Jenkins, man of many ruses, had been tricked.

A federal indictment dated February 23 and unsealed that morning charged Jenkins and the rest of his squad with a series of crimes ranging from RICO Act conspiracy to Hobbs Act Extortion and Robbery—the FBI was using organized crime statutes to take down police.

Commissioner Kevin Davis, whose administration began with a plea to plainclothes cops to do whatever it took to regain control over Baltimore, stood there looking at the monster he had helped create. Davis wanted to look each of the officers in the eyes as they were taken down. One by one, Gondo, Hendrix, Hersl, Rayam, Taylor, and Ward were ensnared in the same trap as their sergeant. Each looked away from their commissioner in shame. Only Jenkins stared back at him.

"He didn't look away, he didn't blink, he didn't show any signs of remorse or regret or embarrassment," Davis said.

BOOK
THREE

– – – – – – – – – – –

"EVERYBODY'S LIFE IS
DESTROYED, MAN."

ELEVEN

IVAN BATES WALKED back to his office with a swift, victorious stride. He could almost feel the reverberations of the GTTF indictments echoing through downtown Baltimore.

Everyone was talking about the dirty cops.

Bates had been in court waiting to ask for a postponement on a case he had with prosecutor Anna Mantegna when the news broke that seven Baltimore police officers had been indicted on federal RICO charges: for allegedly robbing people, filing false affidavits, and submitting fraudulent overtime. One of the cops was also charged in a separate indictment involving a drug crew.

Every lawyer in the room reached for their phones. Mantegna gasped. A public defender named Deborah Katz Levi, who had made her name calling out corrupt cops, flashed an irrepressible smile.

Bates could see the full range of emotion right there—prosecutors were crushed, defense attorneys were elated, and everyone was in shock, except for him. He'd been expecting something like this for months. He'd had a small part in making it happen.

The first thing Bates needed to do was call his clients and make sure they heard about the indictments. He would start filing motions to dismiss their cases. He wanted to see how the State's Attorney's Office would respond. Mosby, famous as the great prosecutor of police because of Freddie Gray, had nothing to do with this sting.

When he got to his office, there was a message waiting for him. Early that morning, a woman called, crying, hard to understand. Through tears and desperate, gulped breaths, she tried to explain how her husband had been arrested and needed a lawyer. Her husband was a Baltimore cop, she said. He had just been arrested. He knew Ivan Bates. His name was Wayne Jenkins.

He told an assistant to call Kristy Jenkins back.

"Tell her I can't take the case, because I have a conflict," Bates said.

LIKE MUCH OF the city, Bates watched the Baltimore Police Department's livestream of the press conference about the indictments. Rod Rosenstein, soon on his way into the Trump administration, stood at a podium in the U.S. Attorney's Office, where two large poster boards behind him read OVERTIME FRAUD and ABUSE OF POWER.

"The charges in this case are extremely serious," Rosenstein said. "And what you see is a lack of respect for the system, particularly the discussions about overtime. The sergeant is away on vacation and the officers are allegedly at casinos and various other places billing overtime."

Bates noticed Assistant U.S. Attorneys Leo Wise and Derek Hines standing silently in the back, looming over Rosenstein and Commissioner Kevin Davis. This was their case.

When Commissioner Davis approached the microphone after Rosenstein, it was with the same intense, almost panicked look he put on his face each time he stood before the public to decry police malfeasance and promise reform.

"Reform isn't always pretty. It's messy sometimes. Reform is not just a word that you use at press conferences, it's not just something we say when we talk about the Department of Justice investigation or the consent decree. It's something that's real," Davis said. "These seven police officers acted disgracefully; they betrayed the trust that we have and are trying to build upon with our community at a very sensitive time in this city's history. They acted in a manner that betrayed their fellow police officers."

Baltimore's reporters, used to Davis's deflections, came at the commissioner hard.

The city overspends on overtime pay every year by millions of dollars, and yet no one flagged this egregious overtime?

How many cases will be dropped or compromised as a result of this?

Will victims get their money back?

"These officers' names, just, you Google them and they come up in lawsuits and misconduct complaints, all sorts of things," Justin Fenton, crime reporter for *The Baltimore Sun,* said. "Why did it take an investigation into a drug organization to sort of backdoor and get into this squad and what they were doing? This is one of your most productive squads."

"Well, Justin, I think police officers—the small number of police officers who choose to engage in criminal conduct—are pretty savvy, and they're pretty smart, and they know the criminal justice system," Davis said. "These officers are 1930s-style gangsters as far as I'm concerned."

The Baltimore Police Department, under a consent decree with the Department of Justice and still reeling from the death of Freddie Gray and the uprising of rage that laid bare the segregated nature of policing in the city, was once again thrust into the international spotlight.

GTTF took on a mythical quality. The department had a history of changing the names of plainclothes squads when they got in trouble. OCD becomes VCID becomes VCIS becomes SET becomes SES. This scandal was of a different order of magnitude. The name GTTF would not disappear.

It was now the name of a gang.

ANNA MANTEGNA SAT with two other prosecutors at the State's Attorney's Office, and behind closed doors, they wept. Their entire careers were precipitated upon the idea that they could trust cops, and the indictment, filled with lurid details of deception—lies on police reports, in sworn affidavits, on time sheets—blew all of that up.

"We were wondering how we could keep doing what we do, how we could keep doing our jobs," Mantegna recalled. "We had been so wrong."

Mantegna recalled having only one case with most of GTTF— the one where the guys had crashed into the steps of a church. She'd had such a hard time trying to get Jenkins and Taylor into court to testify.

She was most shocked by Danny Hersl's involvement. Sure, she saw that he'd changed. He'd gone on and on about the riots and how demoralizing it all was, how they basically had to stand there and hear colleagues screaming over the radio for help and couldn't react. People were getting hit in the head with chunks of concrete and he couldn't move as he watched the destruction of the city, the destruction of property, people being attacked. Ordinarily, a cop would have been charged with cowardice for standing down like that.

After the riots, Hersl just disappeared and quit coming around. He was so sad around Christmas when they'd met for drinks. For a moment, she felt bad for not checking on him more. Then she was furious again. Fuck him and the rest of them. They'd betrayed their badges. They'd betrayed every prosecutor in this building.

"I'm livid right now, but right now, I'm more focused on the fact of what this is going to do to the justice system as a whole," she said. "What it's going to do to the citizens and the people in this city. It's not just about them. It's about all of us."

IVAN BATES CALLED Oreese Stevenson. He knew that Stevenson would not be happy to have his initials—O.S.—appear in a federal indictment. But Bates also had to tell Stevenson that he needed to be ready, because the feds would almost definitely call on him for trial.

He texted Albert Brown. He sent Andre Crowder a link to a story about the charges against the GTTF.

Bates called Jamal Walker. Since 2010, the Walkers had been trying to escape the fallout of their encounter with Jenkins. The cruddy cop didn't like to lose, and Jenkins took it out on Jamal and Jovonne.

Years after the Walkers' arrest, Walker called Bates when he came home from work and found Jenkins sitting in a van in front of his house. Walker called again when he'd paid a service to trace a number that had been texting him and asking about buying drugs. The number texting him was Jenkins's personal cell phone number, and the website's scrape of all publicly available information also featured a photo of Jenkins and his wife wearing Baltimore Ravens gear.

They had already seen the news when Bates called Jamal, who pumped his old lawyer for more information. Bates told Jamal about some of his other cases where Jenkins had used the same sneak-and-peek MO.

"What happened to Gladstone? Where's he at?" Walker said. "He's a part of this too."

Bates didn't have a good answer, though he suspected that it would not end with these seven cops in what was already being dubbed "the GTTF scandal."

Bates noticed that Mosby did not hold a press conference at all. Her office issued a statement instead.

"Today's federal indictment of several BPD officers will have pervasive implications on numerous active investigations and pending cases in our office," the statement read. "Nonetheless, we will continue our strong partnership with the Police Department and U.S. Attorney's Office to identify, prosecute and ultimately eradicate those bad actors who do a disservice to the dedicated and hard-working officers who risk their lives daily to protect and serve our communities."

Bates was getting closer to deciding that he would run for state's attorney and take on Marilyn Mosby, and in this statement, he saw vulnerability—the GTTF scandal happened on her watch.

THE BATTLE IVAN Bates had been waging against Wayne Jenkins was only one small skirmish in the larger war that defense attorneys, and especially the Office of the Public Defender, had been fighting against a system that had allowed dirty cops to get by for decades.

Deborah Levi, a singularly driven public defender was in court that morning too when news of the indictments swept through the courtroom, talking with Anna Mantegna, who looked like she was going to cry when she learned of the allegations against her friend Hersl and six other cops.

Levi, who had seen so many bad officers protected by a veil of secrecy shrouding police misconduct, couldn't hide her excitement. The indictments were a vindication of her work. Police despised her and prosecutors called her gloating and unfair for fighting so hard over what many saw as minor discrepancies. Other defense attorneys, even other public defenders—typically men—thought she was a showboat sacrificing clients' best interests for larger principles tied to transparency and weeding out corruption. She didn't care what anyone said. She was on a mission.

Years earlier, she was out jogging in Utah, where she had decided to go to law school after a stint as a Baltimore City schoolteacher and she had an experience that was almost religious. It felt like the sky had opened up, and she realized that she had to be a public defender in Baltimore City.

She knew what people thought about public defenders—that they were lazy, unambitious, and overworked lawyers of last resort, and she set out to destroy that stereotype. She'd win every award and accolade she could and hang them on her wall so that people would know she'd chosen to be a public defender. The very words precisely conveyed the way she saw herself and her mission. She defended the public.

When she got back to Baltimore, the Office of the Public Defender was filled with people like her, who saw the job as a calling.

On the morning of the GTTF indictments, the office was more alive than Levi had ever seen it, as everyone scrambled to figure out whether any of their clients were affected. Her boss, Deputy Public Defender Natalie Finegar, said that there was a case that morning where a guy named Maurice Stanton—who had been arrested by some of the indicted cops on August 1, 2016, and charged with a gun—was only minutes away from pleading guilty when the indictments went public. They'd already worked out the deal, and Stanton was filling out the paperwork when the prosecutor jumped up and told the judge that the cops involved in the case had been indicted and asked if they could postpone the matter until that issue had been resolved.

Levi asked Finegar what they were going to do to respond to the potentially thousands of other cases out there—all the Maurice Stantons already in jail.

Finegar, a fierce, funny, self-effacing lawyer who had been with the public defender's office for twenty-three years, shared Levi's distress over the clues they may have missed.

"I felt sick to my stomach," Finegar said. "It reminded you of like all the people you remembered telling you and telling all your line attorneys, 'I didn't have that on me.' You hear that a lot. You become immune to it until you realize they're telling the truth."

In a frenzy of Excel spreadsheets and Coke Zero, Levi and Finegar began cataloging all the arrests involving the seven officers. They were almost overwhelmed with questions.

"Who's in prison? Who shouldn't be? Who should we get out?" Levi said. "How should we prioritize? Who do we contact? What do we do? What do we file?"

When she tried to look at one of the seven officers' cases, Levi saw all the other officers they had worked with over the years—a gyre of ever-expanding circles of corruption that had landed people in jails, prisons, halfway houses, and graves over the course of decades that would take years, maybe decades, to address.

"LITTLE BMORE, LITTLE Bmore, did you see that?" an inmate at the Federal Transfer Center, Oklahoma City, said to Umar Burley. "They just locked up a bunch of cops from Baltimore. Was any of them on your case?"

"What was their names?" Burley said.

Nobody knew. They just saw something on the rec room TV about Baltimore cops being arrested scrolling along the bottom of the screen, and Burley was the only guy in FTC from Baltimore.

Over the years, when other inmates asked Burley about his case, he insisted that he was innocent. Everybody in prison says that, so he didn't talk about it much. The death of Elbert Davis haunted his thoughts. Burley had nightmares about the crash and the gnarled plastic and metal crunched up all around the elderly couple. The Davis family had won a wrongful death lawsuit against him because of the crash. He was on the hook for a million dollars. He could not afford anything like hope.

Burley checked his monitored prison email account. He saw a

message from his cousin Brent Matthews, who was with him the day of the crash.

Jenkins was one of the seven indicted cops.

"They finally got them bastards, man. They got Jenkins and them," Matthews's email read. "Hold tight, you should be home soon."

Burley, who had a tear tattooed beneath his left eye, let a few real tears of hesitant joy roll down his face.

DONNY STEPP COULDN'T shake the image of Jenkins, broken and drunk, doing his sad dance at that birthday party—a last dance as a free man. The paranoia that Stepp had always felt when Jenkins's story did not quite fit together magnified now that Jenkins was arrested.

"It was just instant panic for me," Stepp recalled. "Through Jenkins and me using phones, they know me."

He couldn't stop watching the news.

Photos of all seven cops in uniform, official pictures from their academy days, flashed across the screen, their out-of-date, baby-faced academy photos incongruously paired with the details of their corruption. Then the news showed photos of them escorted out of the Internal Affairs building in handcuffs, Jenkins wearing cargo pants and a long-sleeved black shirt, and Gondo, who looked like he'd been out all night and was coming straight from the club, wearing a silky burgundy shirt, tight tailored pants, and narrow dress shoes. Stepp couldn't process Jenkins in handcuffs.

He found the forty-five-page indictment online and printed it out.

Then Stepp found the second indictment that tied Gondo's Alameda drug crew to the GTTF. He reverse engineered his last chat with Jenkins, who had come to the garage and tried to get Stepp to go meet Gondo. Maybe Jenkins had known this was coming and was trying to set Stepp up. Did Jenkins know Gondo's phone was tapped? Was Jenkins sending him to Gondo to be killed because he knew too much?

Stepp told his wife and child to go somewhere else for the next few days.

"You got to go, and you got to give me time to try to figure this," Stepp said.

His house was still lousy with drugs that Jenkins had brought him.

"I am just in complete panic. I am moving things, I am just doing everything that I can. And I'm steady looking because I'm like there's no way that the FBI is not onto me," Stepp recalled.

Stepp, who had not been able to sleep, realized he had the Breitling watch that Jenkins had stolen from Stevenson, who was in the indictment as O.S. The Swiss luxury watch tied him directly to the March 22, 2016, heist. He needed to get rid of it. It was also worth a lot of money, and maybe all of this would blow over. The watch was waterproof, and as long as a storm didn't wash it away, he figured if he threw it in the water behind his house, he could retrieve it when things calmed down.

He walked the watch out to the end of his pier and dropped it down beside one of the pylons jutting up from the dark water, a marker if he ever needed to get it again.

WHEN THE ARRESTED officers appeared in federal court, pleading not guilty, it was the first time that Wise and Hines, the assistant U.S. attorneys who had been working on the case for so long, had actually seen their targets.

All of them asked to be released until they could stand trial and face their accusers. Jenkins's lawyer argued that the Baltimore prison gang the Black Guerrilla Family had a hit out on Jenkins and it would not be safe for him to be incarcerated anywhere in the state.

Wise contended that these men were experts in evading law enforcement and that the witnesses against them were terrified of retaliation. He mentioned that Rayam had threatened to reveal the identity of a snitch if he informed on Rayam—an act of obstruction amounting to a death sentence in a stop-fuckin'-snitching city like Baltimore. He noted that the crew heard about the investigation by other members of the police department and by an assistant state's attorney.

In the city's legal community with Mosby up for reelection, that detail was explosive—someone in Mosby's office tipped GTTF off.

What Bates and other defense attorneys claimed about Mosby, that she was a poor manager who didn't know what was going on in her own office, appeared to be true.

The SAO denied any knowledge of such a leak.

IN THE HOWARD County Detention Center, about twenty-five miles outside of Baltimore, the seven officers, isolated from the general population for their own protection and kept together in a cell, began to sift through what they had learned about the facts of the case against them.

The investigation began back in late 2015, when the DEA and Harford County cops arrested Black. The sheriffs found the tracker Gondo and Rayam had put on Black's car when they'd robbed his house with Wells. That robbery, which had brought together Gondo's two different worlds, led to all of this.

Even with the two indictments, elements of the investigation still didn't make sense. Instead of immediately targeting Gondo and Rayam after finding a tracker registered to Clewell—or investigating Clewell—the DEA and Harford County got a warrant for a tracker on Shropshire's car and a wire on his phone. Then in March 2016, when Shropshire called Gondo about the tracker that was on his car, the FBI heard every word, and then they used that to get a wire on Gondo's phone just before Jenkins took over the unit. Clewell was the only member of Jenkins's GTTF who wasn't indicted. There was something suspicious about all of it. The investigation just didn't quite fit together.

In their cells, Jenkins told them all to hold tight. As a squad, they could beat this. He suggested to Hendrix, Taylor, and Ward that if they had to admit to the Stevenson robbery, they should claim they stole less money—say, $5,000 instead of $20,000—and maintain that the video of the safe was real.

Hersl instructed Gondo to tell the government that they had taken the Chanel bag from April Sims's condo to transport the heroin into evidence.

He asked Rayam about the car.

"Hey, is the Impala, you know, mic'd up? Is it bugged? Does it have a bug in it?" Hersl said.

"I don't know," Rayam said.

THE STATE DROPPED the charges against Albert Brown, and a court-room full of reporters was there to watch. Bates tipped them off.

The judge spoke slowly and kindly to Albert Brown. His approach was conciliatory and hushed. It was almost an apology. He explained that Brown could have his charges expunged.

"Your petition for expungement when granted by the court would expunge, or wipe out—extinguish if you will, sir—all the records regarding the allegations, the charges against the case, the records of the case itself. Do you understand that?" the judge said.

"Yes, sir," Brown said.

"Wish you the very best of health and good luck," the judge said.

Outside of the courthouse, Bates and Brown spoke to reporters.

"The body camera footage was not turned on until after my

client was arrested," Bates said. "The problem I have is, you just can't save these cases."

"I felt disrespected. I'm in a gas station, I'm getting pulled over for not wearing a seat belt inside a gas station, putting air in my tires, it don't make no sense at all," Brown, in a nice black suit, wide-brimmed hat, and long winter coat, told reporters. "I'm just happy to get my life back together and take care of my family."

Bates also gave Hersl's body camera footage of Brown's arrest to the press, explaining that prosecutors knew what was going on and offering a first look of GTTF in action: Jenkins shouting questions at Brown; Rayam with the gun and cocaine; Gondo saying he wanted to hurt Brown; Hersl sitting in the car with Brown, talking down to him, calling Safe Streets "cruddy"—while the other cops entered Brown's house.

"Mrs. Mosby's office is the one who brings the charges. The officers may have made the arrests, but Mrs. Mosby's office is the one," Bates told reporters. "If you do not stop this type of behavior, then it will fester. You have to get rid of the cancer immediately. This type of behavior stops the system from working."

HERSL MAINTAINED THAT he should be free until he went to trial. A week after the squad was arrested, he had a second detention hearing, appealing an earlier order denying his pretrial release.

In front of the judge, Assistant U.S. Attorney Leo Wise stressed the extent to which Hersl and his codefendants obstructed justice.

He brought up the case of Zachary Newsome.

"It was Defendant Hersl's idea, as the intercepted communications make clear, that if they arrested [Newsome] the night before on an outstanding warrant they had found in Anne Arundel County, prisoner transport couldn't get him in front of Judge Peters the next day. And so the trial would be postponed," Wise said.

"And they spent the better part of a day causing this scenario. And working and manipulating other law enforcement officers to effect the arrest of this person to prevent him from having his day in court the next day."

Gondo's car was mic'd up.

Wise pointed out that the stakes in the Newsome case were low compared to those facing Hersl now. And the crimes he'd committed were crimes of violence, and releasing him could endanger the lives of witnesses, who were, understandably, terrified of retaliation. Wise went on to note, as another example of a pattern of obstruction, that Hersl was caught on tape saying he did not intend to use his body camera.

"Instead, he intended to keep it locked up in his truck. And then, as he put it, 'Maybe just one day go out when we're not doing something, since I have it on, and tape some video,'" Wise said, quoting a recording picked up in Gondo's car.

Hersl's lawyer argued that he should be allowed to stay with his sister until trial, wearing an ankle monitor. He also argued the charges, simple robberies, were not actually applicable under RICO and should not be federal. The Racketeer Influenced and Corrupt Organizations Act, concocted by the federal government to take down mobsters who may not directly participate in the crimes they benefited from, required that the defendants be part of an ongoing and illegal conspiracy within a common enterprise. Hersl's lawyer said that there was no common enterprise, so the individual officers should be charged separately in state court.

"The enterprise charged here is the Baltimore Police Department," Wise responded, naming a major metropolitan police department as a criminal enterprise.

The judge ruled that Hersl was both a flight risk and a danger to the community.

When he got back to Howard County, Hersl passed information he gleaned from the hearing about how there was a microphone in Gondo's car.

"They got us," Rayam later recalled Hersl saying.

MARILYN MOSBY FINALLY held a formal press conference to address the GTTF scandal three weeks after the indictment. Her office, she said, had identified about fifty active GTTF cases to investigate. In these cases, the defendants' "fate and liberty were at the mercy of these officers," Mosby said.

There were another 150 convictions that could be vacated.

"This will only happen after a thorough review of each and every case where the case depends exclusively on the credibility of these officers," Mosby said. "This is an important distinction—just because one of the officers was tangentially involved in a defendant's case, this does not constitute and immediate means to be released from incarceration, nor does it mean that we will automatically seek to vacate the conviction."

Levi was reviewing these cases with the SAO's chief counsel. Her office thought the number was far larger. That morning before Mosby's press conference, Deputy District Public Defender Natalie Finegar sent out a statement: "The State's Attorney's consent to dismiss these cases was a necessary response to the allegations against the indicted officers. However, thousands of other Baltimore residents had their lives interrupted, and often destroyed, by these officers' wrongdoing in cases that predate 2015 and in cases where the sentence is over but the conviction still impacts the ability to get a job or a home."

Bates, who was going into court to get the charges against April Sims and Damon Hardrick dropped, thought Mosby was dead wrong on this insistence that GTTF cases continue to go forward. The level of corruption and the inability to believe the officers meant you had to throw them all out, and that was un-fortunate because criminals might get out of jail. Carrying on with the cases wasn't just wrong, it was a political liability, Bates realized. Despite what Mosby stressed—that she would "pursue justice over convictions while simultaneously prioritizing pub-lic safety"—the desire to gain convictions, to keep the stats up, seemed to Bates like it was as bad in the State's Attorney's Office as it was in BPD.

The claim that there was a leak in her office, whose identity was the subject of endless speculation, made this indifference into something more nefarious. And when she said that she still did not have any information about the allegation of a leak, it increased the sentiment of incompetence.

Later that day, after the prosecutor finally agreed to drop the charges against her and her husband, April Sims called out Mosby directly.

"I am happy that those cops were pretty much brought to justice, and again, I have questions," Sims said to news cameras outside the courthouse. "Marilyn Mosby, I want to ask her some questions."

"[There was] overwhelming evidence against the defendants, which included 390 grams of heroin recovered at the scene," Mos-by's office later said. "This is yet another example of hundreds of cases where police corruption has impeded our city's ability to de-liver justice on behalf of its citizens."

ALMOST NOBODY BEATS the federal government, but Jenkins was a gambling man, and, in a matchup between himself and Uncle Sam, he was putting his money on Wayne Earl Jenkins. He advised his squad to do the same. He told his crew again that if they would stand tall, they could beat the charges.

"Stick to the story," Jenkins said.

Gondo, whose phone was the only one tapped, his car the only one bugged, didn't see a way out. And Rayam always rode in Gondo's car, and they talked on the phone all the time. Rayam confessed to his cellmates one day that he "always had a problem with the truth."

Telling the truth increasingly seemed like the only option.

When Rayam met with Wise and Hines to talk for the first time, he couldn't look them in the eyes. Sitting there and having to finally own up and confess his crimes—the robberies, the theft, the overtime scheming—to other law enforcement officers was too much at first. His father was an officer in the Newark Police Department for twenty-five years.

He worried that the prosecutors might think he was lying because he couldn't look at them as all the details rolled out of his mouth. Really, he was just "ashamed," he said.

It was the first time he had tried to tell the whole truth in a long time.

WHILE JENKINS COACHED his crew to stay quiet, he was also trying to work out a way to cover his own ass. As FBI agents transported him from the Talbot County Detention Center to the federal courthouse in Baltimore on April 10, he began to toy with talking, offering information about, Jenkins said, the "assistant state's attorney who leaked the information."

He left it at that, just a taste of what he knew.

Gondo had been telling them everything, dredging up every little detail he could remember. At his first proffer session on March 24, he told the government about the Sims and Hardrick incident, the Chanel bag Hersl gave him, and a white dude who brought a bunch of listening devices to Jenkins out in the parking lot. He also told them he had been robbing with other cops for years.

Ward began cooperating on April 19. Hendrix on May 5. Taylor refused to talk and maintained his innocence entirely. At a detention hearing in May, his lawyers argued "unconstitutional and dishonest policing is system-wide at the BPD, and these systemic problems are not a reason to detain Mr. Taylor."

Hersl was not cooperating. Anxiety ate away at him. Since the indictment, he had lost thirty pounds.

"Since I'm a federal prisoner, I cannot get a job or pretty much do anything but walk around the cell block in circles all day," Hersl wrote in a letter to his family in May. "My mind wanders so much. I am so tired of being scared for my safety and fate."

TWELVE

DONNY STEPP GOT a letter addressed to Lucas Colton, Jenkins's dead son. Stepp recognized the writing.

"I started reading the letter, and he's wanting me to go to different officers," Stepp recalled. "He's wanting me to go ask them to do this, to do that, and he's wanting me to lie to the FBI."

Stepp tried to get a message back to Jenkins: "I ain't talking to no FBI, period."

In July, the government returned a new, superseding indictment against Jenkins, Taylor, and Hersl, adding thirteen new robbery charges, with mandatory time added to each count because the crimes involved the use of a handgun. The inclusion of additional robberies in the indictment publicly indicated for the first time that some GTTF members were cooperating.

The prosecutors' gambit worked. Jenkins began to dance around a proffer agreement with the government. He would have to tell them everything and be absolutely truthful.

The government asked Jenkins again if he had been tipped off about the investigation. He named Anna Mantegna, recasting her warning about Gondo and Rayam into a full-blown leak.

Jenkins also snitched on Stepp, who wasn't, at that time, particularly useful in a corruption probe, though the feds sent word to the Baltimore County police that Donald Stepp of Middle River, Maryland, was selling a large volume of drugs from his waterfront home.

Stepp started to think that Jenkins was cooperating when he heard that the FBI had returned to Jenkins's house looking for a letter.

He held on to the note as yet another piece of insurance.

He did not stop selling cocaine.

RAYAM, WHO WAS in the Kent County Detention Center in Chestertown, Maryland, agreed to set up his friend Eric Snell. Rayam had been away for four months now, and Snell had brought some money to Rayam's wife, which was a good pretext for the call.

"She was like, 'Did you ever thank Snell?'" Rayam said, explaining to Snell why he was calling. "And I was like, 'You know, let me hit him up, yo.'"

"You don't gotta thank me, brother," Snell said.

"I know, I figured I had to hit you up for that, you know what I mean?" Rayam said.

"It's all good," Snell said. "You good, though?"

"In the joint, it came in handy," Rayam said, trying to talk in code again.

"Come on, man. I ain't talking about money. I'm talking about you. Good spirits and everything?" Snell asked.

"For the most part, you know," Rayam said.

He told Snell he would know soon if he would be able to get out on bail. Then he tried to bait Snell again.

"Follow me real quick, yo. Let me know if you cool," Rayam said. "The Orioles game and everything. Everybody cool with that, yo? Like your brother never said anything? Everything cool, yo?"

"Family is family, man. You know what I'm saying?" Snell said.

Rayam brought up money again and asked if they were straight.

"Whatever you need for your fam, I told Cherelle too, yo, if you need some help, you know what I'm saying, I don't mind," Snell said.

"Look, man, like I said, thank you for hooking Cherelle up and the family," Rayam said.

"If you need anything for the kids, tell her to call me and I'll, uh, you know what I mean? I'll try my best to help her out," Snell said. "Especially with me not working, I don't mind driving down there. I think I told her that if she need a break, I'll keep an eye on the kids, you know what I'm saying?"

"She don't need no break, man, get outta here," Rayam said.

"You never know, man, you know what I mean? I got you, brother," Snell said. "I'm just putting it out there."

Rayam assured Snell that he had not said anything about Snell or Snell's family.

"Say less," Snell said.

When Rayam hung up the phone, he was afraid that Snell's promise to "keep an eye on the kids" was a threat to kill them.

INTO THE SUMMER, Hersl was put on medication for his anxiety, 25 milligrams of Zoloft. He had taken up drawing, improving his skills and sending illustrations and detailed pages from coloring books to his son. He would not allow his son to visit. He did not want the boy to see his dad locked up, losing weight, all paranoid and depressed. "I'm sooo lost," he wrote his mother. He put on a good face for his son on the phone and in letters.

"Hi, little boy. I hope you're doing well and being a good boy for Mommy. I also hope your summer vacation is going good. I bet you like sleeping in and going to bed late," Hersl wrote to his son in July.

He congratulated the boy on making honor roll and imagined his ten-year-old's summer of fishing and swimming—freedom. At the bottom of the letter, a PS: "Is your computer running? If so, you better catch it. I hope you like my drawings."

. . .

IVAN BATES WAS relieved when he heard the news that the Office of the Public Defender created a new Special Litigation Section to address the thousands of cases tainted by GTTF, and Deborah Levi was going to be its director. And he was not surprised to find she wasn't stopping at GTTF. She was fighting for every attorney to gain access to the disciplinary files of every officer who charges a citizen in Baltimore.

Her office had recently viewed body camera footage used as evidence against one of her clients—and discovered the footage showed drugs being planted right there on camera.

When a cop turns a body camera on, the previous thirty seconds before it was switched on are recorded too. Here it showed this joker, Officer Richard Pinheiro, placing a knot of pills in a pile of trash, walking away from it, turning his camera on, walking back to the trash and pretending to find the drugs while two other cops looked on.

It was like Albert Brown all over again—and worse. Levi had only just started her job as the director of Special Litigation, and she wanted to try to build some kind of relationship with the SAO, so she extended an olive branch and showed them the footage. Maybe they had just missed it. They saw it and still wanted the defendant to plead guilty.

Levi, a ferocious, rapid-fire litigator, was livid. She released the video to reporters, and the news went national—the latest dirty cop story out of Baltimore City. Commissioner Kevin Davis suspended Pinheiro and defended him, claiming he was likely "reenacting the seizure of evidence," rather than planting it. Only after all of that did Mosby's office drop the charges in the case.

"If you have a case dependent on any of these 3 officers," Levi advised other defense attorneys in an email, "dig your feet in and demand disclosure of their IAD records."

Bates was impressed. Sometimes when a potential client came

in to talk to him and he saw Levi was their public defender, he'd tell them, "Save your money and stick with her."

Now that he had finally made the decision to run for state's attorney, he hoped he would be able to work with Levi from the other side. If he was State's Attorney and Levi brought that video to him, he would have handled it a lot differently. It seemed to Bates like Mosby had ignored the situation until it went viral, and then she overreacted and rashly dropped a whole bunch of cases with Pinheiro just to quash the story. He felt like a top prosecutor had to be thoughtful and methodical about these things. The politically expedient decision was rarely the right one. Just look at how the Freddie Gray case blew up.

Bates felt like he had what it took to do the job. Whether he had what it took to win an election, that was another question. So he hired a couple of campaign managers and started putting a team together. Former prosecutors—like his good friend Jeremy Eldridge, who had left the SAO after Mosby won—were turning out to be his biggest supporters. Hearing their stories was one of the reasons he had decided to run.

He was immediately unsure about the folks he had running the campaign. They were all about raising money before they did anything else, and though they were experienced in politics, they were a white couple, and Bates felt like they didn't understand him and didn't get what it meant to be a black man in the city. They seemed to want to make it a generic campaign.

Lana had helped him learn that his pride could trip him up. He didn't know everything. As much experience as he had in the law, he was new to politics, and he should trust the team he'd hired to help him, even if it didn't feel quite right.

. . .

A GUARD AT the small jail in the small town of Denton, Maryland, where Momodu Gondo was being held, handed the former detective, now an inmate, a packet of papers.

It was a summons dated July 20, 2017, five days earlier. At the top, it read *"Nancy Hamilton v. Detective Daniel Hersl et al.,"* and farther down, it was addressed to DETECTIVE MOMODU GONDO.

Attached to the summons, he found a personal injury and civil rights violation complaint alleging that he, Rayam, Jenkins, and Hersl had caused "humiliation, loss of self-esteem, anxiety, embarrassment, emotional distress, and economic damages."

A civil suit was the least of his worries. Gondo had last sat down with Wise and Hines for a proffer session more than a month ago in the middle of June and signed a deal pleading guilty to Racketeering Conspiracy and Conspiracy to Distribute and Possess With Intent to Distribute 100 Grams or More of Mixture or Substance Containing Heroin. He was looking at a combined fifty-six years on those charges alone. He knew the game, and he understood that he could cut that down significantly by cooperating. He'd told the assistant U.S. attorneys about Allers's involvement, back before Jenkins ran GTTF, detailing four robberies with "Sergeant A.," as he was described throughout the plea deal.

Talking about his fellow cops, that was one thing. For Gondo, it would be hard to talk to the feds about Wells, who would not talk. Gondo seemed to have no other option.

RAYAM'S WIFE, CHERELLE, filed for divorce in August.

The Rayams had three kids together, and Jemell had gone through an ugly battle to gain custody of another daughter from a previous relationship. Since the indictment, Cherelle shielded the kids from the news so they didn't hear about it. Kids at school mentioned it and mocked them. Their oldest daughter together took it especially hard.

"She has frequent meltdowns because of all the praying she is doing—yet Daddy is not back," Cherelle said.

In retrospect, it was clear to Cherelle that Rayam had not been happy with his job. She blamed herself for not being more helpful when he'd told her that he wanted to get out of policing and work as a teacher.

Rayam wanted to be a good husband, a good father, a good son, and a good cop, but he spent the past eight years committing both "on the books" crimes at work and "off the books" robberies on his own time. Now, he was going to be a good witness, setting up Snell, informing on Allers, his friend Tom Finnegan, his cousin David Rahim, and anyone else he could think of.

Cooperating became a form of confessing for Rayam, a way to absolve himself. Being indicted by the United States was a hell of a rock bottom.

"Jemell voiced to me that he felt like a weight was lifted from his shoulders now that the truth is out," Cherelle said. "And at this point, he didn't care who saw all of his dirt because he knew that everything being put out there publicly for all to see, this would allow him to have a clean slate."

IN AUGUST, UMAR Burley, who was still sitting in jail, agreed to talk to the grand jury.

Burley told the grand jury all about April 28, 2010, when Jenkins had chased him. He had picked up Brent Matthews on his way to the courthouse where the man convicted of killing his cousin was going to be sentenced. When his girlfriend called, he pulled over on Parkview Avenue. She was angry because he couldn't drive her to work. He was trying to explain to her why when two cars boxed him in. Then men with guns in their hands and masks over their faces jumped out. All he could see were their eyes. He didn't think they were cops at all. He thought he was about to be kidnapped.

He fled. Parkview Avenue has a lot of speed bumps on it because there is a day care center at the bottom of the street, and his Acura hit the first bump hard and then there was another one right after that and the car was flying. As he approached a four-way stop, he made eye contact with Elbert Davis, who was driving a Monte Carlo through the intersection. Both drivers swerved to try to avoid the collision and instead veered into each other.

Burley got out of the Acura, dizzy. The scene was chaotic. A fire hydrant spewed water. The Monte Carlo rested on the porch of a house. He was worried about the guys who were chasing him. He ran past the crashed Monte Carlo and hid in a garage. He had a big knot on his head. It seemed like his leg might be broken. He heard walkie-talkies squawking and shouts from the police.

Jenkins and a detective named Sean Suiter put Burley in a car and drove him to the hospital. When Burley came out of a CT scan, Jenkins told Burley that Elbert Davis was dead. Now, Burley was going to do a lot of time, Jenkins said. Then Jenkins smiled.

They took him to the Western District station. They told him the person he'd killed was the father of a cop. They shoved him around a little bit. The crash was an accident, Burley said. He'd fled because he had drugs, the cops said. They found the heroin in the car. He didn't have no heroin, he insisted. No one would listen.

Burley wanted to fight the charges. The press was attacking him—to *The Baltimore Sun* and local TV news, he was a dope dealer who killed a cop's dad—and the prosecutor told him if he went to court, she would make sure he never got out. He pleaded guilty to get fifteen years instead of thirty or more.

Burley did his best to explain to the grand jury everything Jenkins had cost him. His girlfriend—the one he'd pulled over to talk to right before Jenkins and Suiter boxed him in—was dead now. His mom was dead. His dad had kidney issues, and if Burley ever got out, he would become his primary caretaker. He had never met his grandchildren. He still felt terrible about Elbert Davis, whose family had won a million-dollar judgment against him that he would never be able to pay.

"I was crying, the grand jury—people in the grand jury—was crying, and it was like, you know, we were at a eulogy or something," Burley said.

After the testimony ended, Assistant U.S. Attorney Leo Wise told Umar Burley that he wouldn't be going back to the federal prison in West Virginia. They would keep him here at the federal detention facility. He would be out of jail very soon.

Wise wanted to talk to Sean Suiter, who was now a homicide detective.

IVAN BATES OFFICIALLY kicked off his campaign for state's attorney on the front lawn of a home in the West Baltimore neighborhood of Park Heights where, in 2015, community activist Kendal Fenwick had been murdered, police said, because he was building a fence to keep drug dealers out of the yard. Bates, who knew the victim's father, had helped organize a crew to come together to symbolically finish the fence Fenwick was working on when he was shot and killed.

Fenwick's murder turned out to be a case of mistaken identity that had nothing to do with the fence. Still, the yard was a powerful place to begin the campaign. It let the city know that Bates was serious about solving the homicide problem, and he wasn't afraid of getting his hands dirty doing it.

Fenwick's father spoke and endorsed Bates, pointing out that Mosby dismissed other murder charges that had been pending against his son's shooter, letting him go free to kill again.

"If the current state's attorney would've done her job, my son may be still living today," Fenwick said. "I don't want anyone else to feel the way me and my family are feeling."

Bates stood off to the side with Lana, who was a reluctant and essential part of the campaign. It had taken Lana some time to come around to the idea of having a husband who would be in the public eye. They had two daughters, and Lana knew that a political campaign would thrust them all into the spotlight. He felt like he needed to do it, and she felt like maybe the city needed him.

It was immediately apparent when Lana took the podium that she would be a strong asset on the campaign trail. The campaign managers insisted on writing Lana's speech. Lana refused and wrote her own.

"Ivan is reflective about everything he does, and I don't mean just the lawyer work he does. He comes home and talks about all the things and people and opportunities that he had that day, and he comes and he thinks and he talks," she said. "And he talks and he talks and he talks and he talks, and he talks."

Everyone laughed. Ivan grinned, clapping his hands. And then Lana came with the kicker: "But it's only because he really, truly wants to be good and do good," she said. "When Ivan comes home, he does not leave the people he encountered that day at the office. He brings them home with him. They are sitting at the dinner table with us, they are sitting on the couch with us. They are putting the girls to bed with us. They are always in his heart and mind."

Lana knew him best, and she still believed in him. She introduced Ivan and the ideal of the successful black couple—a lawyer and a doctor of education—trying to lift as they climbed. They kissed, and he took the podium and thanked her, proudly, as "Dr. Lana Bates."

He told a story about moving to Baltimore in 1995 to work as a law clerk and to help his elderly aunt Edna: "See, back then, I remember seeing how the crime in her community paralyzed her.

She had fear in her eyes. It was that fear that motivated me to be a Baltimore City prosecutor. I see that same fear today in the eyes of so many citizens in our city. As a Baltimore City homicide prosecutor, I was able to put violent people away."

He said, whether as a prosecutor or as a defense attorney, he'd been in the courtroom nearly every day since then.

"You see, I'm a trial lawyer," he said. "I stand up for the people, and I fight for justice."

Bates looked over at Natalie Finegar, who could endorse him now that she had left the Office of the Public Defender and was in private practice. Then he scanned the rest of the small crowd in the yard in Park Heights. The people on the lawn, they really supported him. They were his base, but that wasn't enough.

He would have to find a way to unite the politically disparate groups that disliked Marilyn Mosby: the law-and-order types who despised her for prosecuting the Six, and the people who disliked her for failing to gain any convictions in the Freddie Gray case and were suspicious of any prosecutor, even one with progressive bona fides like Mosby.

Both sides complained that she was an opportunist who was motivated by politics rather than justice. Trying to appeal to all these groups was a conciliatory position that fit Bates's character well. He considered himself a "progressive moderate." So he would hammer home locking up murderers and also talk about not prosecuting cannabis cases. There was a progressive wave of prosecutors—most notably Philadelphia's Larry Krasner—sweeping across the country, and Bates couldn't quite go as far as them, because he also shared the concerns of those who wanted to lock up violent repeat offenders. He really was in the middle. He was the guy who'd defended Alicia White at the same time he'd fought against Wayne Jenkins.

The Gun Trace Task Force seemed like it might be the issue that could unite the various anti-Mosby factions. As far as Bates was concerned Mosby must have known about the GTTF and looked the other way because she just wanted to get convictions, and that caused crime to rise. If she didn't directly aid GTTF, her incompetence and mismanagement resulted in one of her prosecutors leaking information about an investigation into GTTF members. He tested his theory. A sentence or two about the scandal is all the expensive, white campaign managers he'd hired would allow in the speech.

"We have a state's attorney that has enabled police misconduct, who knowingly turned a blind eye by putting corrupt police officers on the witness stand," Bates said.

Bates prepared for another opponent too: Thiru Vignarajah, a former deputy attorney general who was prosecuting postconviction relief hearings in the case of Adnan Syed, which was made famous by the podcast *Serial,* planned on entering the race. They'd battled in court when Vignarajah worked a big case that indicted fifty alleged members of the Black Guerilla Family gang. Bates thought there was no evidence against his client and it seemed to him like Vignarajah was just looking for publicity.

"WELL, I GUESS this is the last letter I'll be sending to you from this facility," Hersl wrote in September. "If you've not heard yet, a few inmates found out who I am and threatened me and hatched a plan to jump me. Luckily, I observed them doing this and trying to come after me with two long white shoelaces which I guess were planned to strangle me or choke me out."

Hersl was put on lockdown, for his protection. He was only able to get out of his cell for showers and phone calls. He slept on a mattress pad on the concrete. He continued drawing pictures for his son and was soon moved to another prison. His anxiety skyrocketed.

"I finally got to go outside yesterday for the first time in over two months," Hersl wrote to his family in November. "I have to admit that I actually had tears in my eyes as I walked around the yard for the whole hour I was allowed to stay out."

GONDO SAT AT the witness stand in the Edward A. Garmatz United States Courthouse in Baltimore and gave up his best friend.

"Mr. Gondo, do you know the defendant, Glen Kyle Wells?" prosecutor Leo Wise asked Gondo.

"Yes," Gondo said.

"And do you see him in the courtroom today?" Wise said.

He sort of pointed at Wells, who had finally been taken into custody in July, after four months on "self-imposed house arrest." Wells regretted that he had befriended Gondo again after his shooting.

"Right there," Gondo said.

"Can you describe what he's wearing?" Wise asked.

"Black sweater, gray collared shirt, dreads, braided to the back," Gondo said.

He had known Wells, he said, "for the majority of my life, over twenty-five years."

"Does the defendant Wells sell heroin?" Wise said.

"Yes," Gondo said.

"And how do you know that?" Wise said.

"Talking to him," Gondo said. "He was like my best friend. So it's not too many things I didn't know about Kyle."

Forced to answer questions about the recorded conversations and the texts with Wells and Shropshire, Gondo led Wise through it all: the call where Gondo told Shropshire to remove the tracker, all the attempts to keep Jenkins from arresting Wells, the conversation at Looney's where Jenkins backed off, and the robbery where Rayam and Wells went into Black's apartment while Gondo waited outside watching a GPS tracker app and listening to his police radio.

It was the public's first up-close look at the inverted world invented by Jenkins. Gondo aided Wells because he did not want his friend to get robbed by Jenkins, who was depicted by Gondo as completely out of control, "like an animal."

There was increased security at the courthouse after one of the scheduled witnesses received an anonymous call with a warning not to take the stand.

"Testify and die," the caller said and hung up.

Shropshire had materials related to the trial confiscated from his cell. He said he did not trust the court-appointed lawyers and was preparing for his defense. He had the right to confront his accusers. Prosecutors argued he was intimidating witnesses.

Rayam also testified, almost solely about the robbery that he and Wells had committed together while Gondo stood watch outside. He confessed that he may have threatened to kill Black's girlfriend, a real estate agent and law student who had been sleeping when they had burst in. She also testified.

"I turned over and there was two masked guys that came in my room," she said.

She said Rayam seemed shocked when he saw her, and he pulled his hood around his face. Then he pointed at his gun.

"You know what this is," he told her and then asked, "Where's the money?"

When she told him she didn't know, she testified, he started "jumping around my room, like going in drawers and closets and tossing stuff."

"I'm-a kill you, and where's the money?" Rayam said.

A rogue cop like Rayam was just a small detail in the ten-day trial that circled around the nationwide panic over the "opioid epidemic," pitting sympathetic white users who had gotten hooked on pills against primarily black heroin dealers waiting for them on the streets.

A number of drug customers testified. One after another, users who had been given immunity took the stand and told tales of the heroin habits that brought them into daily contact with the defendants. Most were white. Rural or suburban. Their faces evoked empathy from the jury, whose members were chosen from all around the state and could imagine their own children, grandchildren, or neighbors preyed upon by remorseless, black drug dealers in the dreaded city of Baltimore.

There was a dairy farmer who could not do his chores unless he drove to the Alameda to score; an operating engineer with MS, who had bought five grams a day for the last two and a half years; a gymnast who started using as a result of an injury; a student; an auto-parts consultant.

John, who had been busted and agreed to work off the charge by serving as a confidential informant, had a different story, one that seemed more like the after-school-special version of a dealer looking to hook young innocents. He testified that he had been sitting at a light in his car one day when Shropshire drove up beside him and asked if he "liked to party." John said yes, and Shropshire threw him a half gram of dope and his phone number and then drove off.

Over the next several years, John bought thousands of grams of heroin from Shropshire, who also offered to trade dope for dirt bikes.

After he got busted, he continued to buy dope from Shropshire. Only now, he handed it over to the cops.

None of the defendants testified.

"Everything was taken from me," Shropshire said. "The only reason why I'm not testifying today is because I don't have my belongings."

He did not deny selling drugs, but he maintained that none of the testimony showed that he had been involved in a conspiracy to sell drugs. He thought he could prove it, but that opportunity, along with his protections under the Sixth Amendment, had been stripped.

In his closing arguments, prosecutor Derek Hines argued that Shropshire alone had personally sold more than seven thousand grams of heroin and claimed that sixty people had overdosed on heroin that came from the Shropshire conspiracy, with fifteen of those overdoses fatal. Wells, Hines said, played another role: He supplied the heroin to everyone else in the organization and acted as enforcer—a role Gondo's presence in the conspiracy greatly assisted.

"The defendants managed to turn the system upside down," Hines said. "For the defendants, this wasn't a game of cops and robbers. To the defendants, the cops became the robbers and robbed people with them. They had a seven-year run and trafficked thousands of grams of heroin."

Hines concluded with J.L, a white woman whose overdose in 2011 sparked the investigation into drug-dealing at the Alameda.

"While J. L. can't tell her story, you were able to hear the stories from fourteen other customers in this case," Hines said. "Unlike J. L., they were able to come in here and tell you their truth. And in a moment, you'll have an opportunity to tell the truth as well. That's what 'verdict' means—'to speak the truth.'"

The jury did not take long to deliberate. They came back with a verdict on the morning of Halloween: guilty.

Shropshire sat there shaking his head when the foreperson read out the verdicts.

As Wells tried to piece together how he'd gotten here, his thoughts traversed his entire life. He would have to sit with Gondo's treachery for a long time.

Wise and Hines had won. Now they turned their focus to the higher-profile public corruption case against Hersl, Taylor, and especially Jenkins.

Users who had testified against Shropshire had been hard to wrangle. Witnesses in the GTTF case would be much more difficult to persuade to take the stand. They would have to get people like

Oreese Stevenson, usually seated at the defense table, to appear now, in court, as witnesses for the federal government.

ON NOVEMBER 15, Detective Sean Suiter drove through the Harlem Park neighborhood in West Baltimore, an area he knew well. He'd just gotten back to town after his son's wedding in Jamaica, and he was working with Detective David Bomenka, not his usual partner, investigating a triple murder that was almost a year old.

Around 4:00 P.M., Suiter's lawyer, Jeremy Eldridge, called him. Suiter was scheduled to appear before the grand jury the next day. He told Eldridge he was driving and couldn't talk.

Eldridge called again at 4:27. Suiter didn't answer.

At 4:30, Suiter ignored another call from Eldridge.

Suiter had recently removed Gondo and Ward from his phone contacts and deleted a bunch of text messages and some entries from his call log. Other cops were starting to fall in the GTTF case. The GTTF sergeant before Jenkins, Thomas Allers, was charged on August 30. Then, on November 14, a Philadelphia cop named Eric Snell had been indicted for dealing drugs with Rayam. There was a chilling line in the press release that the U.S. Attorney's Office put out: "Snell told Rayam to 'stand tall' and said he would 'keep an eye' on Rayam's kids, which Rayam perceived as a threat to harm Rayam's children if Rayam told authorities about Snell's illegal drug trafficking."

Suiter told Bomenka he saw somebody in the alley near Bennett Place, a small residential street that spills into two larger thoroughfares in and out of the West side. They should take a look. Bomenka wasn't sure they had seen anything, but Suiter said he'd wait to see if the guy came back out.

The homicide detectives got out of an unmarked Nissan Altima and set up on different sides of Bennett Place. Then Suiter ran into the alley.

"Stop! Stop! Stop!" Suiter yelled. "Police!"

And then, gunshots.

Suiter fell down in a vacant lot near the alley, his gun under him, his radio in his other hand, bleeding from the back of his head. Bomenka did not have a police radio on him and called 911 on his cell phone. He rolled Suiter over on his back and began chest compressions. A patrol car arrived, and the cops hoisted Suiter up and into the back seat and drove off—Harlem Park was only about a mile from Shock Trauma. They couldn't wait for an ambulance to arrive.

The patrol car carrying the gravely wounded Suiter started careening through West Baltimore. Near Shock Trauma, as it went through an intersection, it crashed into a car and a University of Maryland Police car providing escort.

A text from Eldridge came through on Suiter's phone: "You have grand jury by subpoena at 1 pm in federal court. And a meeting at 11 am at USAO."

An ambulance arrived at the crash and took Suiter to the hospital.

Another text from Eldridge a few minutes later: "Dude, what the fuck is going on."

IVAN BATES CALLED his friend Jeremy Eldridge when he heard that Suiter had been shot.

"What the fuck?" Bates said. "Did they tell someone?"

Eldridge considered Bates a mentor, and since he didn't have a lot of federal experience, he'd been asking for advice in the Suiter matter. Bates had helped explain the process of bringing a client to the grand jury.

Eldridge told Bates he had no idea what happened or who knew what or anything—just that his client had been shot.

It was all over the news as cops swarmed the vacants near

where Suiter was shot, looking for the gunman. It was 5:00 P.M. on a Wednesday. Residents were getting home from work, and they could not get to their houses. One woman who lived in the neighborhood said that when she first walked outside, she saw a line of men on their knees on the street, hands on their heads, cops looming over them, keeping them there, detained.

When Bates and Eldridge talked on the phone the next day, the neighborhood was still locked down. Eldridge had already gone to the U.S. Attorney's Office early to get some answers. Suiter was their witness, and he had been shot in the head. They seemed as surprised as anyone else, and they gave him no information. Bates thought of the clients he had brought to the federal prosecutors and wondered if they were all in danger.

The Shock Trauma doctors had not been able to save Sean Suiter.

A week later, at 5:00 P.M. on the Wednesday before Thanksgiving, Commissioner Kevin Davis held a press conference at headquarters where he said he had "just" been informed of Suiter's impending testimony.

He also announced that detectives had evidence of a physical struggle—and that Suiter was shot with his own gun.

Rumors spreading in squad cars and on the streets overlapped now. Cops and criminals both thought it was a hit. Bates also started to hear people saying that it was a suicide. Suiter was dirty, they said, and didn't want to testify, and he knew how to make a suicide look like a homicide. Eldridge said there was no way that Suiter, who had been a friend as well as a client, would commit suicide.

On November 29, the law enforcement community—with a huge showing of support from civilians—held a massive funeral procession for the slain cop.

Bates, still learning the intricacies of running for public office, hoped that people weren't going to think he was there campaigning when he arrived at Suiter's funeral. He had come to show his respects.

When he tried to speak to an assistant state's attorney he knew, she told him that she couldn't talk to him. Mosby would light her up if she saw them together. That wasn't what he was here for anyway. He sat down with Eldridge.

After the somber, grievous ceremony, Bates stood to the side of the road, waiting for the procession to pass, surrounded by dozens of people, many of whom had not attended the funeral itself. The wife of a former client stood there with her mom, waving.

"The cops killed him," she said to Bates.

The next day, the U.S. Attorney's Office indicted Wayne Jenkins on a number of new charges resulting from the Umar Burley crash: Destruction, Alteration, or Falsification of Records in Federal Investigations and Deprivation of Rights Under Color of Law. The indictment described the chase Jenkins initiated with Umar Burley, the crash with Elbert Davis, and the cover-up using planted heroin.

A $215,000 reward for information on Suiter's killer remained unclaimed.

THE JUDGE STEPPED away from the bench and down onto the floor of a federal courtroom and stood on equal footing with Umar Burley and Brent Matthews.

He shook the hands of the two men who had been pressured to plead guilty to drug charges in 2010, even though they had claimed that the heroin was planted on them.

Matthews, the passenger in the car, had served three years. Burley had remained in jail until August 31, 2017, when federal prosecutors arranged for his release.

Now the federal charges on both their records would be dropped.

"I'm sorry," the judge who had presided over their original case and accepted their guilty pleas said.

He noted that, in their cases, the system had failed.

"This has been a nightmare that doesn't end for me," Burley told reporters outside the courthouse. "To be forced to be involved in a death, which will forever haunt me."

JENKINS'S TRIAL WAS scheduled for January 16. Hersl and Taylor were still standing tall, ready for trial too. And Allers, who had initially maintained his innocence, changed his plea to guilty in December but was not cooperating with the investigation.

Prosecutors knew that if Jenkins testified, he could cause a lot of unnecessary chaos. They needed to keep the pressure on Jenkins, without giving him a chance to grandstand. They decided to go after Stepp, whom Jenkins had given up back in July.

On December 13, the cops stopped a woman who had just left Stepp's house. They said they saw paraphernalia in her car, which she gave them permission to search. They discovered a half ounce of cocaine.

Just after midnight, the FBI and Baltimore County Police executed a search on Stepp's home.

The FBI found 223 bags of powdered cocaine broken up for easy sale. In a box where he'd been hiding the stuff Jenkins had dropped off, they also found 51 bags containing 423 grams of crack.

The crack would get him. In the federal system, as a vestigial result of the racist disparity in sentencing for crack versus powder cocaine, anything more than 228 grams could result in a life sentence, with a mandatory minimum of ten years.

Stepp should have gotten rid of it. He didn't even sell crack. His clients owned clubs and restaurants or worked in real estate or government even, and they didn't want rock. There was no market for it in the waterfront bars of Baltimore County where local partiers hung out. He couldn't bring himself to just get rid of it, on the off chance that some situation might arise where he could move it all at once.

Then they found fourteen grams of heroin he didn't even know was still out there in his shed. And some Molly.

Stepp noticed the FBI paying particular attention to strangely specific items, like the duffel bag Jenkins had delivered the sixty pounds of weed he'd stolen from Belvedere Towers in, and a watch.

"They had such particular interest in that watch," Stepp said.

Stepp was booked in Baltimore County, charged with cocaine distribution. He was swiftly released on $100,000 bail. Then the FBI immediately indicted him for the drugs. He had no choice. He had to give up what he knew about Jenkins. He'd always kept his mouth shut in the past and swore to himself he would still never snitch on anyone from the streets.

Telling on a cop who ratted you out was different—it's revenge.

He told the FBI where in the house he had three more kilos of cocaine that they hadn't found and told them he had read about Oreese Stevenson's stolen watch in the indictment and thrown it in the water.

They wanted the watch for trial.

Stepp drew diagrams of where he thought it would be. An FBI dive team plunged off Stepp's dock looking for Stevenson's watch. They were down there for three or four hours before they found it.

The watch had actually belonged to Ronald Hamilton, not Oreese Stevenson.

"The government was like, 'It's better than Oreese's watch, Donny, thank you.' And I'm like, 'Glad to be some assistance,'" Stepp said.

Stepp joked that the feds should give him a job. Then he handed over all the recordings he'd made over the years. Photos of him and Wayne in police headquarters, at the Super Bowl, or at the site of some robbery; shaky video of crimes and burglaries; quotidian footage of Jenkins partying, doing a weird little dance in the most recent, final bit of footage.

"Once we got inside my phone, they actually celebrated on the fourth floor when they started looking at videos of Jenkins in different jobs and capers," Stepp recalled.

The FBI laughed at Stepp, wondering why he would ever record all of this.

"Things weren't adding up," Stepp said.

Stepp was almost enjoying this. Like Jenkins, he loved the game, and though they had both lost big and were facing federal prison, Stepp would not let his old friend beat him. With Stepp's detailed testimony and years of photos and video to back it up, Jenkins agreed to a guilty plea on January 3.

"Bitch-ass Jenkins thought he was smarter than everyone," Stepp said. "I blowed his game plan straight to hell."

THIRTEEN

WAYNE JENKINS'S FAMILY walked away from the U.S. courthouse in a tight, huddled bunch, gripping one another's arms and looking down at the ground through sunglasses, as if they were leaving a funeral.

Jenkins had just pleaded guilty to illegal searches and overtime fraud; stealing more than $200,000, going back to a 2011 robbery he'd committed with Gondo and including Belvedere Towers, Oreese Stevenson, Ronald Hamilton, and Dennis Armstrong; receiving $250,000 from Stepp for stolen drugs; using GPS trackers and police intelligence to break into houses and cars; bringing Stepp drugs looted during the riot; taking seized drugs from evidence control; stealing and reselling dirt bikes. He also admitted to authoring false reports and depriving Umar Burley and Brent Matthews of their civil rights. Jenkins did not admit to knowing that drugs had been planted on Burley, amplifying the mystery of this case and its connection to the death of Sean Suiter.

In court, Jenkins spoke very little, answering, "Yes, ma'am," to the pro forma questions ensuring that he understood the terms of the plea.

"I am ashamed of myself," he told the judge.

His lawyer, Steven Levin, was a former assistant U.S. attorney who had prosecuted the Rice brothers' case that had sent Oreese Stevenson to prison a decade earlier. Now Levin was defending a client who had just admitted to robbing Stevenson.

"He, along with others, were responsible for seizing hundreds of, if not thousands of, illegal firearms and getting them off the streets of Baltimore," Levin said. "Unfortunately, at some point, things changed. Whether that's as a result of something that happened in the military, something that happened during his time with the Baltimore City Police Department, or as a result of the death of his son remains uncertain. What is certain is that Mr. Jenkins is extremely remorseful."

A lot of guys who knew Jenkins on the job were shocked. They had been sure that he would go all the way and take this to trial. He had always been the last to back down.

ANNA MANTEGNA IMAGINED that her meeting with the FBI would take place in some kind of official setting. Instead, she met Special Agent Erika Jensen, the primary investigator in the GTTF case, and John Sieracki, an Internal Affairs detective working with the FBI's corruption unit, in a crowded Starbucks down the street from the State's Attorney's Office in downtown Baltimore.

Everyone in the State's Attorney's Office had been paranoid ever since Leo Wise had mentioned a leak, and everybody had a theory about who it was. Prosecutors heard Jan Bledsoe, the deputy state's attorney who oversaw police misconduct, announce in the lunchroom that people were blaming her. Bledsoe had been one of the main prosecutors in the Freddie Gray case. If people were suspecting Bledsoe, who had a reputation as a cop hater, then Mantegna knew they must also be looking at her, given her ties to Hersl.

There was nowhere to sit, so they stood at one of the tall tables by the window to discuss Jenkins's accusations that she'd told him about the investigation into the GTTF.

Mantegna immediately wished she had not worn her four-inch heels. She also wished she had brought her lawyer, even as Jensen tried to reassure her that they did not think she was the leak.

"Is this about the phone call?" Mantegna said.

"It is," Jensen said and asked Mantegna to tell her about it.

Mantegna, a maximalist, almost incapable of leaving out a detail, moved through the specifics that led up to her call with Jenkins when she'd warned him about Gondo and Rayam.

She'd needed Jenkins in court for a case tied to a car accident—the suspect's car crashed into some church steps after trying to drive away from Jenkins, and it meant the gun Jenkins recovered from the car was hard to pin on anybody because it was thrown all around the interior. She mentioned how cursed that case seemed to be to her, from the very beginning when Taylor lost the evidence he had recorded on his phone and only later, after much back and forth, retrieved it from the cloud. And then, every time it was set for trial, something would jam it up. Jenkins's sick mother-in-law, Taylor's aunt, then Ward's aunt.

When she finally got Jenkins on the phone, on October 5, 2016, Mantegna said, she thanked him for getting in touch, and they chitchatted a little. During the conversation, Gondo and Rayam came up, and Mantegna warned Jenkins about them—they were up to no good, plenty of people knew it.

Jensen asked Mantegna how Jenkins responded to that warning.

Mantegna realized that her call with Jenkins had not been caught on a wiretap. She'd assumed they had Jenkins on a wire. It dawned on her that there was probably no evidence of what they had talked about. Like so many criminal defendants in Baltimore had done before, Mantegna began to fear it might be her word against the word of Wayne Jenkins.

Then Jensen, who could come across as both friendly and severe, asked Mantegna why Gondo and Rayam came up when they weren't part of the case at all.

Mantegna, under pressure, less than a block from her office with two obvious feds, trying to keep her voice down, her feet hurting, couldn't remember. The call had not seemed very important at the time, beyond the fact that they had finally settled on a court date.

She'd had no idea that Jenkins was dirty. She'd warned him about Gondo and Rayam, not about an investigation.

"If I'd have known I was talking to Satan about his minions, I wouldn't have said anything," Mantegna said.

She took out her phone and offered it to Jensen to scroll through and check her messages with Jenkins. Jensen declined.

Then Jensen said they believed it was possible that what Mantegna had told Jenkins kept changing as the cops passed it around like a game of telephone.

"Knowing BPD, I'm sure that's exactly what happened," Mantegna said.

Jensen asked Mantegna if she could think of anyone in the office who may have known about a federal investigation and leaked information to members of the GTTF. The question scared her. Nobody wanted to talk after what happened to Suiter.

The interview lasted two hours. As Mantegna hobbled back across the street, her feet aching in her heels, she kicked herself again for not bringing her lawyer. She was a prosecutor. She should not have been so naïve.

When Mantegna got back to the office, she told her supervisor about the meeting and summarized it for her lawyer as best she could in a series of texts.

"It was definitely a sizing up, getting a feel for me and whether I was telling the truth, but mixed with a bizarre coffee klatch," she texted. "They are looking for leaks."

KEITH GLADSTONE AND a detective he once supervised, Carmine Vignola, waded around in the YMCA's indoor pool, creating white noise in their wake as they talked.

The water wasn't that deep but Gladstone was sinking. He had

retired from BPD in 2012. He'd gotten away free, and then he returned to BPD for a few retroactively disastrous years that now
threatened to capsize his life.

"Do you have anything to worry about?" Vignola asked. "Do
you have any concerns?"

It was a stupid question. The two men had used their wives'
phones to set up a meeting in a swimming pool, where neither
could possibly be wearing a wire, in rural Pennsylvania in January.

GTTF rattled the entire department. Right after the indictments, Commissioner Davis demoted Sean Miller and abolished
plainclothes units, trying to ward off the inevitable. Then, a couple of
days before Gladstone went swimming, the mayor fired Davis and
replaced him with a longtime BPD veteran, Darryl De Sousa. The
day De Sousa got the job, Deputy Commissioner Dean Palmere
was locked out of police headquarters. People saw officers taking computers from Palmere's office. He couldn't get department
email or use his department phone.

Without naming anyone, De Sousa told the press he had blocked
the access of one particular commander because he had feared
that commander would leak sensitive information. Soon Palmere
was back, but things were not right.

Gladstone didn't need to go into all of that. All he had to say to
Vignola was: "Belair Road."

It was March 2014. Gladstone and Vignola were eating at
Chicken Rico near Canton when Jenkins called, panicked, talking
about how he had run over someone in the front yard of a house
on Anntana Avenue and Belair Road.

Dinner stopped, and a cover-up began. Gladstone looked
across the table and asked Vignola if he had a BB gun. He didn't.
He ordered Vignola to call Robert Hankard, his partner, who was
off that day. They drove to Hankard's house and got a BB gun and
then went to Belair Road. Gladstone got out and dropped the air
pistol on the ground near where Jenkins's car still sat on top of the

man, Demetric Simon. Gladstone told Jenkins where it was and left.

If prosecutors or cops ever questioned them about that day, Gladstone said in the pool, Vignola should say he wasn't there at all.

But he was there. Other cops saw him, Vignola said.

Then, they should say they both showed up to Belair Road for "scene assessment," Gladstone said.

"What about Rob?" Vignola asked.

Leave Hankard out of it. They never went to his house. If anyone asks, Gladstone got the BB gun from his own trunk. That was the best they could do and they still had no idea what to expect as the U.S. government brought its case against the remaining two defendants, Taylor and Hersl, in a three-week trial.

IVAN BATES SAT in court, hunched forward with his elbows resting on his knees, his hands under his chin, watching Leo Wise question his client, Oreese Stevenson, a crucial, unlikely, and barely cooperative witness in the *United States of America v. Daniel Thomas Hersl and Marcus Roosevelt Taylor.*

Hersl, defiant with arched eyebrows that looked like they were painted on, often looked back at his brothers, packed into the crowded stadium-style seating with the rest of their family.

Taylor, befuddled one moment and absolutely calm the next, nodded to his father and closely watched Wise, occasionally scribbling notes to his lawyers or whispering some grievance in their ears.

"Just to be clear, Mr. Stevenson, you are appearing here today under a subpoena, right?" Wise said, tilting his cleanly shaven head in Stevenson's direction and rocking back and forth on his toes.

"Yes," Stevenson said.

"It's fair to say you don't want to be here, sir?" Wise said.

"Not at all," Stevenson said.

Bates had beaten Jenkins in court while Stevenson sat silently to the side in his yellow jumpsuit. That was the best he could do in the position he was in as a defense attorney. Even as he had tried to convince Stevenson to testify, he had been flirting with the other side. Not just playing defense against dirty cops, actively going after them as the next Baltimore City state's attorney. So as he sat there, leaning forward like a coach, he studied both sides as Wise questioned Stevenson. In the Freddie Gray case, he had seen how not to prosecute police. In this case, he could maybe find a more useful model.

"I know this is uncomfortable for you and not something you want to do, is that right?" Wise said.

"Absolutely," Stevenson said.

"Now, you were arrested on March 22, 2016, when you were sitting in a car, right?" Wise said.

"Yes," Stevenson replied.

"Can you describe what happened?" Wise said.

"I was sittin' there, and the police car came up a one-way and blocked me in, and they all jumped out," Stevenson said.

In earlier testimony, Ward and Hendrix had both described the Stevenson robbery in jaw-dropping detail. There were still discrepancies: Hendrix and Ward, two dirty cops turned state's witnesses, testified that they had stolen $100,000 from the safe. Stevenson had always claimed there was more.

"Did you get a notice that money had been seized from your house from law enforcement?" Wise said.

"Yes," Stevenson said.

"And how much did the notice say had been seized?" Wise asked.

"$100,000," Stevenson said.

"And how much did you actually have in the house?" Wise asked.

"Close to $300,000," Stevenson said.

Bates could tell that answering the prosecution's questions was excruciating for Stevenson. It was only going to get worse when Wise sat down and Jennifer Wicks, one of Taylor's lawyers, began her cross-examination.

Taylor, who insisted on his absolute innocence on every charge, left his lawyers with few options outside of trying to tear down the state's witnesses.

"What were you going to do with the cocaine?" Wicks asked Stevenson.

"Not correct," Stevenson said, not really answering the question.

Bates watched carefully, worried that Stevenson might blow.

"My question to you is—" Wicks said.

"I'm answering," Stevenson said, interrupting Wicks. "It's not correct."

"What were you going to do with the cocaine?" Wicks said, trying one more time.

"No plans," Stevenson said.

Taylor's other lawyer, Christopher Nieto, who was one of the attorneys representing Adnan Syed in the case made famous by the *Serial* podcast, questioned Keona Holloway, who had also been subpoenaed—and picked up where Wicks left off.

"Did he tell you what he was going to do with those drugs?" Nieto asked.

"No," Holloway said.

"All right," Nieto said. "Were they for personal use? Was he going to get high?"

"I don't know," Holloway said.

"Had you ever seen him get high before?" Nieto said.

"Never," Holloway said.

"Have you ever seen him snort six kilograms of cocaine before?" Nieto said.

"Never," Holloway said.

Bates went out to meet the shaken couple after they testified. They all walked back toward his office together. Bates could see Stevenson was conflicted.

"These are cops that robbed you and your family," Bates said. "That ain't snitching."

Stevenson had not been happy to find his initials in that federal indictment, and now his full name would appear in newspapers around the world. As they spoke, someone at the *Daily Mail* in England was pulling up the only picture of Stevenson on his Facebook page—a slick shot of him leaning contemplatively against a wall in dark glasses, a black skully, and a kaffiyeh around his neck—to accompany an article titled "Who's the Bad Guy Now? Dealers Take the Stand to Testify Against 'Corrupt Cops Who Faked Warrants to Steal Hundreds of Thousands of Dollars in Cash and Drugs from Them.'"

Bates knew what an ordeal it was for Stevenson and Holloway to testify. He also believed the public needed to hear the stories of the GTTF victims who had not been called on to appear in court. The victims needed some way to tell their stories directly to the city. He called his clients, convincing them to go public with their experiences.

RONALD HAMILTON LOOKED almost victorious as he took the witness stand in the same federal court where he had twice before been sentenced to prison. He had agreed to testify if they would leave his wife out of it—her terror had increased after the death of Detective Suiter, and she didn't want to go anywhere near the witness stand. For Hamilton, being heard was a kind of vindication.

Leo Wise walked Hamilton through the entire story of the robbery. For his final question, he produced the watch that the FBI dive team had recovered from the water behind Stepp's house.

"And was your watch taken that night too?" Wise asked.

"Yes," Hamilton said.

Wise sat down.

Hersl's lawyer, William Purpura, who was also representing Joaquín "El Chapo" Guzmán Loera at the time, stood hunched and bald, with the hard-earned air of an aging tough guy who has seen more shit than everyone else in the room combined. He didn't have a lot to say to Hamilton, who did not fit well into the defense Purpura had been unspooling, since Hamilton had never even been charged with a crime. Purpura's argument was that as a police officer, Hersl had the right to seize property from citizens. When Hersl failed to turn that property over to evidence control, that was theft. It was not robbery. It was more like shoplifting than a holdup—and since Hersl was charged with robbery, not theft, he was not guilty.

Taylor was not accused of being a part of the Hamilton heist, so no one expected his team to engage in a lengthy cross-examination designed to damage Hamilton's credibility.

"You make a significant income from legal gambling. That's what you said?" Nieto asked, looking imperiously at Hamilton.

"I make money from gambling, yes," Hamilton said.

"Right," Nieto said. "Despite the fact it looks like you lose more than your entire family earns a year, you're saying you make money from gambling?"

"Yes, I do," Hamilton said.

"Enough where, for example, you can have $50,000 in cash," Nieto said. "Or $70,000 in cash."

"Yes," Hamilton said.

"In your half-million-dollar house," Nieto said.

"Yes," Hamilton said.

"That sits on two acres in Carroll County," Nieto said.

"Yes," Hamilton said.

Nieto mentioned Ronald and Nancy Hamilton's combined income of $130,000.

"Yet you two buy a $500,000 house?" Nieto said.

"Correct," Hamilton said. "I paid $17,000 down on the house. That's what you want to know? I put $17,000 down on the house."

It seemed for a moment like everyone was looking at Wise, waiting for an objection. He did not move.

"What are your mortgage payments?" Nieto asked.

"Does that makes a difference?" Hamilton said.

When Nieto looked at him with a sarcastic smirk, Hamilton exploded.

"This right here destroyed my whole fuckin' family!" Hamilton shouted. "This destroyed my whole family. I am in a divorce process right now because of this bullshit. This destroyed my whole fuckin' family, man. You sit here asking me questions about a fuckin' house. My fuckin' wife stays in the fuckin' Walmart every fuckin' night until I come home. If you want to know that, worry about that. That's what the fuck's the matter in here, man. Everybody's life is destroyed, man. My house don't have nothing to do with this. The problem is my wife is taking medication because of this."

"Sir, sir," the judge said.

"I'm sorry, Your Honor. I'm sorry to the courts," Hamilton said. "But the fact of the matter is, man, my house don't have nothing to do with this. The fact of the matter is, they came in my house, destroyed my family. I'm in a divorce process because of this. Because of this. This has put so much financial pressure on my family. Kids, man, are scared to go in the house because of this."

ON A FRIDAY, when the court was in recess, Bates gathered some of the GTTF's victims for a press conference where they would be able to tell their stories directly to reporters and the public and he could explain how Mosby's office facilitated the corruption.

"Here are just a few of the faces that have been terrorized by those criminals called the Gun Trace Task Force, and we view them as a gang," Bates said. "It's important that we recognize that these few faces that you see are the individuals that you've been hearing about in the courtroom, but there are so many more people that have been terrorized by these criminals."

Jamal and Jovonne Walker said Jenkins and Gladstone robbed Jamal and then broke into their house back in 2010.

"To have your life turned upside down for almost two years, not being able to work in a field where you're passionate about doing what you do because you have pending charges," Jovonne Walker said. "It's just not something that a person that's never been exposed to should ever have to endure over crooked cops."

And Andre Crowder explained what the GTTF took from him.

"It's a little bit different for me. It didn't just hinder me from work. When this occurred, I was took away from my family for three days, and within those three days, I lost my three-year-old son," Crowder said. "Out of the three days I was gone out of my son's life, I lost him. So, it's bigger than a charge they put on me, the mark they put on my record, the cash that was took, all of that. That doesn't matter because I wasn't there to spend those last moments of my son's life with him because of this situation."

It was hard for Crowder to put his story out there. He wanted the world to understand what these cops did, and he wanted to publicly honor his son Ahmeer and wanted everybody to know how much Ivan Bates had done for him even though he considered himself a bottled-up person who would not normally talk publicly about anything, much less something so emotional.

Crowder ended his tragic story with an endorsement for Ivan Bates as state's attorney.

Natalie Finegar was there too and passed out paperwork about Rayam's Franks hearing—proving, she explained, that Mosby's office was aware of the problems with GTTF cops.

The press conference got enough play—all the local news

outlets were there, plus the BBC—that Mosby had to acknowledge Bates's campaign.

"I realize this is campaign season for those seeking elected office. I fully understand that my administration will be attacked, and while people are entitled to their own opinion, they are certainly not entitled to their own facts," she said in a statement.

Thiru Vignarajah, also running for state's attorney, saw the viability of the political issue and released a list of 2,322 GTTF cases that he thought should be reviewed.

ALTHOUGH HERSL AND Taylor were the only two defendants in the trial, much of the testimony centered around the diabolical actions of Wayne Jenkins, who seemed to hover over the proceedings like an evil genius.

When Leo Wise laid the big black bags of burglary equipment, grappling hooks, and skull masks out on the courtroom floor, it awakened in the spectators the same frightened awe that Ward experienced when Jenkins put on the mask, did a little dance, and proposed robbing Oreese Stevenson again.

And when Hendrix testified that Jenkins taught them when "you hurt someone and you need to cover yourself, it's easy to put the BB gun down as if they had a handgun," he confirmed the horror stories about Baltimore police that had been circling the streets for decades—police really did drop guns on people.

Taylor watched Ward and Hendrix, his eyes brimming with disgust. They had all risked their lives together, and now, he insisted, they were willing to lie about him to save themselves and get less time. Even what they said about Jenkins, he said, was not true. Taylor didn't think that his sergeant had betrayed him, even if he had pleaded guilty.

For Taylor, the only ones who were really guilty of the kinds of crimes the government accused them all of were Gondo and

Rayam. They were the ones robbing people and dealing drugs. When they got caught, they came up with a plan and blamed everyone else.

"Dirty, dirty motherfuckers," Taylor called them.

RAYAM LOOKED LOST and broken, his dark eyes both empty and darting in the middle of his now bloated face. Ward and Hendrix were playing the game, doing what they had to do, but Rayam was somehow trying to purge his sins.

He confessed to countless crimes and then turned on his old partner. He said that Gondo had helped a friend buy a gun that had been used in a murder, adding that when Gondo was shot in 2006, it was drug related.

When prosecutors played the muffled audio of a car crash, Rayam really broke down. There had been a microphone hidden in Gondo's car that rainy night in August 2016 when a chase resulted in a car crash and now Rayam had to sit here in public and listen as he and his coconspirators decided not to give aid.

"How about we just go and see and just act like, 'Oh, is everything okay?'" Rayam said. "You get what I'm saying?"

"Yeah," Gondo said.

"He wants to sit here and see how they handle it in case they get on the air saying they pull Citiwatch up," Hersl said. "He's saying we gotta stay in the immediate area."

Finally, Hines stopped the audio and continued to question Rayam, who stumbled through his answers, conflating details, unsure who was in the car with him and Gondo that night.

"There was so many car accidents," Rayam said, almost crying. "Could you just refresh my memory as far as the location of this one?"

"Were there multiple other car accidents like this one which your unit was involved in?" Hines said.

"Yeah," Rayam said, tears in his eyes. "Chases and everything, yes."

Hines highlighted a particularly cruel line from the recording.

"When Taylor said, 'That dude unconscious. He ain't sayin' shit,' what did you understand that to mean?" Hines said.

"Meaning he won't say police was chasing him, you know, and he may forget, or, you know, we don't have anything to worry about," Rayam said.

Taylor tried to tell his lawyers that Hines and Rayam were lying. That was Rayam who'd said that, not Taylor. He wasn't even in the car. He'd hopped out of Jenkins's car to take a piss and was walking toward the gas station when he spotted a guy sitting in his car with a bag of weed on his lap. Taylor reached for the guy's door, and the car sped off and almost ran over Taylor's foot. Jenkins hit the gas and left without him. Gondo followed. The squad left him at the gas station.

And now no one would listen to him.

There was no disputing Hersl's East Baltimore twang.

"These car chases, it's a crapshoot, you know," Hersl's disembodied voice said.

His recorded chuckle filled the quiet courtroom. Only Hersl's family—who came as a group each day, always with a cooler full of sandwiches for lunch—could fathom the true horror of that moment captured by the FBI. Danny's brother Matt had died in 2013 when a car fleeing from the state police jumped a curb and crashed into him as he'd stood there smoking a cigarette.

The family had been prone to thinking of Danny's persecution in the light of Matt's death. The closest they ever came to admitting Danny's misdeeds was to say that something had changed in him since his brother's death. Now this audiotape pushed the catastrophic moments close together, blending the two calamities.

From a legal standpoint, the next moment, when Hersl suggested that they falsify their time cards so it would like they weren't working when the crash occurred, was even worse.

"We could go and stop the slips at 10:30 before that happened," Hersl said.

It was probably the only time GTTF conspired to make it look like they worked less than they actually did—and it was clear evidence of a conspiracy.

WHEN MOMODU GONDO took the stand, he seemed inexplicably chill. It was nothing to sit here and tell the court about the crimes of Hersl and Taylor after the ordeal of betraying his lifelong best friend, Kyle Wells.

Gondo had answered Shropshire's call about the GPS tracker and intervened in Jenkins's investigation of Wells out of a sense of loyalty. In the Shropshire trial, when he sat on the stand and pointed out his friend, he had moved beyond loyalty, and now here he was, ready to give up anybody. Under cross-examination, he said Rayam had confessed to the murder of a man named Sean Cannady in 2009.

"Didn't you tell federal agents that Rayam told you, 'Fuck it, I just didn't want to chase him'?" Nieto said.

"Absolutely," said Gondo.

"And that Rayam also told you that Baltimore Police Department colonel Dean Palmere had arrived at the scene and coached Rayam on how he should sort of explain the shooting, right?" Nieto said.

"He coached everybody who was at the scene," Gondo said. "People in command coached, yeah."

Later that day, Palmere announced he was retiring from the police department. Palmere denied Gondo's allegations and said his retirement had nothing to do with the testimony. He had put in his two weeks' notice right after De Sousa took over the department.

DEBORAH LEVI, WHO was tasked with evaluating every case that may have been tainted by GTTF and looking into all the police misconduct in Baltimore, had followed the trial in the news, but she wanted to be in the courtroom for the testimony of Donald Stepp.

It was strange for her as she sat in the gallery waiting for Stepp to be called, looking down on Hersl and Taylor both sitting there in the defendants' seats. She almost always felt a sense of empathy for the defendant.

"Even in Freddie Gray, the officers became defendants," she said. "And so you feel a sort of kinship toward the position that they're in or the space that they're in because you want to make sure that they're represented well and they're not falsely accused and that they still are presumed innocent."

She could not see Hersl and Taylor that way.

"I had seen too much of what I thought they had done to people over a long period of time," Levi said. "That connection for them as criminal defendants—I didn't feel it."

She sympathized with the lawyers and was fascinated by the challenge of a case in which everyone was an accused criminal.

"You had to figure out, how do I relate to this criminal sympathetically, and how do I relate to this criminal non-sympathetically?" she said. "How do you play all those cards?"

When Stepp walked into the courtroom, he sported a slick, tailored suit and thick-framed glasses that gave his shining baldness an air that was more intellectual than intimidating and, when he stepped up to the stand, he flashed an involuntary, elfin smile. He was geeking to share his role in this incredible tale, as eager now to help Wise and Hines as he had once been to please Jenkins.

"Did he say anything about what the Gun Trace Task Force did?" Hines asked Stepp of his many conversations with Jenkins.

"It was a front for a criminal enterprise," Stepp said.

He added that Jenkins "was supplying men within his unit and men within other parts of the Baltimore Police Department."

"And did you find it unusual that he was coming to you to order equipment rather than getting it from the Baltimore Police Department?" Hines asked.

"It was obvious to me that when I'm taking millions of dollars' worth of drugs from the Baltimore Police Department and selling them, that these are not a—this is not a normal police department," Stepp said.

This voluble, hyperbolic bail bondsman was living proof of everything that Levi had been trying to show for years. And he had photos to prove it. Prosecutors showed the jury a picture of Stepp standing in police headquarters with a BPD vest, a gun, and a wicked smile.

In the gallery, watching the testimony with savage concentration, Levi could only imagine how much Stepp knew. He seemed to be trying to make amends for his work with Jenkins, and William Purpura, Hersl's lawyer, shut him down at every turn.

"If you didn't want to sell it, why didn't you just throw the damned stuff out?" Purpura asked Stepp about the crack that accounted for much of the sentence he could be facing.

"That's a good question," Stepp said.

"That is a good question," Purpura said. "Can you answer it?"

Levi laughed out loud. She admired Purpura's pugnacious performance and stored that line away for a future cross-examination of a cop.

Even Levi, after a year spent looking through hundreds of GTTF cases, wasn't quite ready for some of what she heard.

"It was during the riots of Freddie Gray that he called me again and told me to, woke me up and says, 'I need you to open the garage door.' So I went downstairs, opened the garage door. Same routine: pulls in, police-issued car, undercover car, popped his trunk," Stepp said. "This time he come out with two trash bags, large trash bags. And he goes, I go, 'What's this?' And he says, 'I just got people coming out of these pharmacies. I've got an entire pharmacy.'"

This revelation fundamentally changed the version of reality that had been agreed upon since the uprising in 2015.

"There's some argument that these guys robbed drug dealers, some people say that, right, and that these guys, you know, committed crimes against other alleged criminals," Levi told reporters out in front of the courthouse at the end of the day. "But when you're taking prescription medication that the citizens of Baltimore, and in impoverished neighborhoods, really needed, that shows a level of callousness that rises all the way to the top."

IN CLOSING ARGUMENTS, Taylor's lawyers tried, one last time, to discredit the witnesses who had testified.

"The government has gone to the depths of the criminal underworld in Baltimore. And what have they found, ladies and gentlemen? They have found convicted criminals who are authorized, with immunity, to come in here and testify," Wicks said. "It's deplorable, and it's nauseating."

Both Wise and Hines lived in Baltimore and, in fulfilling one of the federal government's promises to protect citizens from the tyranny of their town or city, they argued with the passion of men defending their home.

"Ms. Wicks just told you that in the course of this investigation, the United States went to the depths of the criminal justice system, and she's right. And what we found in those depths were Daniel Thomas Hersl and Marcus Roosevelt Taylor," Wise said. "And what is deplorable and nauseating is not that it was exposed in this courtroom but that they did those things."

Wise, who had come to the U.S. Attorney's Office from the Office of Congressional Ethics, had sounded increasingly radical as the trial progressed.

"The badges and the guns they carried were powerful, power they chose to abuse," Wise told the jury in his final statement. "But now, now you have the chance and the responsibility to speak truth to power."

After two days of deliberations, the jury returned a verdict: Guilty of racketeering, racketeering conspiracy, and robbery. Not guilty on use of a firearm in commission of a robbery.

Taylor looked down, like he still wasn't sure what was happening, his world quietly swirling into what he later described as a nightmare.

Hersl got red and rubbed his head with his hands. His family wailed when they put handcuffs on him.

"I love you, Danny!" Hersl's brother Steve cried out.

Outside, Steve, a former firefighter, was cornered by news cameras.

"My brother Danny Hersl wasn't a part of this gang," he said, his cheek glistening with tears. "He tried to get out of this gang. He begged. He cried. He cried to the family. He cried to everybody to get out of the gang. He didn't want a part of it."

Steve Hersl blamed former commissioner Kevin Davis and Deputy Commissioner Dean Palmere.

"When you got guys resigning, walking out the door with their head down—the commissioner, Palmere, all of them. Why are their heads down?" he asked. "Hey, is there an unsolved murder of a police officer? They know what the hell happened. They know. My brother Danny Hersl knows what happened."

FOURTEEN

ANTONIO SHROPSHIRE DID not plead for mercy at his sentencing.

"I've reviewed this discovery from top to bottom. As you can see, I'm still here today reviewing discovery," Shropshire said to the judge, papers laid out on the defense table in front of him. "It's a lot of things that's just been said today that's just simply not true."

"Court's indulgence," Shropshire's lawyer said, interrupting his own client, trying to get him to slow his roll.

The two bent in, put their heads together, and whispered.

Shropshire looked at the judge again.

"I don't want you to take what I have to say as a sign of disrespect, because it's not directed towards you," Shropshire said. "It's some things that need to be said that I don't think you are aware of."

He pointed out that McDougall had testified that he was arrested with $8,000, when it was actually $5,000.

"Science now tells us that the view of human memory is fundamentally flawed. The mind not only distorts and embellishes memories, but a variety of external factors can affect how memories are retrieved and described," he said. "It's a number of reasons that I can think of why Corporal McDougall testified falsely under oath, but I'm going to give him the benefit of the doubt and assume, like science now tells us, that the human mind fundamentally distorts and embellishes memories."

He did not extend the same benefit of the doubt about faulty memory to the prosecutors.

"Also, Mr. Wise and Mr. Hines are liars," he said.

Shropshire accepted responsibility for the seventy-one grams he'd had on him when he was arrested but denied that what he was doing was grand enough to be considered a conspiracy. He ended his speech with a condemnation of the Chesapeake Detention Facility, where federal inmates are held prior to sentencing.

"I would also like to respectfully ask Your Honor to credit me more time due to the inhumane conditions of the Chesapeake Detention Facility," he said. "The unit I was on smelled like urine and sometimes feces. Mold was everywhere, and the jail didn't do nothing about it. The other inmates told me that the jail has an asbestos problem, and I am truly concerned and would like to be tested."

The judge showed no mercy. A black man convicted of selling heroin to white people in the county was not going to get much sympathy in an age of heightened opioid panic.

"Mr. Shropshire was involved in distributing many kilos of heroin over many years over the course of this conspiracy. Heroin kills people," the judge said. "We heard a lot of testimony about overdoses in this case. Heroin destroys people's families."

His sentence was enhanced because of the conversation he'd had with McDougall and Kilpatrick in the car after they arrested him—an attempt to bribe a police officer to obstruct justice as far as the government was concerned. The judge also increased Shropshire's sentence because of his leadership position within the "organization," which Shropshire said did not even exist.

"The evidence in front of me is that Mr. Shropshire continued to sell this poison to other people's parents and other people's children, affecting many, many other lives during the course of his criminal activity. Does that mean he's a monster? Of course not," the judge said. "But it is also just inescapable that he, again, has participated in a very dangerous and destructive activity for many years."

Shropshire was sentenced to twenty-five years.

ANNA MANTEGNA HAD been ordered to report to the tenth-floor conference room in the State's Attorney's Office at the end of the day. She had a sense of what was coming and had already started packing up her desk.

"So 5:00 comes, I got upstairs and honestly, I have put my sneakers on at that point, took my heels off, because I just wasn't going to bother since I was packing," Mantegna recalled. "And I was met at the door by Camille, the human resources person, who led me down the hall toward the conference room. And as we're going down the hall, she's explaining to me that I serve at the pleasure of the state's attorney."

When they reached the conference room, Marilyn Mosby was not there. Mantegna's division chief was not there. Deputy State's Attorney Michael Schatzow, the chief prosecutor of the Freddie Gray case, sat in the room looking at the floor while the HR official explained that the state's attorney thought it would be best if Mantegna was separated from the office. She was not given a reason why except that all attorneys were at-will employees serving at the pleasure of the state's attorney and they could be fired at any time.

Schatzow did not say anything and took occasional notes. They had written a resignation letter for Mantegna to sign, to save her reputation, to make it easier to get another job.

"I have a hundred dollars in my checking account right now," she said. "What am I going to do? How am I going to afford my medication?"

If she resigned, she couldn't get unemployment. That was when she started crying.

"Even if I want to resign, I don't have a choice. I'm not financially in a position where I'm able to do so. I'm going to file for unemployment," she said.

HR agreed that they would not fight her claim and agreed to give her copies of her most recent evaluations.

Mantegna was escorted back to her office by Mosby's security detail. She looked at fourteen years' worth of books and research materials and started hyperventilating. Security comforted her and said they would help her carry her stuff and arranged for her to pull up to the loading dock.

"There I am sitting next to the dumpster, packing up fourteen years of my life into my car," she said. "I remember sitting there thinking I feel like I'm being thrown in the trash, and here I am next to the dumpster."

She looked over and saw Michael Schatzow and her former friend Jan Bledsoe walking away. They would not look at her.

When word of the firing got out the next day, the SAO acknowledged that they had "separated" from Mantegna and that they had spoken to the U.S. Attorney's Office about the leak. They did not say Mantegna was the leak, but, to her, the implication seemed intentional. Bates, who had gone up against Mantegna plenty of times in court, praised Mantegna.

"I had a number of cases with Mantegna. She was a good lawyer, she was fair," Bates said to the press. "To lose a person like that concerns me."

Bates noted that more than ninety prosecutors had left the SAO during Mosby's term. He said that Mantegna was one of the few prosecutors willing to drop a case if a dirty cop was involved in the arrest. He suggested that Mosby chose the politically expedient course of action over the right one.

Levi, who rarely had anything nice to say about a prosecutor, came to Mantegna's defense. Mantegna could not be the leak.

"It wasn't her," Levi said. "I saw her face when the indictments came out."

DEBORAH LEVI SAT in a conference room inside the Baltimore Police Department's Internal Affairs surrounded by IAD files on a Sunday afternoon.

Internal Affairs was an anonymous brick building in East Baltimore, a chain-link fence with barbed wire on top of it wrapped around its perimeter. There is nothing to mark it as a police building. There is a sign for a Baltimore Stationery Co. and another, on a black awning, that reads *Total Office Interiors*. When GTTF was arrested and reporters caught the handcuffed cops being led out, it was this building the public saw on the news, not the sleeker, brutalist police headquarters or even one of the homey-looking district stations.

It had taken Levi a long time to get to this room. Because there was no legally acceptable procedure for the State's Attorney's Office to review the files of officers involved in a case and then give them to the defense, Levi had to ask a judge to rule that she could get the files directly from the police department and review them herself. BPD reluctantly agreed and said that she could come to the IAD offices on Sunday to see them.

The detectives assigned to assist her kept coming in with more and more papers, which overwhelmed the table and threatened to engulf the entire room.

She was working on the last active GTTF case to be prosecuted: Charles Smith, who had been arrested on July 21, 2016, and charged with attempted murder. He had been in jail since then and still had not gone to trial.

Smith was nabbed by Hendrix and Taylor after a shooting outside a liquor store on a particularly hot and violent night in a hot and violent month. Jenkins, Hendrix, Ward, and Taylor were driving around doing door pops, looking for trouble, when they heard the shots. They were the first officers on the scene. Hendrix and Taylor tackled Smith. They Mirandized him, they took a statement, bagged his hands, and ordered the test for gunshot residue—a test that came back negative.

After the GTTF indictments, BPD created a new statement of charges against Smith that removed all references to Hendrix and Taylor and just mentioned "Baltimore Police detectives" arriving on the scene after a shooting. Later, the charges referred to Hendrix and Taylor as witnesses "who will remain anonymous at this time." This was a perfect example, Levi believed, of how the BPD and the SAO collaborated to cover for officer misconduct.

A couple of weeks earlier, Levi had argued in a lengthy motions hearing that her client deserved the right to challenge his accusers and so she should be allowed to subpoena Hendrix, Taylor, Jenkins, and Ward and get them transported from jails around the county to the Baltimore City courthouse so she could question them. She wanted to ask the GTTF officers if they were high the night of Smith's arrest. It was hardly a stretch to think that these guys who had been busted for stealing and dealing drugs might also be using them. Jenkins was yelling, "There's blood everywhere!" and there is a photograph of him leaning back on the curb, his neck supported by his interlocked fingers cradling the back of his head, kicking back like some fucked-up frat boy outside a house party.

The judge ruled with Levi, and she began making the complex arrangements required to transport the officers who, because of the nature of their crimes, could not be in Baltimore City at the same time as one another, requiring an intricate ballet of prison transport vehicles.

In this conference room, she viewed the IAD files for GTTF

members involved in Smith's arrest and every one of the other twenty or so officers who'd signed into the crime-scene log. Levi was such a good litigator because she was an even better researcher.

Surrounded by thick files, flipping through page after page of police perfidy with her law clerk as more and more were plopped on the table, Levi would likely learn more about police misconduct than anyone in the city when this was all over.

"We just sat there and pored over every single document and said, 'Copy this, give us that, copy this, give us that,'" Levi said.

DRESSED IN A long black overcoat and flanked by several defense attorneys, including Natalie Finegar, Bates held a press conference in front of Marilyn Mosby's office and again accused her of knowing about GTTF corruption and looking the other way.

He'd split with his campaign managers and taken a chance on an energetic, young black man named Marvin James to run the campaign. Bates felt like James understood him and brought a new energy to the campaign, along with new tactics, and so here they were, at James's suggestion, out on the sidewalk in front of Mosby's office in what could be seen as a stunt on this cold winter day.

Campaign staffers put poster boards featuring blown-up documents on easels behind Bates as the cameras set up and the wind blew and people passed by on the sidewalk.

"What we have here is a State's Attorney's Office that knew what was happening," Bates said, his voice rising over the traffic into the tone he sometimes employed in closing arguments—earnest and outraged like a preacher condemning sin. "The documentation we had is there."

Bates turned to the boards behind him just as a big gust of wind came and blew them over. After fussing with the easels, he abandoned the display and grabbed ahold of a poster-size blowup of the disclosure about Rayam's 2009 complaint for making a false statement.

"The Baltimore City State's Attorney's Office said he was an officer you could believe in every time they put him on the witness stand," Bates said.

He held up a second letter, where a prosecutor alerted the SAO's front office about the Franks hearing where Judge Williams ruled Rayam was not credible.

"What happened was in this case, an officer broke into the house of Mr. Clayton's girlfriend looking for Mr. Clayton. That officer was none other than Officer Rayam," he said. "What is even deeper, there was a white, male sergeant who put a handgun to the head of the victim in this case. And yet the State's Attorney's Office did nothing."

Then he turned to the Charles Smith case that the SAO was prosecuting at that very moment, even though Taylor and Hendrix were the arresting officers.

"For me, it's simple—if those officers are involved, let's go ahead and move on and dismiss the case," Bates said. "Because now the defense has a right to call those officers to the witness stand. So now what you've done is made it a circus."

He settled on metaphor to describe the legal bind created by corruption.

"It's almost like a piece of moldy bread. See, what they want to do is take the mold off the bread, but they want you to eat the rest of the bread," Bates said. "However, we don't know if the other mold is inside the bread."

THE CASE AGAINST Charles Smith fell apart when it turned out that the police had failed to disclose nearly thirty minutes of surveillance footage. Neither the defense nor the prosecution had seen more than ninety seconds of tape, and both sides would have to watch and study the footage while Smith continued waiting in jail, so the judge dismissed the case.

As all of that was going on, one of the BPD witnesses sexually harassed the judge's clerk in the hallway. For Levi, it was the same kind of sexist bullshit that suffused the entire legal system, an example of the hypermasculinity that allowed people like Jenkins to thrive.

Levi had been through it all before. The city's chief judge had been forced to step down a few months earlier after Levi had filed a complaint because he'd spoken to her using demeaning gendered terms, calling her both "child" and "mother hen." Nothing would happen to this creepy cop. Another day in Baltimore City's Circuit Court.

Still, it was a victory for Charles Smith, the last man to be prosecuted on the word of these particular corrupt cops. He was free.

Levi dove back into the case files of the men still suffering as a result of GTTF corruption, preparing to battle the State's Attorney's Office, which seemed to be stalling and slowing down the number of GTTF cases they were willing to drop, especially when they weren't high-profile cases.

She was always searching for the next Wayne Jenkins.

THE FAMILY OF Elbert Davis stood in the back of the courtroom watching the chief counsel for State's Attorney's Office call the case of Umar Burley.

The SAO joined with Burley's lawyer to reverse the guilty plea Burley entered seven years earlier for the heroin planted in his car. Now they announced they would not pursue charges against Burley for the crash, killing Elbert Davis. It was a tough call because Burley had suffered an injustice, but Elbert Davis was still dead.

Burley stood outside the courtroom in a wide, pin-striped

suit, the sun shining down on his bald head, and said this was the first time he had felt free since Wayne Jenkins rolled up on him in 2010.

"I've lost practically everything behind this," Burley said. "They totally destroyed my life to this point. So, I'm happy on one hand and angry on the other, and even through all this, I still feel as though nothing has really changed."

Burley's lawyer said he was planning to file a civil rights suit against the Baltimore Police Department and that Jenkins and the other officers involved—which included Suiter—should face additional criminal charges.

"These officers should be charged with felony murder," he said. "It's incredulous to me that no one from the State's Attorney's Office has even considered that."

Albert King, one of Elbert Davis's ten children, stood in the hallway outside the courtroom, conflicted.

"I understand how the justice system works," he said. "I'm glad Umar got the justice he deserved."

Then he shook his head.

"But I lost my father," he said.

BATES HUNG UP the phone. Another client wondering what he was doing running for the position of top prosecutor.

"You gonna try to put me in jail now?" the client asked. "You're supposed to get me out."

His clients did not want to hear about structural reform, and voters suddenly seemed less interested in GTTF than he'd anticipated. Once Mosby fired Mantegna, she'd neutralized the "leak" controversy. There was no use explaining its intricacies and how Mantegna wasn't actually a leak and should not have been fired and how it was another cynical move by Mosby. That story line was dead.

His duties as a defense attorney were another reason to back off GTTF. The more he highlighted specific cases, the more he was blasting out his clients. Some of them were talking to the grand jury, others had lawsuits against BPD, and some didn't want their names out there in the news. Oreese Stevenson had called him up, angry when a paper pulled his Facebook photo and put it in an article about his trial testimony. Local news rolled the body cam footage of Albert Brown's arrest every time they did a story on GTTF. For these victims, the nightmare returned every time their names were mentioned.

So Bates finally backed off the GTTF as an issue, and his campaign turned its attention on prosecuting homicides. Even more than when the campaign first started, he stressed his record as a homicide prosecutor more than a decade earlier, when he'd never lost a murder case.

"I'M GONNA DIE, I'm just gonna fucking die," an inmate heard Hersl say in his neighboring cell. "They're going to fucking kill me."

He was back in Howard County, in protective custody, waiting on sentencing. Taylor was there too. There was some hope that there would be a mistrial, because one of the witnesses against Hersl had been arrested as part of an ongoing drug investigation. If the U.S. attorneys knew that and didn't disclose it, it was enough to throw the whole thing out.

Taylor, who spent a lot of time in the law library, had a long list of grievances against the prosecutors. He believed that his phone had evidence that would show all the witnesses perjured themselves, and they would not give it back to him.

Other cops used to call Taylor stupid, but in prison, he came across as a genius. He helped other inmates file motions.

One of their fellow inmates said that in his hopeful moments, Hersl would tell Taylor how they were going to get a yacht when they got out and sail down to Florida and live on the boat and bring a different set of women on board every night.

Most of the time, that optimism was impossible, and, looking at his federal sentencing guidelines, Hersl disappeared into a panic, pacing frantically around the cell.

"They're going to fucking kill me. I'm going to die," Hersl would say.

ANNA MANTEGNA SAT in the back of a microbrewery not far from prestigious Johns Hopkins University, watching Ivan Bates and Thiru Vignarajah verbally spar while Marilyn Mosby, her former boss and the incumbent, was a no-show.

Vignarajah was muddying everything up. He would only split the anti-Mosby vote. Bates had told Mantegna he was not going to attend any debate or forum that Marilyn Mosby skipped out on. Now, it was a month and a half from the election, and he had to do something to show the city who he was.

He decided to participate less than twenty-four hours before the debate. Mantegna stayed up all night helping prepare for the debate. It felt like prepping for trial. She was happy to be doing meaningful work again.

The brewery where Bates was debating Vignarajah was full as the two candidates took to the makeshift stage, stacks of canned beer behind them. A chair—empty but for a card with Mosby's name printed on it—sat between them as they debated violence in the city, police corruption, and who was better at putting people in jail.

DONNY STEPP TYPED furiously away on his new Double D Bail Bonds Twitter account, @DoubleDBailBond.

He was on home detention with an ankle bracelet awaiting

sentencing. He'd moved out of his million-dollar house on the water, the place with the shed and the dock, and bought a much smaller house down the road.

His garish Double D truck sat out in the driveway of the new house, parked in the grass. His old life was over, and he was trying to invent a new one. He filed a motion so that he could go to church while on home detention. He still wore that big gold cross on a thick gold chain around his neck. He cast his trial testimony as a victory for social justice and a chance at redemption.

"Wow!!! Larry Krasner is the TRUE MESSIAH," he tweeted of Philadelphia's newly elected progressive prosecutor. "Can Larry send a clone to Baltimore!!!!! Imagine if Baltimore had someone like LARRY!"

One afternoon, he tweeted out something between an endorsement of and a challenge to Bates.

"Ivan Bates is qualified probably best bet but the reason he can win is he has extreme DIRT on Mosby. Trust me extreme dirt. That's why he ran," Stepp tweeted. "He had dirt which is political capital. If he would go more to the left progressive Krasner approach I would endorse him and provide him the real dirt to unseat her!"

Soon, Stepp was praising Levi—she was Baltimore's Krasner.

"She should run for STATE'S ATTORNEY! A real Baltimore hero!" Stepp later tweeted.

WAYNE JENKINS TRUDGED through the halls of the Chesapeake Detention Facility, where he was held, waiting to be sentenced, escorted by guards, the tiers temporarily closed off for his protection.

"There go Jenkins, there go Jenkins," the murmur rose up, passing from block to block.

Inmates in maroon jumpsuits pressed against the glass and

yelled at the cruddy cop holding his head high as he was led through the brick building, almost on display.

"We gonna get you!" one man yelled out.

Everyone was screaming and pounding on the glass.

He pointed his fat finger at other jeering prisoners.

"Man, you're hot!" Jenkins yelled and pointed at another man, pressed up against the glass, accusing everybody of snitching. "And you're telling."

Threats and insults swirled past Jenkins's head, now fitted with a bad prison buzz cut.

One of the prisoners, Thomas Linwood Jones, had a big smile on his face. He was serving a ten-year sentence on a drug conspiracy charge as a result of a Jenkins raid. When he was arrested, he'd claimed Jenkins had stolen $300,000 from him. Nobody had listened.

Now, the feds had called him back to Baltimore to talk about his case.

"Thank you," Jones mouthed at Jenkins through the glass, seeing in Jenkins's crimes a chance to get back a whole decade.

"Yeah, fuck all y'all," Jenkins said to no one in particular.

IVAN BATES WOULDN'T be able to come to court for Wayne Jenkins's sentencing. It was scheduled at the same time as the first—and only—state's attorney debate that included incumbent Marilyn Mosby.

The debate at the University of Baltimore featuring all three candidates was cosponsored by a local TV news station and would air live. The primary that would decide the new state's attorney was less than two weeks away.

"When we sit down and look at the criminal justice system and where we are, it's broken, and we need new leadership," he said to close out his opening remarks, feeling good and confident in a blue suit and yellow tie. "My name is Ivan Bates, and I am that leadership."

None of the candidates mentioned GTTF when they were asked about the relationship between the State's Attorney's Office and the police department, even though Jenkins would be sentenced that day and the investigation was still going on. Mosby referred to the fact that, since she had been in office, she'd had to deal with four police commissioners—Darryl De Sousa, who had replaced Kevin Davis, had resigned in May, after Wise and Hines charged him with tax fraud.

"Baltimore is in a crisis, and we do not have the luxury to fight with our partners at the Baltimore City Police Department," Bates said, casting Mosby's comment as finger-pointing.

He focused on his experience on both sides of the bar.

"I'm the only person who's been on both sides. Prosecutors see things with one eye, defense sees with the other eye, I see the whole picture," he said. "I won every murder case I was involved with."

Mosby accused him of lying about never losing a murder case.

"These are lies. Unfortunately, that's what people do when they're running for office. They lie," Mosby said.

Then she disparaged the role of the defense attorney in the criminal justice system.

"I didn't become a defense attorney and defend robbers and rapists," she said.

After the debate, Bates was annoyed. Mosby had called him a liar, attacking both his record and his character—and the defense bar. He hadn't expected her to go so low.

Still, he had done well. It was a strong showing. Some people said he won. Lana congratulated him backstage. Wayne Jenkins was being sentenced, possibly at that very moment, he thought. His final conversation with Jenkins had been about his wife and kids, and he knew the sentencing would be hard on them.

He was running for state's attorney, but he was a defense attorney at heart.

WAYNE JENKINS ENTERED the courtroom in a maroon prison jumpsuit.

Led by a marshal, he made his way to the defense table, quickly looked at his family sitting in the gallery, and, when he sat down, wiped tears from his eyes.

This was the first time Jenkins had appeared in public since his guilty plea, and the actual man standing there, broken in his bad prison haircut and teary face, seemed small and almost inconsequential after all the stories that had been told about him over the course of the trial, where he'd taken on a larger-than-life quality. He was off the chain, out of control, unpredictable, on a whole different wave; like letting an eight-year-old drive; like an animal, a Rottweiler with the pink thing hanging out; protected, untouchable, a golden boy—the prince of the city.

His friends and family tried to counter that impression, writing letters to the judge presenting him as "an incredible father and husband," the wild uncle who maybe even had "too much fun" with the kids, "a rock" to his wife, a devoted son, a reliable friend, "a great male role model."

He was not, they insisted, "a monster."

When Jenkins used the word *monster,* he was talking about scale. A drug dealer was a monster in the same way a truck was a monster. Something bigger, better, extraordinary.

Structural and systemic problems allowed Jenkins to thrive, yet he was truly of a different order from the other corrupt cops caught up in this case. A lot of cops fall into corruption through peer pressure, moral laziness, or situational greed. Jenkins was something else with his double- and triple-cross schemes, always expanding in new directions. His corruption was a crusade, his career a police picaresque, plundering with a degree of technical

proficiency and a criminal mind that distorted the debate on police reform beyond recognition.

"When we first learned of this video, it was after the debate
that had been had about body cameras, right? And the body cameras were seen as a solution to misconduct, as a way to monitor,
in an objective sense, what was going on," Leo Wise said of the
recording of Oreese Stevenson's safe. "And if you step back and
think about that for a second, I mean, what chance do we have
when you've got people like Jenkins and his codefendants fabricat-
ing video evidence?"

Jenkins's lawyer likened him to the biblical King David, claiming that Jenkins suffered from the "Bathsheba Syndrome"—he
was not prepared for his own success and so it brought about his
downfall.

To the family of Elbert Davis, Jenkins was the coward who lied
about their father's death. They practically had to bury him a second time when they learned the true circumstances behind Davis's
death.

"What I want to say this morning is that my father was killed
in a fatal car crash," Davis's daughter Shirley said at Jenkins's sentencing. "So now we have no father to share our lives with. We
miss our dad. We no longer have the special occasions, birthdays,
holidays that we spent with my dad."

She paused and collected herself so the great absence threatening to overwhelm her wouldn't.

"And then to find out seven years later that Officer Jenkins was
involved in the accident that took my father's life, that he is no
more than a common criminal," she said, still stunned. "My dad
would be alive today had it not been for his actions on that day."

Shirley's sister, Dolores, stood up to speak next.

"On that day, I told my dad I would see him later on that
night. And that would be the last kiss I got from my father, 'cause
I wouldn't see him no more. That was it. I'm trying to keep, keep

myself together," she said, breaking up into heavy-breathing tears. "I hope Mr. Jenkins know how much he hurt my family."

Jenkins leaned his weight in Dolores's direction without looking at her directly.

When it was his turn to speak, Jenkins stood up, his legs shaky and uncertain, and addressed the Davis family directly.

"To the Davises, who lost their loved ones, from the bottom of my heart, I wish I could take that day back and not stop that vehicle," he said.

The same nervous energy he had in his voice when he started talking about one of his monsters over the phone was still there, though now tempered by bursts of blubbering and a bit of a stutter.

"I'm so sorry about your father," Jenkins said. "I sat at the University of Maryland and held the woman's hand for over an hour in the bed. I held her hand for over an hour with her, the passenger in that vehicle."

He turned toward the gallery. His family sat huddled together. They seemed to be holding their breath as he spoke.

"Mr. Umar Burley," he said, returning to the formerly professional court voice he had used for years when lying on the stand, lying again. "I am truly sorry for, after finding out what happened with the drugs being planted, I didn't speak up. I didn't come forward after I found out about that. I should have came forward, and I didn't."

Then Jenkins broke out into a big, weeping, operatic howl that seemed at once ecstatically real and methodically rehearsed.

He always was good in court.

"I've tarnished the badge," he bellowed, his voice, like everything else in his life, cracked and distorted.

He apologized for letting down the Marine Corps. He turned to the Davis family once again and told them he understood their loss because he couldn't imagine losing his own father and he knew now when that time came, he would not be there for his dad—sick with cancer—because he would be in federal prison.

He could no longer visit Lucas Colton's grave with his wife. He mostly saw the older kids and Kristy through glass. He could not comfort them.

"I have a one-and-a-half-year-old son I don't even know. And when he comes into the room to see me, he won't even get close to me," Jenkins said.

He turned back toward the judge.

"Your Honor, I've been alone mostly for this year and a half because I can't be around people in jail, obviously. And it's playing mental parts on me," he said. "But again, it's my fault. I know it's my fault because I did it. And I deserve to be punished. I deserve to go to jail."

And jail, he said, had been good for him.

"I've never read the Bible a day in my life. I'm one of the people who went to jail to find God," he said. "So I finally went to jail, and I read the Bible over thirty-one times, and I can't stop reading it and asking for forgiveness. I can't stop reading it."

He would be a senior citizen by the time he got out of prison. He hoped he could be a good grandfather.

"I'm so sorry, Your Honor. I'm so sorry to the citizens of Baltimore," he said. "Mr. Umar Burley, God forgive me. I wish I would have came clean when I found out that drugs were planted. I should have came clean, and I didn't."

He may have been broken, but he was not reformed. In his final words before being sentenced, Jenkins still did not come clean.

He did not apologize to Walter Price, Oreese Stevenson, Ronald Hamilton, Dennis Armstrong, April Sims, Damon Hardrick, Albert Brown, Andre Crowder, or any of the others he'd terrorized in the years since he'd helped frame Burley.

The judge sentenced him to twenty-five years.

"I just want to apologize again about the Davises' father," Jenkins blurted out.

Then he just stood there for a moment, stripped of all his power and legitimacy, frozen beneath bad fluorescent light. As a police officer, Jenkins had been invisible, shrouded by the power of the state, able to move about the city undetected, to disappear. Now he was exposed, forced into full visibility for one more moment, before being hauled off again, hidden in a hole, away from the other prisoners who wanted to see him dead.

He put his hands behind his back. The handcuffs clicked. A U.S. Marshal in a blue sport coat put his hand on Jenkins's shoulder and ushered him forward.

Wayne Jenkins looked once more at his family, turned, and walked away.

IVAN BATES PULLED his Lexus SUV out of the police training academy building, where he had just spent an hour shaking hands and reminding folks to vote for Ivan Bates for state's attorney.

Today, the building, which was the same place where the Hamiltons had been detained two years earlier, was a polling station.

It was Election Day, June 26, 2018.

The last few weeks had been rough. A couple of days after the first debate with Mosby, *The Baltimore Sun*'s editorial board endorsed Bates. Then he made some missteps when he got baited into debating his own record instead of Mosby's. Vignarajah echoed the claim that Bates had never won a murder case. And then it felt like the entire political establishment came out against him, calling him a liar.

He was being crushed by the Machine.

Now there were only three hours until the polls closed. Lana and Brielle were with him, which made it all easier, better. He steered the SUV up Northern Parkway, passing Jonquil Avenue, where Oreese Stevenson had been stopped, toward the next polling place, the League for People with Disabilities building, right off the Alameda, once Shropshire territory.

When he arrived, a pickup truck with a huge *Ivan Bates for SAO* sign in its bed was blasting Public Enemy's "Rebel Without a Pause," with samples from Bates's campaign spots laid over the instrumental track replacing Chuck D's booming voice.

Bates pumped his fist to the beat, to his own voice, and dapped the dude in the truck—an old client helping the campaign.

Polls closed in just two hours.

In the parking lot, an older man in a porkpie hat confronted Bates.

"I think you're an FOP sycophant," the man said. "And I can't vote for that, I'm sorry."

"You know what, bruh," Bates interrupted. "Three hundred forty-two murders. Go ahead, go ahead, I want you to vote. You like the murders."

"It's not about that," the man said.

"I know you got to make that decision, you thinking about it, right?" Bates said, trying one more time to flip a vote. "We fighting the system."

This fight was winding down. With one hour before the polls closed, he could hit one more polling place—a straight shot up the Alameda. Bates backed his Lexus SUV out of the parking lot and drove up the same roads Gondo, Wells, and Shropshire cruised all their lives. The Northeast neighborhood's two-story homes and row houses whipped by.

There weren't too many voters outside the Baltimore Collegiate School For Boys, just a few desultory volunteers standing around holding signs, including an awkward cluster in THIRU shirts. Vignarajah would split the anti-Mosby vote. Bates knew that. Whatever mistakes he made, he would ultimately lose because of Vignarajah.

Bates began pulling his signs off the grass in front of the school. Brielle looked on, finally bored after a long day of eager assistance. Lana waited in the SUV.

An hour later, Bates, Lana, Brielle, and London arrived at the Mexican restaurant that was hosting his campaign party.

Anna Mantegna, her hair dyed purple, paced around the party, nervous, excited, in a big blue IVAN BATES shirt. She was still unemployed, working on a lawsuit against Mosby, and doing some temp work to get by.

A Mosby victory was starting to feel inevitable.

An hour later, precincts reported that Mosby garnered 49.2 percent of the vote. Bates came in at 28 percent. Vignarajah mustered 22 percent. The race was over.

Bates stepped to the podium, his family up there with him. He congratulated Mosby and then started swinging.

"Now I'm not a politician, I'm a lawyer, and I'm one of the best in the city. And politicians, they like to lie, and not tell the truth. So right now, the citizens, they deserve better," Bates said. "One thing I will definitely say is I'm not going anywhere. I will continue to defend individuals in this city on their constitutional rights."

In his unscripted speech, he finally found the progressive message that had eluded him much of the campaign. He attacked her treatment of the family of Tyrone West, a man killed by police in 2013, which Mosby had promised to look into and then hadn't; and demanded she drop the charges against Keith Davis Jr., a man shot by police and later charged with a murder, activists said, to cover up the shooting. He told Mosby to stop prosecuting weed possession.

"Let's follow the lead of Philadelphia if you really want to be a true criminal justice reformer," Bates said. "That is just a start of where we are going."

Bates's concession speech made no mention of the Gun Trace Task Force.

He went for a drive alone, attempting to come to terms, in his own mind, with the feeling of loss. He'd put himself before the people, and the people said they didn't want him.

He reflected on his campaign and took some small solace in his role in Jenkins's downfall, but he knew that kind of monster would return in some other form. He resolved to reorient and focus on keeping people out of jail again. He had to build the practice back up after neglecting it during the campaign. There would be no shortage of work.

That forlorn night and every night thereafter, men in cargo pants with guns on their hips and tactical vests and badges on their chests steered unmarked Malibus and Impalas down the same narrow Baltimore streets, prowling overtime on the city's dime, hunting men they call monsters.

They are out there right now.

EPILOGUE

SINCE HIS SENTENCING, Wayne Jenkins has bounced around federal prisons, his life in constant danger.

Ivan Bates continues to practice criminal defense law.

After testifying in three separate trials, Jemell Rayam was sentenced to twelve years and Momodu Gondo to ten. Daniel Hersl and Marcus Taylor each got eighteen years. Both maintain their innocence although they lost appeals. Evodio Hendrix and Maurice Ward were each sentenced to seven years. Thomas Allers received fifteen years.

Despite the vast quantity of drugs he was caught with, Donny Stepp's cooperation cut his sentence down to five years. At his sentencing, Stepp mourned his daughter, who died of an overdose, and alluded to more corruption, referencing "dead souls" surrounding Jenkins. Eric Snell was sentenced to nine years—changing his plea from not guilty to guilty halfway through his trial. Kyle Wells was sentenced to eighteen years. He and Shropshire, who got twenty-five years, are both appealing their convictions on the grounds that there was no conspiracy and the "Shropshire Organization" was a fiction.

In March 2019, former BPD sergeant Keith Gladstone was federally indicted for planting a BB gun on Demetric Simon after Jenkins ran Simon over and for obstruction of justice—tied to that meeting at the YMCA with Carmine Vignola days before

Hersl and Taylor's trial. Gladstone pleaded guilty in May 2019. In September 2019, Vignola pleaded guilty to lying to the grand jury. In January 2020, Robert Hankard was indicted for lying to the grand jury.

Former police commissioner Darryl De Sousa pleaded guilty to three misdemeanor charges related to tax evasion and was sentenced to ten months in federal prison. Former police commissioner Kevin Davis is teaching criminal justice at American University and writing a book about police consent decrees around the country.

The Commission to Restore Trust in Policing—a six-member committee of lawyers, judges, and former cops put together by State Senator Bill Ferguson to try to explain how GTTF happened and what could be done to make sure it never happened again—was established in the fall of 2018. Both Bates and Levi testified at commission hearings. It will investigate GTTF into 2021.

The American Bar Association gave Deborah Levi the 2018 Dorsey Award, which "recognizes exceptional work by a public defender or legal aid lawyer." The Office of the Public Defender has accused the State's Attorney's Office of slowing down the review of GTTF-related cases. They have also accused BPD of expunging police officers' Internal Affairs files to avoid handing them over to defense attorneys.

Anna Mantegna filed a suit against Marilyn Mosby for defamation of character because of the State's Attorney's Office's implication she leaked information to Jenkins.

The City of Baltimore has maintained that it is not financially responsible for any wrongdoing committed by members of GTTF, but City Solicitor Andre Davis has engaged in a complicated legal strategy to push a couple of cases to the state's highest court to receive some definitive guidance. As part of the deal, Davis acknowledged that GTTF planted guns on civilians. William James, whose civil suit was serving as a test case, was murdered on April 29, 2019. Davis has since resigned.

Gregory Harding was murdered on February 21, 2019.

Umar Burley and Brent Matthews filed suit against Wayne Jenkins and BPD for $40 million.

The state police and the independent review board (IRB) investigating Sean Suiter's death ruled it a suicide. Many people, both inside and outside the department, disputed the ruling. Suiter's family has claimed that it was an "inside job."

New Baltimore police commissioner Michael Harrison—Baltimore's tenth since 2000—has encouraged the use of plainclothes police in Baltimore and told the public that the Baltimore Police officers were being "extremely aggressive," going after shooters and trigger pullers. There were 348 people murdered in Baltimore in 2019.

BPD is operating under a consent decree.

The federal investigation into police corruption in the Baltimore Police Department is ongoing.

ACKNOWLEDGMENTS

First and foremost, we'd like to thank all the people who spoke to us for this book, sometimes at personal risk. Just as the case against GTTF could not have gone forward without people sharing their experiences, this book would not have been possible without the people who trusted us with their stories. Ivan Bates was particularly generous with his time and insight and was patient with our repeated requests to tell us something just one more time. We are grateful to Lana Bates for her trust, opening her life to us as well and essentially sharing her husband with us for more than a year.

Donald Stepp endured months of questioning and badgering, and while he did not always respond with answers to our countless inquiries, he did always respond with patience and humor. Umar Burley, Brent Matthews, Ronald Hamilton, Levar Mullen, Antonio Shropshire, Kyle Wells, Jamal and Jovonne Walker, Andre Crowder, Charles Smith, Sakinah DeGross, Blanton Roberts, Kenneth Bumgardner, Alex Hilton, and others who were not comfortable seeing their names in print courageously opened up to us about some of the most traumatic moments of their lives, and for that, we are forever grateful. Long before Daniel Hersl was indicted, Kevin Evans and his son Young Moose tried to help us see how the corruption worked.

Joe Crystal has been an advisor, always willing to explain some facet of police procedure or practice, and he has saved us from numerous blunders. His help has been essential to this project. Larry Smith has been essential in helping us understand the psychological toll of policing on police officers and the procedures of IAD. Neill Franklin has also been a valuable advisor, who not only has helped us understand how policing works but has also served as an example of how former cops can use their knowledge to help reform the profession. Former mayor Sheila Dixon, former police commissioner Frederick Bealefeld, and former deputy commissioner Anthony Barksdale all helped us understand the origins and the purpose of the Gun Trace Task Force.

Anthony Gioia showed us that it is possible to fulfill a Maryland Public Information Act request within the time dictated by law—he is the only one we have encountered. Other law enforcement sources wished not to be named. They know who they are, and we thank them. The people who work at both the federal and state courts' clerks' offices have always been extremely helpful, as have the folks in the court reporter's office. We'd like to thank them and also thank Nicolas Riley and Daniel Rice, of the Institute for Constitutional Advocacy and Protection at Georgetown University Law Center, and Adam Holofcener, of Maryland Volunteer Lawyers for the Arts, for helping us sue the courts to gain greater access to videos of court proceedings. Thank you to David Wright, who helped us obtain ownership of our GTTF trial reporting. Senator Bill Ferguson's Commission to Restore Trust in Policing helped shed light on the subject.

We could not have completed this project without the support of the team at Alpine Labs, who almost immediately gave up their lives and came to Baltimore to report a documentary version of the story alongside of us. Kevin Abrams, Jamie Denenberg, Auriell

Spiegel, and Lauren Deacon all contributed insight and support to the project. Kevin helped conduct many of the interviews that made the book come alive.

We wouldn't have understood anything about the case without the patient help of dozens of lawyers over the years. Richard Woods (no relation) helped us see how Hersl worked in 2014. Since then, Deborah Levi, Natalie Finegar, Jeremy Eldridge, Joshua Insley, Anna Mantegna, Justin Brown, Christopher Nieto, Erin Murphy, Steven Silverman, Jenny Egan, Todd Oppenheim, Neel Calchandani, Latoya Francis-Williams, Dwight Pettit, Andre Davis, Mandi Miliman, Steven Levin, Leo Wise, Derek Hines, and Stephen J. Beatty have all helped us understand various aspects of criminal law. Even more important, many of these lawyers have arranged for us to meet with their clients, and that has been essential.

But none of that would have cohered into a book without the assistance of our editor, Marc Resnick, assistant editor Hannah O'Grady, copy editors Sara Ensey and Chris Ensey, and the whole team at St. Martin's Press, who helped us carve a story out of the massive mountain of facts. Brandi Bowles, our agent at United Talent Agency, believed in us and took a chance on the book when it was little more than the rough idea of a stunning descent set against the big sprawling backdrop of Baltimore's dysfunction.

Brandon Block waded through all those documents, transcripts, videos, and wiretaps, assisting with fact-checking, and we sleep better at night because of his diligence.

D. Watkins first put us onto Hersl and, through many years of conversations, helped us understand the dynamics of East Baltimore. Laura Wexler, Karen Houppert, and Wil S. Hylton provided crucial notes on early versions of the manuscript. Damien Ober also offered insight into the project. Clay Risen and Jennifer Parker of *The New York Times* helped us clarify our thinking surrounding the implications of GTTF. Jessica Lussenhop shared notes and

"WTF" responses to the GTTF revelations with us during the trial, and her BBC story "When Cops Become Robbers" was the first long-form story to try to make sense of GTTF. We've spent many hours discussing the case with Justin Fenton, whose *Baltimore Sun* story "Cops and Robbers" provided a few last-minute details.

The discussions and arguments about GTTF and Baltimore policing were always welcome from Keesha Ha, Lawrence Brown, Justine Barron, Amelia McDonnel-Parry, and Alec McGillis.

J. M. Giordano shot photos for the book and spent years racing around Baltimore with us covering this crazed city. Thanks to Evan Serpick, Rebekah Kirkman, Anna Walsh, and Brandon Weigel of *Baltimore City Paper* for assigning, editing, fact-checking, and encouraging our reporting. We are grateful to Lisa Snowden-McCray and Maura Callahan for their work with us at *City Paper* and *Baltimore Beat*. Eddie Conway, Marc Steiner, Jocelyn Dombrowski, Eze Jackson, Dharna Noor, Jaisal Noor, Tracey Beale, Kayla Rivara, Bashi Rose, Soldier, and Darryl, all of whom either worked or work at the Real News Network and have encouraged our reporting and offered insight. Mary Finn helped us both sharpen our thoughts.

Baltimore Bloc, Open Justice Baltimore, Black Leaders Organizing for Change, and other activists and organizers helped our thinking evolve much quicker than it would have without them.

We would especially like to thank Nicole King and Frank and Kim Soderberg for accommodating and hosting the extended discussions about abstruse and unpleasant material that cowriting a book like this requires. Nicole tolerated our conversations and scattered notes and evidence on the daily, and the Soderbergs put us up at a crucial moment when we needed to hide from ordinary life to finish the manuscript.

And thank you to the citizens of Baltimore.

Baynard Woods: Nicole King is a constant source of love, support, and inspiration. She believed in me as a writer and, over the last two decades, has consistently helped me have the courage to make the decisions necessary to become one. She has also regularly kicked my ass into being a better person, and has served as a daily reminder that the world is not always as bleak as it appears in these pages. For all of that, I am deeply grateful. I'd also like to thank John and Martha Woods and Frances-Earle King for all their support. Aaron Henkin, Dan Pavlick, Michael Shank, Beth Harper, and Albert Garcia helped me forget the book on Friday nights.

Brandon Soderberg: Thank you for all your love, advice, support, and emotional labor, Jen Mizgata, Adam Holofcener, Bernie, Frank Soderberg, Kim Soderberg, Shannon Soderberg, Dan Soderberg, PFK Boom, Ethan Brown, Lawrence Burney, Shorty Davis, Andy Holter, Patrice Hutton, Nicole King, Margot Kniffin, Wally Holofcener, Ethan McLeod, Sean McTiernan, Lisa Cassidy, Reginald Thomas II, Tariq Touré, Ryan Dorsey, Andrew Wichmann, and Cecilia Wichmann.

NOTES

Because we rely heavily on the indictments and trial of GTTF members, we cite *United States v. Kenton Gondo et al.* and the superseding indictment that followed as "GTTF indictment" and *United States of America v. Daniel Thomas Hersl and Marcus Roosevelt Taylor* as "GTTF trial." We similarly use "Shropshire indictment" and "Shropshire trial" to cite the case against a number of codefendants in *United States v. Shropshire et al.*

Indictments of individuals and plea agreements are cited with the defendant's name. All civil and criminal state cases, which are used less frequently, are cited with the name of the case.

FBI surveillance recordings are labeled as *wiretap* if they are recordings of Gondo's phone and as *Chevrolet Mic* when referring to the bug in his car.

In the case of conflicting accounts of events, we have gone with the most plausible and noted the alternative versions here. To verify stories and confirm details, we have interviewed some of the people who appear in this book multiple times over the course of several years, including the frequent textual exchanges on text, email, or direct message. When you see *Interviews* cited in the endnotes, it means we spoke to them frequently over an extended period of time.

Additionally, we conducted many interviews with our film partners at Alpine Labs. Alpine's Kevin Abrams interviewed Donald Stepp, Erika Jensen, Leo Wise, and Derek Hines. We made extensive use of the Stepp interview and used the interviews with Jensen, Wise, and Hines as references.

ONE

The account of the Oreese Stevenson robbery comes from a wide range of sources, including the sworn testimony of Maurice Ward, Evodio Hendrix, Donald Stepp, Oreese Stevenson, Keona Holloway, and DEA agent Ethan Glover in the GTTF trial; interviews and other personal communications with Taylor, Stepp, and Bates; testimony of Jenkins in *State v.*

Stevenson; testimony of Demetrius Brown's former partner Lillian Ramirez in *State v. Brown;* evidence photographs of the van and inside the house; photographs taken by Stepp; cell phone videos made by Taylor; interviews conducted by Orrin Henry, Bates's investigator; photographs taken by Bates to prepare for trial; personal observation of the locations; federal GTTF indictment; charging documents, including statement of probable cause, and affidavit for search warrant in *State v. Stevenson,* which has been expunged.

7 *He steered a silver Malibu full of plainclothes cops against traffic:* Marcus Taylor, who claims to have been ignorant of anything illegal that happened, said that the squad was coming from a meeting with their lieutenant, Marjorie German. "We left the academy from meeting with Lt. German. During which time we went towards liberty heights, during which time we observed a male jogging from the house on Jonquil Ave, down the slight hill with a book bag. During which time Jenkins who was driving turned the vehicle around and headed down the street, we were all wearing our vests with the words Baltimore Police affixed on them, driving an untinted vehicle, which you can clearly see through," he wrote the authors via prison email. When asked why they were meeting the lieutenant, Taylor replied, "I think Jenkins had to go meet her for something administrative. I think we was going to areas where there was shootings, homicides."

8 *an arcane set of rules:* The various rules about why to stop people are based on Hendrix's and Ward's testimonies, GTTF trial. Former BPD detective and whistle-blower Joe Crystal helped us understand the ways these rules worked in the context of ordinary policing.

8 *Jenkins hit the gas:* There is a tension throughout this and the book as a whole between the justifications that Jenkins gave to the courts, his coworkers, and his other purely criminal coconspirators. Because Jenkins was often playing multiple angles and pitting people against one another or using them for different purposes, it is difficult to accurately describe a situation from all the various angles. Ward and Hendrix both testified that seeing a man with a backpack had something to do with the stop. But both the statement of probable cause and Jenkins's testimony in *State v. Stevenson* make it seem as if the rationale for the stop were a subsequent throwing motion performed by Stevenson. Ward testified in the GTTF trial that they never saw anyone throw anything at all. The account Jenkins provided later to Ward, Rayam, and Stepp showed that he had researched and

prepared for the stop but did not necessarily share that knowledge evenly with his coconspirators.

8 *Oreese Stevenson, the van's driver, saw SES detectives fanning out:* Stevenson testimony, GTTF trial.

9 *"How much money you have in the box between your feet?":* Statement of probable cause, *State v. Stevenson.* Brown's lawyer suggested in motions hearings for *State v. Brown* on October 31, 2016, that Jenkins never said this because the money was not in plain sight to be commented upon. But he also pushed to have the statement removed because Brown had not been Mirandized.

9 *no legal reason for this stop:* Jenkins and his crew provided various reasons to justify the stop, but a judge ultimately overturned them in motions hearings for *State v. Stevenson* and *State v. Brown.*

9 *city was at war:* Jenkins worked with the BPD's War Room, which had been created the previous summer and made the whole notion of policing as war official. Kevin Rector and Natalie Sherman, "Baltimore Police, Partners Create Around-the-Clock 'War Room' to Address Crime Surge," *Baltimore Sun,* July 12, 2015, www.baltimoresun.com/news/crime/bs-md -violence-strategy-20150712-story.html.

9 *People said police had been lying low since Freddie Gray:* Many social scientists and law enforcement officials espoused the "Ferguson effect," or similar explanations, that argued that police were reluctant to make arrests after Gray's death either because they didn't want to be "the next viral video" or, as one former police commander explained to the authors, because they legitimately felt they didn't understand what would count as probable cause anymore. This pullback of police resulted, the argument goes, in an emboldened criminal class, which began settling scores and making moves, thereby increasing the murder rate. Much of this book shows how Wayne Jenkins and other plainclothes detectives both utilized this mythology and showed its fundamental lack of truth.

9 *Hendrix said something about how Stevenson's windshield was tinted:* Statement of probable cause, *State v. Stevenson;* Stevenson testimony, GTTF trial.

9 *about the Steelers:* Jenkins testimony in *State v. Stevenson;* Marcus Taylor, emails to authors.

9 *"Don't move; put your hands up":* Statement of probable cause, *State v. Stevenson.*

10   *Taylor filmed the ritual with his cell phone:* Taylor, Ward, Hendrix, and Jenkins all said either in testimony, charging documents, or personal communication that Taylor filmed this as well as subsequent statements. But when discovery evidence was provided to the defense, prosecutors said there were no recorded statements by the defendants and this video was unavailable. Taylor was known for losing his phone, but we have seen other footage that he recorded that day.

10   *A woman came out of the house:* Lilian Ramirez testified about the officers running into her house in *State v. Brown,* where she said that Brown had just told her he was going out for a minute, and she got curious and pulled the blinds back and watched from the window and saw it all: Brown got in the van, the cops pulled up, blocked the van in, and then swarmed. "I've never seen them stop a car and run right into the house like that," Stevenson testified in the GTTF trial.

10   *Jenkins had studied up on Stevenson:* Although Stepp was not in on planning the Stevenson heist with Jenkins, he said in interviews that Jenkins had been watching him and debriefed him on Stevenson's background. Ward testified in the GTTF trial that Jenkins told him about Stevenson. Jenkins later told Rayam about the Stevenson robbery and said that his crew shouldn't have gotten the cut he'd given them because "I put all that time and work," as Rayam recounted the conversation on Chevrolet Mic, September 22, 2016. Accidentally happening upon a coke deal is not putting in time and work.

10   *"This is a big one":* Hendrix testimony, GTTF trial.

10   *He followed a procedure: Tell Stevenson he could go free if he'd flip and give them another name—his plug or a rival dealer:* Police officers who worked with Jenkins have described the general procedure, which can also be seen in the Hersl body cam video of Albert Brown's arrest. Ward and Hendrix testimony, GTTF trial; and emails to authors with Taylor confirm that he applied it in this case.

11   *Stop Fuckin' Snitching and Zero Tolerance:* During Martin O'Malley's mayoral administration, BPD was committed to Zero Tolerance policing, in which the quantity of arrests was deemed more important than their qualitity. In 2006, BPD made more than 100,000 arrests. Wayne Jenkins made at least 244 of those, according to Maryland's online database. In Oreese Stevenson's 2006 drug conspiracy indictment, a coconspirator was prominently involved in the underground video "Stop Fuckin' Snitching." Crooked cops William King and Antonio Murray also appeared in the video and were ultimately indicted by the U.S. Attorney's Office.

11 *after getting out of prison for manslaughter:* Stevenson was charged with the death of his older brother in 1996.

11 *Howard and Raeshio Rice and their crew funneled $27 million in heroin into the city:* Federal indictment. The Rice crew had numerous high-powered political affiliations, which were centered around the Southern Blues restaurant. According to Hendrix and Ward testimony, GTTF trial, Jenkins was obsessed with this crew.

11 *the case against Stevenson began in 2003:* As court documents show, the state case that ultimately went federal began with 2003 observations made by Detective Christopher O'Ree, who was, in 2016, the lieutenant in charge of Wayne Jenkins's SES unit.

12 BALTIMORE POLICE MAKE LARGEST-EVER DRUG SEIZURE: WBOC TV 16, February 20, 2009, www.wboc.com/story/9880616/baltimore-police-make-largest-ever-drug-seizure. Police turned in only $11,000 from this arrest. The sentence was reduced by five years in federal court in early 2019.

12 *"If you could put your own crew together and rob the biggest drug dealer you know, who would that drug dealer be?":* Hendrix and Ward testimony, GTTF trial. People Jenkins has robbed have confirmed this to us.

12 *one of his most common lies:* Jenkins is caught on a wiretap telling Gondo to call him the U.S. attorney, Chevrolet Mic, July 8, 2016. Ward and Hendrix testimony, GTTF trial, claimed that Jenkins regularly told people he was a U.S. attorney when he wanted to rob, rather than arrest, them. Sometimes he used DEA and, in at least one scheme, was planning to pose as ATF, according to Stepp interview.

13 *"Where do you live, sir?":* Affidavit for search warrant, *State v. Stevenson.*

13 *"I got a monster":* Stepp interview; Stepp testimony, GTTF trial. Others have confirmed that this was one of Jenkins's favorite phrases. We engaged in a wide variety of conversations with Stepp from June 2018 through early 2019, including hundreds of text messages, several telephone calls, and dozens of email messages. Stepp agreed to be interviewed by our documentary partners at Alpine Labs but would not allow either of the authors to be present, because his legal team was concerned we would push him for information beyond the scope of the plea agreement and jeopardize his situation. So, with his knowledge, we helped Kevin Abrams, the director of the documentary, to craft questions for Stepp, but Abrams asked them all, providing us with video, audio, and transcripts. The team also went with Stepp as he turned himself in to prison in October 2018.

13 *They'd had this kind of arrangement for years:* Stepp testimony, GTTF trial; Stepp interviews; and charging documents inform all descriptions of Stepp's role in this chapter.

14 *"There's a quarter million dollars on top of a safe in the bag, there's $500,000 inside the safe, and there's ten kilos in a closet six feet from it; I got the whole squad here so they don't know":* Stepp testimony, GTTF trial.

15 *"sneak and peek":* Ward testimony, GTTF trial.

16 *Taylor took out his phone and began recording:* Taylor's recording informs this scene. Taylor recalled the scene: "She was a nice older lady, I recorded her after I came from the rear of the house, where everyone was at. I was the only one in the rear of the dwelling. I didn't go in the house until after they cleared the house to make sure no one else was in the house due me seeing the boy running from the rear. I was suppose to secure the rear just in case someone exited out the rear," Taylor emails to authors.

19 *sneak-and-peek purgatory:* Ward testimony, GTTF trial informs the descriptions of his time inside the house.

19 *Ward happily accepted:* The account of Ward's early time in SES and the robbery of Belvedere Towers, Ward testimony, GTTF trial. Taylor denies any involvement.

19 *It was an honor when Jenkins wanted to work with you:* Justin Fenton, "Cops and Robbers," *Baltimore Sun,* June 12, 2019, https://news .baltimoresun.com/cops-and-robbers/part-one/.

19 *he and Taylor had lifted a little cash:* Taylor was convicted of robbing Shawn Whiting with Ward in 2014.

20 *"You guys willing to go kick in the dude's door and take the money?":* Fenton, "Cops and Robbers."

21 *Ward asked Jenkins what he was going to do with the weed in the trunk of his car, and Jenkins said he was going to take it home and burn it:* Ibid.

21 *"teatime":* interview with police department sources, which coincides with the U.S. attorney's evidence of Jenkins and Daniel Hersl drinking Twisted Tea together.

21 *robbed a stripper:* Superseding GTTF indictment. In the GTTF trial, the court tried hard to make sure that the information about the lap dance did not make its way to the jury, but such conversations are abundant in the bench conferences, which are available in the transcripts. We have also interviewed an attorney about a deposition with the woman.

21   *He imagined the guys they robbed were undercover or that it was all caught on camera somehow:* Ward testimony, GTTF trial.

21   *He would be blackballed:* Ward testimony, GTTF trial.

22   *sister of Stevenson's wife:* Ward testimony, GTTF trial.

22   *"Oreese sent us here":* Holloway testimony, GTTF trial.

23   *"I don't know why your son ran":* This entire scene comes from Taylor's recording.

24   *"Ma'am, do you understand your rights?":* Taylor video informs this scene. Everything following this moment, Taylor denies. We went to great pains to try to verify his claims of innocence, but he is alone in his version of events, which relies on a vast conspiracy that turned his purely innocent behavior into something criminal. We find his account mostly incredible, but we provide his version of the events in the following notes. Taylor says: "The only person that was in the rear of the house was the young boy, which I observed upon me going into the rear alley. Yes but then I stopped chasing because I wasn't sure if anyone else was still in the house so I just secured the rear of the location and made communication on the radio, to my supervisor. Which calls into question the total case of the government due to the witnesses lying under oath multiple times in order to get a good deal. Which you will soon find out more to the story, that contradicts everything," Taylor emails to authors.

24   *"How much did he say was in there?":* Hendrix testimony, GTTF trial.

25   *"Hey, Sarge?":* Taylor video; Ward and Hendrix testimony, GTTF trial.

25   *It was a convincing act:* Taylor claims that the video was not staged and actually recorded the first popping of the safe. "The Oreese case that was a shocker because the time I was recording was the first time that safe was breached, it popped open," he wrote. "I took pictures of the money serial numbers and its position due to Jenkins said that he had to call HIDTA to pick up the large U.S. currency. I been locked up with some people who are pretty good with opening safes and they have told me that was not no re-enactment as what witnesses testified. Once that safety mechanism is broken you can't close it up period. My thing I asked myself and attorneys where is the safe at if it was allegedly fake. There could of been a demonstration on the safe in questioning, but such evidence was destroyed or lossed. I did chase a little boy from the rear of the house while he ran towards the nearby school. Where the GF/Wife of Mr. Stevenson was sitting nearby the school," email to authors, October 2, 2018.

26 *they met at his new three-story town house in:* Ward and Hendrix testimony, GTTF trial. Taylor denies that such a meeting occurred. "I don't know when or who took the money due to the fact that I was told to go with Detective Glover from HIDTA to submit the money while everyone else was still at the location, I personally seen the door be locked upon leaving," he wrote. "They never came to my house, which the agent said no phones pinged at my house or any other location," email to authors, October 1, 2018.

26 *Taylor was all about spending the cash on home improvements:* Ward and Hendrix testimony, GTTF trial. Taylor denies that he took money, although the FBI evidence showed that he did have a new deck built.

27 *Ward opened the bag and heaved it:* The FBI admitted to suspicions about the truth of Ward's account and noted that its agents did not look for the money. We did look for it, several months after the trial. We did not find it, but neighbors told us that his house had been raided, more than a year after he had been arrested, by men in FBI jackets. The door was busted open, but the FBI denied the raid.

TWO

The accounts of Ivan Bates's meeting with Keona Holloway and his background come from Bates interviews.

31 *he was obsessed with the calls Oreese Stevenson made from jail:* Ward testimony, GTTF trial; Stepp interviews.

31 *Holloway tell Stevenson how the house looked the morning after the robbery:* Holloway testimony, GTTF trial; Bates interviews.

32 *Wayne Jenkins was a hardscrabble county boy and the pudgy-cheeked baby of his large family:* The details of Wayne Jenkins's background are largely derived from letters sent by various family members to the court at his sentencing and internal police department documents detailing his hiring and his pre-police career. Additional details are derived from Jenkins's testimony in a variety of cases, including *United States v. Byers et al.*

33 *In 2008, he was going after a guy named Antonio Lee:* The account of the Smithee's bar raid and its aftermath comes from court filings; video of the trial in the civil suit; and transcripts of *United States v. Oakley.*

35 *Walter Price:* The account of the arrest of Walter Price is derived from surveillance video; Brian Mobley interview; and Sakinah DeGross interview; BPD Internal Affairs file.

36 *"Have we raised the possibility of a wire?":* Justin Fenton, "Cops

and Robbers," *Baltimore Sun,* June 12, 2019, https://news.baltimoresun
.com/cops-and-robbers/part-one/.

36   *Darryl De Sousa, a powerful Baltimore Police commander, had intervened on his behalf:* Fenton, "Cops and Robbers."

36   *He was already working with Stepp:* Stepp testimony, GTTF trial; Stepp interviews.

39   *Jenkins called a sergeant to bring an ounce of heroin to plant on Burley:* Wayne Jenkins indictment, November 30, 2017. Jenkins pleaded guilty to the incidents surrounding the Umar Burley crash, while noting that he quibbled with the U.S. attorney's characterization of the planting of the drugs. "He was aware that another officer planted drugs—and he knowingly wrote a false report," his lawyer, Steve Levin, told *The Baltimore Sun.* Justin Fenton, "Baltimore Gun Trace Task Force Leader Pleads Guilty, Expresses Remorse," *Baltimore Sun,* January 5, 2018, www
.baltimoresun.com/news/crime/bs-md-ci-jenkins-pleads-guilty-20180105
-story.html.

39   *Jenkins called Gladstone:* Keith Gladstone plea agreement.

40   *Jenkins told her he didn't believe in God anymore:* Interview with the victim, who wished not to be named.

40   *He took the plan to his squad:* The story of placing the note on the door comes from Ward testimony, GTTF trial. Characteristically, Taylor claims that he never returned to the house again after the arrest and that Jenkins never wrote any letter. Neither Stevenson nor Holloway ever told Bates about this event—until the trial, they would have had no way to know that the note was left by Jenkins.

41   *Jenkins wrote a long letter commending Stepp's impeccable character:* Fenton, "Cops and Robbers."

41   *now carried brass knuckles:* When the FBI searched Jenkins's van, they found a pair of brass knuckles.

42   *"front for a criminal enterprise":* Stepp testimony, GTTF trial.

THREE

43   *opposite sides of the Alameda:* The description of the neighborhood surrounding the Alameda here and throughout the book comes from interviews with people, who requested anonymity, who grew up there and had been at some point engaged in the drug trade. Shropshire's emails and letters to authors provided further information on the workings of the neighborhood.

43 *Like Gondo, he had been shot:* Shropshire, letter to authors.

43 *"What's up, brother?":* The entire phone conversation between Gondo and Shropshire is from the DEA wiretap on Shropshire's phone, detailed in Shropshire indictment. Gondo testimony, Shropshire trial added details.

44 *The trackers had been in the news:* Dan Morse, "Robbers Hid GPS Device on Casino Patron's Car to Find His Md. Home, Police Say," *Washington Post,* March 7, 2016, www.washingtonpost.com/local/public-safety/montgomery-county-police-make-arrest-in-home-invasion-robbery/2016/03/07/ff25f972-e4bb-11e5-bc08-3e03a5b41910_story.html.

45 *Six months earlier:* The following account of the Aaron "Black" Anderson robbery and the planning of the robbery, including obtaining trackers from Clewell comes Shropshire indictment; from Gondo, Rayam, McDougall, and Teana Cousins testimony, Shropshire trial; and Rayam testimony, GTTF trial.

45 *robbed the owners of a bird supply store:* GTTF indictment; Rayam testimony, GTTF trial.

46 *a former marine:* Biographical information about Clewell here and throughout comes from Justin Fenton, "One Officer Left Standing After Indictments of Baltimore Gun Trace Task Force Members," *Baltimore Sun,* September 7, 2017, www.baltimoresun.com/news/maryland/crime/bs-md-ci-clewell-gun-task-force-20170905-story.html.

46 *GPS trackers:* Clewell is the only person who was a member of GTTF between 2015 and 2016 who was not indicted. The Shropshire indictment and Gondo and Rayam testimony, GTTF trial, said Clewell was using personal GPS trackers for police purposes, which was against police protocol.

47 *had stolen enough money:* Allers guilty plea. Among Allers's supporters, there is a persistent claim that Allers only pleaded guilty because the U.S. attorney's threatened to charge his son, who, according to Allers's indictment, was involved in a robbery with Allers, Gondo, and Rayam. One of Allers's former informants told us that he may have been the one who went along on a raid and was mistaken for Allers's son. The informant denied stealing money. That claim doesn't make sense because both Gondo and Rayam were familiar with this informant and would not have mistaken him for Allers's son. Allers's son has not been charged with any crimes related to GTTF.

47 *Hersl had been a terror in East Baltimore:* We began reporting on Hersl in 2014, and the following paragraphs are based on years of accounts provided, sometimes with physical evidence, by residents of East Baltimore. Some of this information was published in Baynard Woods and Brandon Soderberg, "The Detective and the Rapper," *Baltimore City Paper,* October 14, 2014, www.baltimoresun.com/special/fallartsguide /2014/bcp-the-detective-and-the-rapper-20141014-story.html and Brandon Soderberg, "A Cop's Aggressive Behavior," *Baltimore City Paper,* March 8, 2017, www.baltimoresun.com/citypaper/bcp-030817-mob-hersl -20170308-story.html.

47 *Hersl was transferred out of his beloved district and into the GTTF:* Hersl told Mantegna that no official reason was given for Hersl's transfer, and he maintained a grudge about his sergeant, John Burns, transferring him with no notice, via email. But Hersl's notoriety was the generally assumed reason both in the department and on the streets for the transfer.

47 *Gondo didn't fully trust Hersl:* Gondo testimony, GTTF trial. Rayam testimony, GTTF trial claimed Allers had said, "Hersl's not part of it. I don't trust Hersl."

48 *"Fuck it, I just didn't want to chase him":* Gondo testimony, GTTF trial. Rayam contests he said this.

48 *"You know you murdered that dude?":* Gondo testimony, GTTF trial. Gondo also testified that Rayam confirmed it was a murder. "Yeah, I did," Gondo claimed Rayam said. Rayam denied this and in his testimony, Snell trial, emphasized that there was nothing wrong with this shooting and two other shootings he was involved in as a police officer around the same time.

48 *Colonel Dean Palmere had come on the scene:* Gondo testimony, GTTF trial. The pattern of claiming that someone the police shot was about to run them over has been common among plainclothes squads in the BPD. Palmere maintains that he was not involved in any cover-up and no action has ever been taken against him.

48 *Rayam had no choice but to shoot him:* In March 2009, Rayam shot and killed Sean Cannady. A typo-ridden email from homicide detective Kendell Richburg described the shooting as follows: "Upon arrival this detective spoke to detective Ram and detective Edwards had observed two males in the odd side ally in 4900 block of Pimlico Road. As they approached the males in the ally they identified themselves as police and began to exit their unmarked vehicle. The unknown males then got into a Lexus and pull off striking detective Giordano. Detective Ram then fire on shot from his service weapon striking the driver, the vehicle continued down the ally were it came to rest." In 2013, Richburg pleaded guilty to conspiracy to distribute heroin and possession of a firearm in furtherance of drug trafficking. He was still a police officer at that time.

48 *Rayam understood it as a drug beef:* Rayam testimony, GTTF trial. Gondo testimony, GTTF trial, maintains the shooting was a robbery and had nothing to do with him being a police officer or his connections with drug dealing.

48 *Wayne Jenkins looked bloated, bored, and above it all:* Photographs of BPD's Meritorious Conduct Awards Ceremony 2016 by Gino Inno-centes.

48 *BPD's Meritorious Conduct Awards Ceremony:* This ceremony was recorded by BPD, and details and quotations come from "BPD-Meritorious Conduct Awards Ceremony (Part 1)," YouTube video, 33:40, posted April 21, 2016, by Baltimore Police Department, www.youtube.com/watch?v =QJvZaRKFZ5M and "BPD-Meritorious Conduct Awards Ceremony (Part 2)," YouTube video, 30:25, posted April 21, 2016, by Baltimore Po-lice Department, www.youtube.com/watch?v=f3vKdv-8LD8.

48 *"gay training":* Anonymous source, who spoke to Jenkins in prison.

48 *Darryl De Sousa, who'd helped Jenkins with his IAD issues in 2014:* Justin Fenton, "Cops and Robbers," *Baltimore Sun,* June 12, 2019, https:// news.baltimoresun.com/cops-and-robbers/part-one/.

49 *After Commissioner Davis took over the department:* Eric Kowal-czyk, *The Politics of Crisis: An Insider's Prescription to Prevent Public Pol-icy Disasters* (Oceanside, CA: Indie Books International, 2018), 132–137.

50 *Donny Stepp knew the rest:* The remainder of this scene comes from Stepp testimony, GTTF trial, and Stepp interviews.

51 *Stepp knew, if anything, the stolen pills kept the county hard for a few weeks:* The revelation that Jenkins stole drugs during the April 27 ri-oting was a bombshell, locally, adding a whole other dimension to post-uprising Baltimore and the homicide spike. If police officers stole drugs and resold them into the city and the police commissioner at the time, Anthony Batts, connected the uptick in violence to an increased prolifera-tion of street drugs stolen during the riot ("There's enough narcotics on the streets of Baltimore to keep it intoxicated for a year," Batts said), then po-lice were directly responsible for the homicide spike. Interviews with Stepp make it clear that a lot of what was stolen wasn't pills likely sold on the street and also suggest that little of what was stolen ever made its way back to Baltimore City (Stepp's clientele base was not in the city). Stepp interviews also make it even clearer how exaggerated Batts's claims were. If you imagine many looters leaving pharmacies with bags of drugs just like Jenkins, it's likely they too were digging through bags of pills with little or no street value. *Baltimore City Paper* reporter Edward Ericson Jr. challenged Batts's claim immediately after it was made, crunching the numbers based on what the DEA said was 175,000 dosage units stolen during the riot: "If Baltimore has but 20,000 addicts (and not three times that many, as earlier estimates claimed), then the 175,000 units work out to less than nine doses for each of those 20,000 people. If they cop once per day, that's a little more than a week's supply. If it's three times a day, that would be a three-day supply. If there are three times as many addicts, then that's a one-day supply." Edward Ericson Jr., "Checking Batts' Fuzzy Math," *Baltimore City Paper,* June 4, 2015, www.baltimoresun.com/blogs/the-news -hole/bcpnews-checking-batts-fuzzy-drug-math-20150604-story.html.

51   *reliving their own personal version of 2015's trauma, including Ivan Bates:* The account of Ivan Bates in April–May 2015, during the uprising, in San Francisco, his conversations with Sergeant Alicia White, the harassment he endured when he began representing White, and more comes from Bates interviews and Lana Bates interview.

55   *April 28, GTTF was out early:* The robbery of Davon Robinson comes from the statement of probable cause and the Allers indictment. Obviously, these two documents contrast with each other greatly. We prioritized details in the indictment over details in the probable cause, but the simplest way to understand the documents is that the indictment picks up where the probable cause ends. Claims by Gondo and Rayam as well as the FBI during the GTTF trial and Allers's sentencing were that the GTTF under Allers robbed while doing otherwise legitimate investigations. We worked off the assumption that the account of how the raid and arrest operated as described in the probable cause is accurate—but with details about robbing Robinson omitted. Additionally, Hersl wrote the probable cause here, and all accounts claim he was not involved in this robbery.

56   *Allers didn't trust Hersl yet, he told Rayam:* Rayam testimony, GTTF trial. According to Rayam, Allers told Rayam, "Hersl's not part of it. I don't trust Hersl." GTTF trial testimony and Allers indictment said that Hersl was initially left out of the robberies along with Clewell, and it wasn't until the end of May that Hersl was let in on the robberies.

FOUR

57 *their first meeting:* The description of this GTTF meeting is based on Taylor, emails to authors, and Gondo wiretap, June 14, 2016, where he discusses the events with Ward.

57 *"Yo, Gondo, you ain't even come over to listen, man":* This dialogue comes from Gondo recounting the encounter in a wiretap conversation with Ward.

58 *"Yo, old boy, he definitely know how to lie to a nigga, huh?":* Gondo wiretap with Ward, June 14, 2016, which also provides the remainder of dialogue in this conversation.

59 *Ward explained that Jenkins met:* Ward testimony, GTTF trial.

59 *"That nigga say, 'Y'all can work whenever y'all want to work'":* Gondo wiretap with Rayam, June 14, 2016.

60 *GTTF's first raid on June 15:* The exchange between Rayam and Hersl about not finding money was recounted in Rayam testimony, GTTF trial. The arrest and what was seized is described in "Guns and Drugs Seized in Southwest Baltimore Raid," Eyewitness News WJZ Channel 13 CBS Baltimore, June 16, 2016, https://baltimore.cbslocal.com/2016/06/16/guns-and-drugs-seized-in-southwest-baltimore-raid/.

60 *"Hey, if there's any money, you know, we'll split it":* Rayam testimony, GTTF trial.

60 *Ryan Guinn:* Ward testimony, GTTF trial. *The Baltimore Sun*'s Justin Fenton later uncovered documents that show that Guinn came forward in 2013 and told the FBI that "Gondo and Rayam were taking money and stealing drugs during traffic stops while on duty." Justin Fenton, "Baltimore Police Whistleblower Flagged Gun Trace Officer, Helped Launch Racketeering Case, Documents Show," *Baltimore Sun*, November 19, 2018, www.baltimoresun.com/news/crime/bs-md-ci-gttf-whistleblower-20181117-story.html.

61 *On June 24, Jenkins, Gondo, Rayam, Hendrix, and Ward entered Milton Miller's row house:* GTTF indictment; Ward plea; Ward testimony, GTTF trial.

61 *Jenkins called Gondo:* Gondo wiretap, June 29, 2016, also the source of subsequent dialogue in the scene.

62 *"A couple of nights a week, we would just go out to hot areas, we would drive around":* Hersl testimony, *State v. Holmes.*

62 *A group of black men:* The scene at this corner is based on the statement of probable cause *State v. Holmes;* observation of this corner; and

Google Street View history, which verifies what the corner looked like in
June 2016.

62 *Clewell lost him:* Clewell testimony, *State v. Holmes.* The rest of this
scene comes from testimony in that trial.

62 *The door pop was a new strategy for the GTTF:* Gondo testimony,
GTTF trial; Taylor, emails to authors.

63 *An informant Allers had used:* This anecdote comes from informant
interview. Informant is also the second source to mention Jenkins's use of
the word *nigga.* Anonymous source who spoke to Jenkins in prison also
said Jenkins frequently used the word.

63 *Davon Robinson was posted up:* This physical description, general
scene, and all dialogue is from video of *State v. Davon Robinson,* specifically Robinson's arraignment on July 1, 2016.

63 *caused plenty of problems:* Allers indictment.

64 *Rayam called Gondo, geeked up about overtime:* Gondo wiretap,
July 1, 2017.

65 *The Southwest District put him on a snitch:* Justin Fenton, "Cops and
Robbers," *Baltimore Sun,* June 12, 2019, https://news.baltimoresun.com
/cops-and-robbers/part-one/.

65 *Around 3:00 P.M., Davon Robinson sat in his car:* The account of
Robinson's murder comes from charging documents and testimony from
Robinson's girlfriend in *State v. Frasier.* There are conflicting claims about
why Robinson was shot. The U.S. Attorney's Office suggested that there
was a connection between the robbery and murder of Davon Robinson.
"Allers stole over $10,000 during the search. Following the search, D.R.
was shot and killed because he could not repay a drug-related debt," they
wrote in Allers's indictment. One year later, a motion filed by the Baltimore
City State's Attorney's Office in *State v. Frasier* challenged the USAO's claims
and argued that GTTF's robbery of Robinson should not be allowed to
be brought up during the trial. "The motive in the present was allegedly
because the victim was going to pay $200 for a debt his cousin owed . . .
and word on the street was that the defendant was just supposed to scare
him but not kill him." Antwan Frasier was acquitted of Robinson's murder.
The homicide remains unsolved.

66 *"Wooda had a smile like no other":* "Davon L. Robinson Obituary,"
Legacy.com, www.legacy.com/obituaries/name/davon-robinson-obituary
?pid=180614565.

FIVE

67 *Jenkins started to target Gondo's friend Kyle Wells:* Gondo testimony, GTTF trial; Wells, letters to authors.

67 *"We had several high-speed chases every day":* Justin Fenton, "Cops and Robbers," *Baltimore Sun,* June 12, 2019, https://news.baltimoresun.com/cops-and-robbers/part-one/.

67 *"He normally targeted people for money in, like, robberies":* Gondo testimony, GTTF trial.

67 *he called Jenkins to try to figure out where he was:* This entire incident comes from a number of sources: Gondo and Ward testimony, GTTF trial; Shropshire indictment; Gondo testimony, Shropshire trial; and Gondo plea deal.

68 *"Stew Love":* Given the way Gondo and Wells mock Jenkins with sexual innuendo, Stew Love sounds like a silly R&B crooner to us. Wells did not respond to questions about the name, and so this interpretation could be wrong.

68 *Gondo and Wells had never talked about Jenkins being racist:* Wells's written correspondence to the authors. Wells's emails and letters to authors inform this entire section characterizing Gondo's feelings about being a cop post–Freddie Gray, the shift in their friendship when Gondo joined BPD, how they reunited after Gondo was shot, and Gondo's worry that Jenkins knew Wells was his friend.

68–69 *"Wells's connection with Gondo didn't really protect him from other cops":* Wells previous interactions with Jenkins and Gladstone were described by Wells in emails and letters to the authors. The 2014 arrest also comes from watching *State v. Wells.*

70 *One night, they boxed in a man in front of a sub shop:* Ali Bey interview. Bey was arrested by Jenkins, Hendrix, Taylor, and Ward on July 7, 2016.

70 *prepping to take down Ronald Hamilton:* The account of the Ronald and Nancy Hamilton robbery and the surrounding drama comes from a wide range of sources: Hamilton interview; GTTF indictment; Gondo, Hamilton, Rayam testimony, GTTF trial; wiretap, July 8, 2016; *Hamilton v. Hersl et al.* Dialogue that is not from wiretap, July 8, 2016, is reconstructed from Hamilton interview, and Gondo, Hamilton, Rayam testimony, GTTF trial.

70 *"He at this big-ass mansion with a pool in the backyard":* Fenton, "Cops and Robbers."

71 *Jenkins told Rayam that he saw Hamilton get out of his car with a bag:* This is yet another example of how hard it is to believe anybody's complete version of events because of Jenkins's lies and a lack of oversight in GTTF. Jenkins is the only person who claimed to see Hamilton do anything illegal, which is something Jenkins would likely lie about to get the rest of the squad on his side when it came to planning a robbery or pursuing an investigation. We know that Rayam's approach to this investigation was haphazard. Clewell said he did not see anything, according to Rayam.

71 *"Man, I know it was money in there":* Jenkins dialogue via Rayam testimony, GTTF trial.

72 *The Hamiltons had closed on the half-million-dollar house:* Financial information about the Hamiltons and their home in Westminster comes Hamilton testimony, GTTF trial.

72 *"We pull them over, bring them back to the academy, that's per Sergeant Jenkins":* The phone conversations as GTTF detained the Hamiltons quote wiretap, July 8, 2016. Dialogue between Ronald Hamilton and Gondo, Rayam, and Jenkins in the car and later at "the barn" comes from Hamilton's recollection during Hamilton interview and Gondo, Hamilton, and Rayam testimony, GTTF trial.

73 *$3,400:* There is a lot of back-and-forth later on about who stole money from Hamilton's bedroom that was not split up among the four of them—either Gondo or Hersl. This initial $3,400 Rayam took from Hamilton was not commented upon later.

73 *She believed they were crooks impersonating cops: Hamilton v. Hersl et al.* provides insight into Nancy Hamilton's mind-set.

73 *Gondo called Jenkins:* Dialogue from wiretap, July 8, 2016.

74 *The training building used to be:* John Fritze, "New Police, Fire Training Facility Opens," *Baltimore Sun*, July 31, 2008, www.baltimoresun.com /news/bs-xpm-2008-07-31-0807300143-story.html.

74 *"the barn":* Information about the barn and its appearance and function comes from a former BPD detective who wished to remain anonymous. *Hamilton v. Hersl et al.* has additional details about the barn.

74 *Hamilton thought he would probably get the shit beat out of him if he resisted:* Hamilton testimony, GTTF trial.

75 *He hit Hamilton up for the names of dealers:* Gondo testimony, GTTF trial. Hamilton testimony, GTTF trial, confirms he was asked to give up people, but Hamilton denied he gave up the names of dealers. Gondo testified Hamilton tried to give people up. "He actually attempted to make a phone call in our presence, but it didn't go through. Person didn't answer the phone," Gondo said under oath. "I believe it was a person that he was using as a supplier, basically." This introduces the question of who was lying, who knew they were lying, and who believed the lies they were told. Jenkins and his squad(s) often claimed someone they robbed gave them information. In this case, both Gondo and Hamilton would have reason to lie, but we've chosen to go with Hamilton's version of events that he did not provide them with any names because it does not seem like they acted on any potential information related to Hamilton after the robbery and, because Hamilton was not arrested, there's not even a statement of probable cause that claims Hamilton made these calls.

76 *The floors of the Hamiltons' house*: Description of the Hamiltons' home exterior comes from personal observation. Descriptions of the interior comes from Zillow.com photos introduced as evidence during GTTF trial.

77 *They interrogated the Hamiltons*: Dialogue reconstructed from Hamilton interview and Hamilton, Gondo, and Rayam testimony, GTTF trial.

77 *everyone was on edge, especially Nancy*: Hamilton v. Hersl et al.

78 *"Yo, G, I'm taking it"*: Gondo testimony, GTTF trial.

79 *no name, just the letter J beside a phone number*: Hamilton interview.

80 *"Justice for Alton Sterling, Philando Castile, & All Victims of Police Terror" march*: We covered this protest for *Baltimore City Paper* and observations including the "Fuck Hersl" moment comes from our reporting. See Brandon Soderberg, "A Cop's Aggressive Behavior," *Baltimore City Paper,* March 8, 2017, www.baltimoresun.com/citypaper/bcp-030817-mob-hersl -20170308-story.html.

80 *"Hersl'd"*: Anecdote comes from a former Baltimore Police detective, who followed a suspect into the Eastern District where he stopped him and made an arrest. The commander asked if it was legit or if he'd "Hersl'd him." The broader sense in this same paragraph that Hersl became a sort of metonym for dirty cops comes from extensive conversations with East side residents and other cops aware of Hersl's reputation.

81 *It was 10:35 P.M. when Gondo called her*: Wiretap, July 8, 2016. When Gondo called Lee, she was watching *What Now?* a BET and MTV town hall tied to recent police shootings, and the audio came over the wiretap as well. Rapper Killer Mike was on the show talking about investing in black banks as a form of protest. "Eh, that one person probably doesn't have a good amount of money," Gondo said of Killer Mike, whose net worth is an estimated $5 million, before going on to dispense some financial mansplaining.

82 *There was $17,000:* Dialogue with Jenkins comes from Gondo testimony, GTTF trial. It isn't clear who took the $3,000. Hersl may have lifted it off the $20,000 under the assumption that they weren't going to steal all the money. It is also unclear whether Hersl ever got his share from Jenkins, who could have kept Hersl's share. The GTTF indictment implies Gondo stole it by noting that he deposited $8,000 in the bank days after the Hamilton robbery. His split of the $17,000 plus $3,000 extra would be close to $8,000. But it is difficult to imagine that Gondo would be so worried about missing money on a phone call with Lee if he stole it. There is also the $3,400 Rayam stole, which goes unaccounted for at all during all this back-and-forth about money.

83 *"You know, there's plenty of other people out here you can target":* Gondo's confrontation with Jenkins and his call to Wells about the confrontation are described in Gondo testimony, GTTF trial, and Shropshire indictment.

83 *"You robbed me":* Hamilton interview.

84 *Before he left for vacation:* Jenkins's overtime scheme is described in GTTF indictment and Ward testimony, GTTF trial. The rest of this scene comes from a number of sources. Letters from family and friends to Judge Catherine Blake contained in Jenkins's sentencing documents were a major source for biographical information and the characterization. These documents, and especially Jenkins's sister Robin's letter, describe the death of Lucas Colton Jenkins and the ways the family dealt with that loss. Additional details came from interviews with former Baltimore City Police detectives.

85 *Jenkins told Stepp that he was still managing the criminal operations of other crews:* Stepp interviews.

85 *On the morning of July 15:* Bates interviews.

86 *Wells called Gondo:* Dialogue from Shropshire indictment.

88 *Bates went to see Stevenson in the jail:* Bates interviews.

SIX

91 *"There's blood everywhere!":* This account is based on Charles Smith interview; Deborah Levi interviews; *State v. Smith* trial, in which security camera video of the aftermath of the shooting and Smith's arrest appeared as evidence.

92 *"Two days later":* Jenkins's and Gondo's night of door popping, including the dialogue, is based on wiretap, July 24, 2016, where Gondo describes

the events to Rayam. For additional detail, we used the statement of probable cause for Darrell Hill's arrest.

94 *"What's up, Wayne?":* Wiretap, July 24, 2016.

94 *spot to work surveillance for Jenkins:* Jenkins's appreciation of Canton comes from an interview of a former BPD detective who wished to be
anonymous.

95 *The condo should have at least forty to fifty thousand dollars in it:*
Jenkins dialogue from Gondo testimony, GTTF trial. Gondo also testified
that Hersl mentioned he could use the money because of his house. Hersl
had just settled on his house during this time. Hersl's lawyer, William Purpura, challenged the validity of Gondo's claim.

95 *At 2:30 A.M.:* The account of the April Sims and Damon Hardrick incident comes from a number of sources. The phone dialogue comes from
wiretap, July 25, 2016. Descriptions come from security camera footage
showing Jenkins, Gondo, and Hersl entering the lobby of the condominium
with Sims and Hardrick in the lobby. Accounts of the entrance into the
condo come from interviews conducted by Orrin Henry, Ivan Bates's investigator, with Sims's daughter and Timothy Owens. Additional detail
comes from interviews with Bates and Joshua Insley. Biographical information was compiled in *The April Sims Project* plot summary, www.imdb
.com/title/tt3377130/plotsummary. Sims's Instagram account was used for
details on the interior of the condo and specific information about Sims's
and her daughter's lives. Dialogue that is not from wiretapped calls is reconstructed based on Gondo testimony, GTTF trial; Henry's interviews
with Sims's daughter and Owens; Bates interviews, and the statement of
probable cause, which was written by Hersl. The probable cause and
charging documents were consulted when necessary—information included
that was verified by other recollections was prioritized—though again, the
probable cause was written by Hersl and as a result is typically melodra-
matic and used sparingly. Issues with the veracity of the warrant GTTF
used to to enter Sims and Hardrick's condo are described in Chapter 12.

96 *The three-bedroom, three-bathroom condo:* Description of the condo
comes from images on Sims's Instagram account.

96 *He grabbed a pink Chanel bag:* Gondo testimony, GTTF trial; GTTF
indictment. Hersl denies stealing the bag.

97 *"Hey, you can just give this to your girl":* Gondo testimony, GTTF
trial. During GTTF trial, Hersl's lawyer, William Purpura, pointed out
that when Gondo initially talked to the FBI about this robbery, he did not
mention Hersl's involvement in the theft. Following Gondo's arrest, there

was an FBI search for the Chanel bag, and eventually they found it and took it from the woman who had it—a woman Gondo was seeing at the time.

97 *Ivan Bates was back in a courtroom with Sergeant Alicia White:* This scene in the courtroom and the two press conferences come from Bates interviews and Woods's reporting at the time. Baynard Woods, "Freddie Gray Death: Remaining Charges Dropped Against Police Officers," *Guardian,* July 27, 2016, www.theguardian.com/us-news/2016/jul/27 /freddie-gray-police-officers-charges-dropped.

97 *"He said to tell you hello":* Bates interviews.

99 *Hersl turned his body camera on:* This scene comes entirely from footage recorded by Hersl's body-worn camera of Albert Brown's arrest.

101 *In December 2013:* Levar Mullen interview. Brown's arrest mirrors Mullen's in many ways, and so perhaps all it took for Jenkins to find a way to stop Brown was the Safe Streets connection.

101 *Jenkins and Gondo placed Brown:* When this body-worn camera footage was released to the media after the GTTF indictment, a few reporters referred to Gondo as Taylor. This is likely because Taylor's name is on the paperwork for this arrest, and in Maryland Case Search, Jenkins, Hersl, Rayam, and Taylor are listed as being involved in the arrest. Gondo is not listed at all. Taylor is not present at all in the nearly thirty minutes of body camera footage.

102 *"You can see the cocaine up in the visor":* More accurately, when Hersl filmed the contraband, which Brown maintained was planted, it was stuck above the visor in a lip where the windshield meets the ceiling.

103 *Hersl fielded a phone call:* By enhancing the audio, we were able to hear glimpses of the phone call Hersl takes while he sits in the car with Brown.

104 *Jenkins called Stepp and told him:* Stepp interviews. Rayam testimony, Snell trial.

104 *The Jenkinses' house on Cunning Circle:* Personal observations of the Jenkinses' residence (and yes, Jenkins really did live on a street named Cunning Circle).

104–105 *Jenkins had approached Rayam and Gondo about selling drugs for him:* Gondo and Rayam testimony, Snell trial. We could not determine the exact date when Jenkins approached Gondo and Rayam about selling drugs for him, so we have referenced it at the moment where Rayam decided to act on the offer. Likely, Jenkins ran this by them some time after the Hamilton robbery.

105 *Having Rayam and Stepp at his house at the same time made Jenkins nervous:* Stepp interviews; Rayam testimony, GTTF trial.

105 *Rayam left Jenkins's house with the heroin:* All the details of Rayam's subsequent attempts to sell the heroin were presented as evidence, including an extensive series of text messages and cell tower tracking data, in Snell trial.

SEVEN

The chase and robbery of Dennis Armstrong primarily comes from Armstrong, Gondo, Rayam, and Stepp testimony, GTTF trial; and Stepp interviews. The statement of probable cause in Armstrong's case was cross-referenced with Armstrong's own version of events from GTTF testimony, but Armstrong's version of events was prioritized—especially because GTTF made up a minor in the car to charge Armstrong with driving with a minor in the car without a seat belt. Evidence photos from GTTF trial showed the damage to the storage locker. All the dialogue in this scene is reconstructed from Armstrong, Gondo, Rayam, and Stepp testimony, GTTF trial; and Stepp interviews.

109 *Taylor wasn't even in the country:* Erika Jensen testimony, GTTF trial. Taylor, emails to authors.

109 *"It was Danny's score":* Hersl's alleged involvement with dealing drugs here comes from Jenkins who also told Stepp Armstrong was related to Thomas Wilson, Jenkins's old partner. Jenkins's lies here are especially hard to parse and Hersl's involvement doesn't make much sense.

110 *Bates sat in his office studying the evidence:* Bates interviews; investigative notes, Orrin Henry.

112 *"Change is painful, growth is painful":* Davis would also later adapt this quote from his comments on the day of the GTTF indictment.

113 *This gave Stepp cover when he came by the GTTF office:* Stepp interviews.

113 *"They think that you're a fed":* Jenkins dialogue from Stepp interviews.

113 *William James:* Account of James's arrest comes from Tiffany Coby interview and Andre Davis interview. For more details, see Baynard Woods, "The Cash Value of Truth: One Gun Trace Task Force Victim's Case Will Help Decide If the City Is Responsible for the Actions of Dirty Cops," *Baltimore Beat,* July 12, 2019, http://baltimorebeat.com/2019/07/12/the-cash-value-of-truth-one-gun-trace-task-force-victims-case-will-help-decide-if-the-city-is-responsible-for-the-actions-of-dirty-cops/.

114 *dirt bikes—which Jenkins sometimes stole and sold on Craigslist:* Jenkins guilty plea.

114 *"This is your gun right here":* Jenkins dialogue from a stipulated set of facts that the City of Baltimore and the estate of William James agreed upon. The statement of facts came from depositions of James and Coby. With this statement of facts, the City of Baltimore officially acknowledged that GTTF planted guns. Taylor disputes this. "Where is all this planting shit come, that's ridiculous," Taylor wrote over a prison email system. "Please show me valid physical proof, because I can show proof that nothing like this ever happen involving me, I wouldn't even put myself in that position and I would not ethically or morally allow that to happen."

115 *Zachary Newsome:* This scene, including dialogue, is based on the response to Hersl's motion for review of his detention order, which included extensive wiretap evidence.

116 *Later that night, during a car stop:* These two robberies are detailed in GTTF indictment.

116 *Jenkins hit the gas:* The U.S. Attorney's Office contended in GTTF trial that Taylor was present and attributed some of the dialogue heard on Chevrolet Mic August 31, 2016, to him. Taylor, in this case, presents a relatively compelling argument for why he was not there. At present, we simply avoid mentioning him here. But in Chapter 13 and the related notes, we discuss the issue at great length.

118 *Jenkins had gotten away with plenty of crashes before:* Jenkins received his first departmental citation for an avoidable accident in 2004, a year after he joined the force, according to his Internal Affairs file on the Walter Price case.

118 *Back in the spring of 2010:* The account of the Umar Burley and Brent Matthews / Elbert Davis car crash in April 2010 is reconstructed from Burley interview; Matthews interview; lawsuits filed against the Baltimore Police Department by Burley, Matthews, and the Davis family; the federal indictment of Wayne Jenkins on November 30, 2017; and brief interviews with the Davis family.

118 *jumped out gripping a gun and wearing a black mask:* This claim comes from Burley interview, Burley's lawsuit, and statements made by Burley, Matthews, and their lawyers. Suiter's estate was later removed as a defendant in Burley's lawsuit, but the claim that he wore a mask was not repudiated and fits with the other accounts provided by Stepp and others about Jenkins's use of masks during robberies.

119 *a sergeant who had "the shit":* Jenkins indictment.

119 *"You're definitely going to jail for the rest of your life now":* Jenkins dialogue from Burley interview.

120 *"Hey, yo, Wayne, Wayne, Wayne!":* The following scene comes from Chevrolet Mic, August 31, 2016.

EIGHT

121 *Rayam just didn't get the point of street rips:* Scene and dialogue from GTTF indictment and Rayam's contemporaneous account of it to Gondo, Chevrolet Mic, September 22, 2016.

121 *They had recently rolled up on a homeless guy:* Sergio Summerville was robbed but not arrested on September 7, 2016. GTTF indictment; Summerville testimony, GTTF trial.

122 *Sitting on a curb in handcuffs:* The arrest of Andre Crowder comes from Crowder interview; Bates interviews; statement of probable cause in *State v. Crowder*; and bodyworn camera of Crowder's arrest.

123 *Hersl, who had Always loved being a cop, more or less quit coming to work:* Jensen testimony, GTTF trial, provided a number of receipts and cell phone records to show that Hersl was working on his house while he was supposed to be at work throughout the month of September.

124 *Ivan Bates always picked up the phone when Andre Crowder's family called:* This scene comes from Bates interviews Crowder interview.

125 *"How stupid would I be":* Bates interviews.

125 *It was September 29:* This scene comes from Crowder interview.

126 *Wayne Jenkins pulled into a lane of oncoming traffic beside Gregory Harding:* The Gregory Harding robbery comes from Gondo's body camera; Gondo and Rayam testimony, Snell trial; Bates interviews.

127 *"This is my life. Don't lie on me like that":* Gregory Harding was murdered on February 21, 2019. When Ivan Bates testified before the Commission to Restore Trust in Policing on June 11, 2019, he told the commission he believed Harding, like Davon Robinson, was murdered because of the drug debt he'd accrued when the cocaine was stolen.

127 *Jenkins called Rayam the next morning:* Scene comes from Rayam testimony, Snell trial; Rayam's text messages and phone records from Snell trial.

128 *Jenkins got a call that day from Bates:* Bates interviews.

NINE

130 *Assistant State's Attorney Anna Mantegna:* The scene of Mantegna's call with Jenkins is reconstructed from Mantegna interviews; phone records; text messages between Jenkins and Mantegna; Maryland Judiciary Case Search for Maurice Hill hearing dates; interviews with other SAO employees who wish to remain anonymous; Mantegna notes; and a letter from then acting Maryland U.S. attorney Stephen Schenning to Marilyn Mosby's State's Attorney's Office.

130 *Jamal Johnson and Maurice Hill:* Mantegna interviews; statement of probable cause and charging documents for *State v. Johnson, State v. Hill.*

130 *Jenkins had given Mantegna all kinds of excuses for why his detectives couldn't make it to trial:* Text messages between Jenkins and Mantegna.

131 *Taylor lost the phone he had filmed evidence on:* Mantegna interviews; Mantegna text exchange with defense attorneys in the case.

131 *In the video:* Justin Fenton, "Cops and Robbers," *Baltimore Sun,* June 12, 2019, https://news.baltimoresun.com/cops-and-robbers/part-one/.

131 *"They're dirty as shit":* Dialogue reconstructed from Mantegna interviews, Schenning letter.

131 *Rayam's Franks hearing:* Mantegna had recently learned of Rayam's Franks hearing when her friend and colleague had a retrial of a case that involved both Gondo and Rayam, *State v. Zachary Newsome.* Public information requests revealed that the prosecutor had concerns about going forward with the case and forwarded those concerns to the front office.

131 *Gondo was there with Jenkins as he talked to Mantegna:* Schenning letter.

131 *he had not mentioned it to Gondo:* Gondo testimony, GTTF trial. The following rumors that came back to the squad also come from Gondo testimony.

132 *Gondo spotted someone in a car:* Jensen testimony, GTTF trial; Jensen Alpine interview.

132 *He told Rayam:* The following conversation comes from GTTF indictment, which quotes wiretap, October 5, 2017.

132 *Jenkins told Hersl about his talk with Mantegna:* Ward testimony, GTTF trial.

132 *During leave, they could work full-time on a heist, he told Stepp:* Stepp interviews.

133 *When Andre Crowder came by to visit Bates:* This scene comes from Bates interviews; Crowder interview.

133 *"U got something":* The text messages for this scene were all evidence in Snell trial.

134 *On a Sunday in October:* Bates interviews.

134 *Bates had sent his investigator out:* Bates interviews; subpoena. A very brief phone recording of the footage also verifies that Bates's investigator did see the footage. In *State v. Brown,* Bates tells Judge Peters and ASA Brian Pritchard about the security footage disappearing.

135 *"You don't take money, and you don't put stuff on people":* Kostoplis testimony, GTTF trial.

135 *Kostoplis was serious about his work:* Characterization of Kostoplis and biographical information comes from Kostoplis testimony, GTTF trial; Mantegna interviews.

136 *pushing Rayam about the heroin:* Rayam testimony, Snell trial; texts between Jenkins and Rayam, evidence in Snell trial.

136 *The morning of the Stevenson suppression hearing:* The court proceedings pertaining to *State v. Stevenson* and *State v. Brown* on October 31 were videotaped. All dialogue and descriptions of actions within the courtroom come from that video but are supplemented by information from Hendrix, Holloway, Stepp, Stevenson, and Ward testimony, GTTF trial; Bates interviews; and Jenkins plea deal.

143 *"You need to call me":* This line of dialogue is not recorded but from Bates interviews.

143 *Jenkins joked that Bates had finally beat him in court:* The following dialogue is reconstructed from Bates interviews and is partially, independently corroborated by Stepp. "Great conversation with Ivan & Jenkins in elevator on way out of courthouse," Stepp texted us. Stepp added that Jenkins told him, "Bates was boasting that he finally won a case against Jenkins."

TEN

145 *The Jenkins family had taken its hits:* Description of the Jenkins family history from Jenkins, sentencing letters.

145 *Kristy placed a flower arrangement:* Photo on Kristy Jenkins's personal Facebook page.

145 *Jenkins texted Rayam:* Jenkins and Rayam text messages, evidence in Snell trial.

146 *Rayam wrote to Hood:* Hood and Rayam text messages, evidence in Snell trial.

146 *Snell had deposited:* Rayam testimony, Snell trial; PNC bank security footage, evidence in Snell trial. All Rayam text messages in this section were presented as evidence in Snell trial.

147 *Jenkins spent his free time with Stepp hatching an ambitious heist:* Stepp interviews.

148 *Jenkins told Stepp that he should work out a deal with Gondo:* Stepp interviews.

148 *Since the Hamiltons had been robbed by GTTF in July:* Hamilton testimony, GTTF trial; Hamilton interview; *Hamilton v. Hersl et al.*

148 *"It was only fifty":* Dialogue from Hamilton interview.

149 *"This is a setup," Hamilton told his lawyer:* Dialogue in this scene from Hamilton interview.

149 *In the hallway outside the courtroom, Rayam took out his phone and started photographing Hamilton:* Hamilton interview. *Hamilton v. Hersl et al.* includes this story, but it names Jenkins, not Rayam, as the officer who showed up to court. This is not accurate. Ronald Hamilton showed us the photos he took of Rayam in the courthouse.

149 *On November 21, the FBI approached Oreese Stevenson:* Stevenson testimony, GTTF trial.

150 *he did not want to talk to the FBI:* Bates interviews. The rest of this scene is derived from Bates interviews as well.

150 *Walter Price and his wife:* Sakinah DeGross interview. The details of this scene, unless otherwise noted, from DeGross interview.

150 *With Jail Mail:* Stephen Babcock, "This App Helps Inmates Stay Connected with Friends and Family. Its Founder Knows the Struggle," *Technical.Ly Baltimore,* January 25, 2016, https://technical.ly/baltimore/2016/01/25/jail-mail-app-walter-price-prison-letters.

151 *men in black masks:* Former homicide detective familiar with the investigation, interview. Bates also mentioned this during his testimony at the Commission to Restore Trust in Policing, June 12, 2019.

151 *Later that day, a homicide detective knocked on DeGross's door:* Entire exchange with detectives from DeGross interview.

152 *Wayne Jenkins was especially involved in the holiday festivities at his kids' school:* Jenkins's involvement in school and community from Jenkins sentencing letters and Wendy Kraft, who spoke at Jenkins's sentencing.

152 *Antonio Shropshire pulled his car:* The scene of Shropshire's arrest is reconstructed from Shropshire, email to authors; McDougall testimony,

Shropshire trial; Kilpatrick testimony, Shropshire sentencing. Shropshire admits to possessing the drugs they found him with but denies being part of a conspiracy.

153 *"Yo what's good bro?":* Rayam and Snell text messages, evidence in Snell trial.

154 *Anna Mantegna reached out to Hersl at the end of the year:* Mantegna interviews; Mantegna and Hersl text messages.

155 *the Bates family spent Christmas with a new baby:* Bates interviews; Bates photographs.

155 *Gondo's father died of pancreatic cancer:* "Albert Momodu Samuel Gondo Obituary," Legacy.com, www.legacy.com/obituaries/name/albert -gondo-obituary?pid=183406111. Church Facebook post.

156 *Wells was there at the funeral:* Wells, letters to authors.

156 *During Jenkins's leave, no one did much work:* This entire scene comes from Kostoplis testimony, GTTF trial.

157 *After the FBI visited Stevenson in November:* This entire scene comes from Bates interviews; Stevenson testimony, GTTF trial.

157 *When Wayne Jenkins returned to work:* Jenkins's request for transfer from Justin Fenton, "Cops and Robbers," *Baltimore Sun,* June 12, 2019, https://news.baltimoresun.com/cops-and-robbers/part-one/.

158 *most of the squad was desperate to escape Jenkins:* Hendrix, Ward testimony, GTTF trial.

158 *"Let's go for a ride":* This entire scene comes from Kostoplis testimony, GTTF trial.

159 *Bates was late to Albert Brown's hearing on January 30:* This entire scene comes from video of hearing in *State v. Brown;* Bates interviews.

160 *"He said he was on the lieutenant's list":* Kostoplis testimony, GTTF trial.

161 *He told his family:* Steve Hersl interview.

161 *Anna Mantegna was shocked by the transformation:* Mantegna interviews.

161 *On February 2, Stevenson and Holloway met Bates at his office:* This entire scene was reconstructed from Bates interviews.

162 *No one could find the warrant:* This entire scene comes from video of hearing in *State v. Sims, State v. Hardrick.*

163 *In the back of the van:* Characterization of Jenkins during this time and the scenes of Jenkins showing the gear and proposing robberies comes from Hendrix and Ward testimony, GTTF trial; evidence, GTTF trial; and Stepp interviews.

163 *in the garage one day:* Hendrix and Ward testimony, GTTF trial, diverges at some points in their descriptions of the bags. Hendrix said that he locked his keys in his car and Jenkins pulled the gear out to get into Hendrix's car without having to call a locksmith. According to Ward, they were just in the garage passing by the van.

164 *Hendrix wanted a transfer:* Hendrix testimony, GTTF trial.

165 *new van was going to play a crucial part:* Stepp interviews.

166 *Just go over to the Alameda Shopping Center:* Jenkins's proposal was described in Stepp interviews.

166 *When he walked in, he was not comforted:* Jenkins's behavior at this party described in Stepp interviews.

167 *Miller said Jenkins had nothing to worry about:* Fenton, "Cops and Robbers."

167 *Wayne Jenkins parked his minivan in the lot of Internal Affairs:* The scene of Jenkins and the rest of GTTF's arrest comes from Gondo, Hendrix, Rayam, and Ward testimony, GTTF trial; Wise and Hines Alpine interview; Jensen Alpine interview; Fenton, "Cops and Robbers." The description of Jenkins's clothing comes from news photos and news footage of Jenkins being led out of the Internal Affairs building in handcuffs.

167 *He checked in his firearm:* Jensen Alpine interview. During a December 17, 2017, motions hearing for Hersl, Jenkins, and Taylor, Special Agent Matthew Vilcek discussed why GTTF were brought to Internal Affairs when they were arrested. "It was a place where police officers routinely respond for training or for inquiries. They were required to remove their firearm upon entering the building. It was a matter of safety, so I believe this is why that place was selected," Vilcek testified.

168 *Davis wanted to look each of the officers in the eyes:* Jessica Lussenhop interview; Fenton, "Cops and Robbers."

168 *"He didn't look away, he didn't blink":* Fenton, "Cops and Robbers."

ELEVEN

The account of Kristy Jenkins's call to Bates's office comes from Bates's father-in-law and office manager, Valentino Ascension, interview, and Bates interviews. Bates ultimately recommended Andrew Alperstein, the lawyer Jenkins eventually hired, to the family. Jenkins later hired Steven Levin, a former federal prosecutor, to represent him.

171 *Every lawyer in the room:* Bates, Mantegna, Levi, and another attorney, Joshua Insley, were all in the same courtroom, and we interviewed them each about this scene and also watched it on the video recording of the proceedings in the court reporter's office in the Circuit Court for Baltimore City.

174 *Anna Mantegna sat with two other prosecutors at the State's Attorney's Office:* Mantegna's account of the aftermath of indictment, Mantegna interviews.

175 *Walker called Bates when he came home from work and found Jenkins sitting in a van in front of his house:* This account of Jenkins's postarrest harassment of the Walkers comes from Jamal and Jovonne Walker interviews and Bates interviews.

176 *Deborah Levi, a singularly driven public defender:* Levi's account of the aftermath of the indictment and all biographical information in this scene, Levi interviews.

177 *Her boss, Deputy Public Defender Natalie Finegar:* Natalie Finegar interviews described the conversations inside Office of the Public Defender after the indictments and Finegar and Levi going through spreadsheets of cases, along with Levi interviews. We also viewed the reception court proceedings of *State v. Stanton* to confirm Stanton was about to plead guilty and that an ASA Vanea Morrell interrupted the proceedings to prevent Stanton from pleading guilty.

178 *"Little Bmore, little Bmore, did you see that?":* Burley recalled this scene in an interview.

182 *if they had to admit to the Stevenson robbery:* Ward testimony, GTTF trial.

182 *"Hey, is the Impala, you know, mic'd up? Is it bugged? Does it have a bug in it?":* Rayam testimony, GTTF trial.

185 *"They got us":* Rayam testimony, GTTF trial.

187 *"Stick to the story":* Jenkins plea deal.

187 *When Rayam met with Wise and Hines to talk for the first time, he couldn't look them in the eyes:* Rayam sentencing.

188 *"Since I'm a federal prisoner":* All Hersl letters that we cite come from his sentencing.

TWELVE

189 *"I started reading the letter":* Stepp interviews. Stepp showed the letter to our colleagues at Alpine Labs but would not allow them to film it.

189 *He named Anna Mantegna:* Schenning letter.

189 *Jenkins also snitched on Stepp:* State v. Stepp search warrant; Stepp federal indictment; Stepp interviews.

190 *Rayam, who was in the Kent County Detention Center:* Wiretap, Rayam testimony, Snell trial.

191 *"keep an eye on the kids":* Rayam testimony, Snell trial. The government made much of this conversation when announcing Snell's arrest on November 14, 2016, citing as a fact that Snell had threatened Rayam's children.

191 *Hersl was put on medication:* Hersl sentencing.

194 *A guard at the small jail in the small town of Denton:* Handwritten note on files for *Hamilton v. Hersl et al.*

194 *Rayam's wife, Cherelle, filed for divorce in August:* The information and quotations from the following scene come from Rayam, sentencing letters.

195 *who was still sitting in jail:* Burley interview; November 30 indictment of Wayne Jenkins.

201 *"Mr. Gondo, do you know the defendant, Glen Kyle Wells?":* All dialogue comes from transcripts, Shropshire trial.

202 *"Testify and die":* Shropshire trial; Shropshire sentencing.

202 *"I turned over and there was two masked guys that came in my room":* Teana Cousins testimony, Shropshire trial.

205 *Detective Sean Suiter:* The following scene depicting the shooting of Sean Suiter comes from a wide variety of sources, including the medical examiner's report; evidence collected the independent review board's report (IRB), which includes audio and video; Jeremy Eldridge interview; and numerous interviews with current and former law enforcement officials. The IRB's conclusion that the death was a suicide has been quite divisive and has been rejected by many, including Suiter's family and then commissioner Kevin Davis.

206 *Then Suiter ran into the alley:* Reporter Justine Barron argues that Suiter was shot before or as he moved toward the alley. Her analysis provides valuable insight into all the questions left open by the investigation. Justine Barron, "The Impossible Story: An Investigation into the Shooting Death of Baltimore Police Detective Sean Suiter," *Jewish Times,* July 20, 2018, https://jewishjournal.com/blogs/n_the_case/236270/impossible -story-investigation-shooting-death-baltimore-police-detective-sean-suiter -part-1-commissioner-story/.

208 *The judge stepped away from the bench:* Burley interview; Justin Fenton, "Judge Vacates Conviction of Man Who Feds Say Had Drugs Planted by Gun Trace Task Force Officer," *Baltimore Sun,* December 19, 2017; Jayne Miller, "Judge Overturns Convictions of Men Involved in 2010 Drug Case," WBAL TV Channel 11 NBC Baltimore, December 19, 2017,

www.wbaltv.com/article/judge-overturns-convictions-of-men-involved-in
-2010-drug-case/14458116.

209 *executed a search on Stepp's home:* The account of the raid of
Stepp's home comes from Stepp interviews; Stepp indictment; search warrant for *State v. Stepp;* Stepp sentencing; Jenkins arraignment; Stepp testimony, GTTF trial.

THIRTEEN

212 *Jenkins had just pleaded guilty:* Jenkins plea deal; video of family
leaving court from Brian Kuebler, "Supervisor of Gun Trace Task Force
Pleads Guilty," WMAR Channel 2 ABC Baltimore, January 5, 2017, www
.wmar2news.com/news/crime-checker/baltimore-city-crime/another-gun
-trace-task-force-officer-expected-to-plead-guilty.

213 *Anna Mantegna imagined that her meeting:* Mantegna interviews,
contemporaneous notes and correspondence with her attorney; Schenning
letter to Mosby.

216 *"Do you have anything to worry about?":* The scene of Gladstone and
Vignola in the pool comes from Gladstone guilty plea and Vignola guilty
plea. Gladstone was indicted for his involvement in planting a BB gun on Demetric Simon on February 27, 2019, and later pleaded guilty. In this pool scene
from January 2018, Gladstone is coaching Vignola on the lie to tell the prosecutors, police, or a grand jury if he were to ever have to discuss the BB gun
planted on Demetric Simon. On February 13, 2019, Vignola appeared before
a grand jury and provided them with a false account of what happened, claiming that when he called Robert Hankard his partner, Hankard did not have a
BB gun on him so Gladstone got one out of his trunk instead. Actually Hankard did have a BB gun and Gladstone and Vignola went to Hankard's house
and got a BB gun. Vignola was charged with false declaration before a grand
jury on September 10, 2019, and later pleaded guilty. Hankard was charged
with false declaration before a grand jury on January 15, 2020.

216 *Deputy Commissioner Dean Palmere was locked out of police headquarters:* Kevin Rector, "Confusion Rampant Within Baltimore Police HQ
After Commissioner's Firing, as Other Commanders Have Access, Phones
Cut," *Baltimore Sun,* January 18, 2018, www.baltimoresun.com/news
/crime/bs-md-ci-headquarters-confusion-20180119-story.html.

217 United States of America v. Daniel Thomas Hersl and Marcus Roosevelt Taylor: The scenes of the trial come from transcripts, GTTF; author observations and notes; interviews with Wise, Hines, Taylor, Stepp,

Check Out Receipt

Sylvan Way - Bremerton
360-405-9100
http://www.krl.org

Saturday, September 5, 2020 3:51:17 PM

Item: 39068030773438
Title: I got a monster : the rise and fall
 of America's most corrupt police squad
Call no.: 364.1323 WOODS 2020
Material: Book
Due: 09/26/2020

Total items: 1

Choose your own adventure, something new
Read 10 to 100 hours, it is all up to you!
Visit KRL.org weekly for more summer fun
Virtual events to enjoy, out in the sun.
Dive in to Summer Learning 2020!

Hamilton, Bates, Shawn Whiting, Christopher Nieto, Jennifer Wicks, Steven Hersl, and others. Associated Press and Ashley Coolman, "Who's the Bad Guy Now? Dealers Take the Stand to Testify Against 'Corrupt Cops Who Faked Warrants to Steal Hundreds of Thousands of Dollars in Cash and Drugs from Them," *Daily Mail,* February 1, 2018, www.dailymail.co .uk/news/article-5340101/Drug-dealers-stand-testify-against-cops.html.

220 *being heard was a kind of vindication:* Hamilton interview.

226 *He wasn't even in the car:* Whether or not Taylor was involved in the car chase was one of the most vexing questions we faced in this reporting, despite the Chevrolet Mic, August 31, 2017. Taylor, who has denied any involvement in any crimes, claims not to have been in the car. In most cases, like the jury, we found the evidence against him overwhelming, but we concede the possibility that he may not have been in the car.

It is clear in GTTF testimony that Rayam could not remember who was in the car with him. "Was Hersl in your vehicle, or is that radio chatter coming over into your vehicle?" Hines asked.

"I believe it could have been radio chatter," Rayam answered. "I—I don't think Hersl was in our vehicle—in our vehicle. I, I just—I know I was in the front seat and Gondo was driving. But I can't recall if he was in our vehicle."

"And then when Hersl says, 'Get in, Taylor. Get in,' was Taylor also involved in the episode?" Hines asked.

"Yeah, he—he must have—that must have been another voice from the vehicle saying, 'Get in,' get into the other vehicle."

After this, Hines asked a question that presumed that Taylor was in the car. "When Taylor—directing your attention two-thirds of the way down the page, when Taylor said, 'That dude unconscious. He ain't sayin' shit,' what did you understand that to mean?"

"Meaning, like, he's not going to say anything," Rayam responded, without saying whether it was Taylor or not.

Taylor wrote to us: "So if you listen to the whole tape, Rayam is the one speaking the whole time, and he testified under oath that it was me who was speaking, when if fact that is a total disregard to the truth. The prosecutors knew that wasn't me, which they continued to assert that it was me. I was outside of the car the whole time and everyone left me there, I then went into the gas station with the two employees working. Which time I purchased a drink and waited until Jenkins came back. They were two vehicle which we operated Jenkins drove one vehicle and Gondo drove his but mostly Gondo and Rayam be gone doing who knows what. I have no idea what happen to the vehicle because I was advised that the vehicle got away, I was out there for about 15-20 minutes at that Exxon gas station by myself. Then I was asked what did I see, it was a black unidentifiable male who had his head looking down into his lap with his hands moving something, when I looked into his vehicle I seen him with a numerous amount of green plant looking objects which I know resembled weed. At which time he looked up and took off as I was attempting to open his door. I was in my full vest uniform with the words Baltimore Police."

There are other reasons to believe Taylor was not in the car. He and Gondo and Rayam were not friendly. He also got carsick in the back seat and always rode in the front with Jenkins. "Jenkins didn't allow me to ride with them, but allowed Hendrix or Ward to," Taylor wrote. "As if he was shielding me from them, I didn't see it at the time but, now I believe that he was keeping away from them"; Taylor, email to authors.

Although the U.S. Attorney's Office had much more tape than they played, they declined to explain why they believed Taylor was in the car.

In our account of the crash, we simply did not mention Taylor, since we do not know which of the alternative accounts is more plausible and it was, likewise, not an issue that the jury had to rule on.

226 *The family had been prone to thinking:* Mike Hellgren, "Brother of Indicted Officer: 'The Charges Are Bogus,'" Eyewitness News WJZ Channel 13 CBS Baltimore, March 5, 2017, https://baltimore.cbslocal.com /2017/03/05/brother-of-indicted-officer-the-charges-are-bogus. "Jerome says that traumatic event changed the way Detective Hersl approached his job," Hellgren reported.

227 *Palmere denied Gondo's allegations and said his retirement had nothing to do with the testimony:* "It's not true. I would not coach somebody," Palmere said. "I've always taken pride in my ethics and integrity." Kevin Rector, "Top-Ranking Baltimore Police Official Retires, Denies He Coached Gun Task Force Officer on How to Avoid Punishment," *Baltimore Sun,* February 5, 2018, www.baltimoresun.com/news/crime/bs-md -ci-palmere-retiring-20180205-story.html.

FOURTEEN

232 *Antonio Shropshire did not plead for mercy:* Shropshire sentencing transcripts; Shropshire emails and letters to authors.

234 *Anna Mantegna had been ordered to report:* Mantegna interviews; Schenning letter to Mosby.

236 *Deborah Levi sat in a conference room:* Levi interviews; court proceedings in which she got permission by a judge to go to Internal Affairs.

236 *Charles Smith, who had been arrested:* The account of the Charles Smith case comes from Smith interview; Levi interviews; charging documents; and observation of numerous motions hearings.

240 *demeaning gendered terms:* Levi interviews; Tim Prudente, "State Panel Finds Demeaning Remarks Cause for Judge Nance to Be Expelled," *Baltimore Sun,* October 15, 2017, www.baltimoresun.com/news/crime/bs -md-ci-judge-nance-20171019-story.html.

240 *The family of Elbert Davis stood in the back of the courtroom:* Personal observations and notes; court documents.

242 *"I'm gonna just fucking die":* The prison scenes come from an anonymous inmate interview.

242 *Taylor, who spent a lot of time in the law library:* Taylor emails to authors.

242 *Other cops used to call Taylor stupid:* In Chevrolet Mic, July 27, 2016, Gondo and Rayam have a long conversation about what they consider Taylor's stupidity after he did not arrive at work at the time indicated by Jenkins, who, according to Gondo, said, "I don't understand this stupid motherfucker." The exchange between Gondo and Rayam is indicative of the distance between Taylor and the two detectives. "Yo, Taylor is a stupid nigga, yo," Gondo said.

242 *He helped other inmates file motions:* Anonymous inmate interview.

243 *Anna Mantegna sat in the back of a microbrewery:* Mantegna interviews; Bates interviews.

244 *Wayne Jenkins trudged through the halls of the Chesapeake Detention Facility:* This account is based on Thomas Linwood Jones interview.

245 *Ivan Bates wouldn't be able to come to court:* The account of the state's attorney's debate comes from a livestream and Bates interviews.

248 *"Bathsheba Syndrome":* In Jenkins's sentencing memorandum, Levin wrote: "Like David—who lost the child he bore with Bathsheba, who lost the respect of his kingdom that led to future leadership problems, whose conduct lowered morale among his troops, and who had to deal with the extreme personal guilt of his conduct—Mr. Jenkins lost a child, has lost his job, his reputation, his retirement benefits and, of course, has lost his freedom." He was referring to Dean C. Ludwig and Clinton O. Longenecker, "The Bathsheba Syndrome: The Ethical Failure of Successful Leaders," *Journal of Business Ethics,* no. 12 (1993): 265–273.

251   *Ivan Bates pulled his Lexus SUV out of the police training academy building:* Observations about the race and Election Day were reported by us, in real time, and these scenes are derived from that reporting.

EPILOGUE

255   *Wayne Jenkins has bounced around federal prisons:* We frequently checked the Federal Bureau of Prisons website to see which prison Jenkins was in and noted its many changes over the past three years.

255   *Jemell Rayam was sentenced to twelve years and Momodu Gondo to ten:* All sentencing data for comes from observation of sentencing hearings and court documents.

256   *City Solicitor Andre Davis has engaged in a complicated legal strategy to push a couple of cases to the state's highest court to receive some definitive guidance:* Baynard Woods, "The Cash Value of Truth: One Gun Trace Task Force Victim's Case Will Help Decide If the City Is Responsible for the Actions of Dirty Cops," *Baltimore Beat,* July 12, 2019, http://baltimorebeat.com/2019/07/12/the-cash-value-of-truth-one-gun-trace-task-force-victims-case-will-help-decide-if-the-city-is-responsible-for-the-actions-of-dirty-cops/.